FLASH™ deCONSTRUCTION

FLASH deCONSTRUCTION
THE PROCESS, DESIGN,
AND ACTIONSCRIPT OF JUXT INTERACTIVE

JUXT INTERACT

FLASH deCONSTRUCTION

FLASH™ deCONSTRUCTION

AUTHORS
TODD PURGASON
PHIL SCOTT
BONNIE BLAKE
BRIAN DRAKE

DESIGN
PAUL VENAAS

New Riders

JUXT

New Riders

FLASH DECONSTRUCTION: THE PROCESS, DESIGN, AND ACTIONSCRIPT OF JUXT INTERACTIVE

International Standard Book Number: 0-7357-1149-6

Library of Congress Catalog Card Number: 2001094085

Printed in the United States of America

First Printing: November 2001

05 04 03 02 01   7 6 5 4 3 2 1

Interpretation of the printing code: The rightmost double-digit number is the year of the book's printing; the rightmost single-digit number is the number of the book's printing. For example, the printing code 01-1 shows that the first printing of the book occurred in 2001.

TRADEMARKS

WARNING AND DISCLAIMER

Publisher
David Dwyer

Associate Publisher
Stephanie Wall

Executive Editor
Steve Weiss

Product Marketing Manager
Kathy Malmloff

Managing Editor
Sarah Kearns

Acquisitions Editor
Theresa Gheen

Development Editors
Nancy Sixsmith
Robin Graham

Project Editor
Jake McFarland

Copy Editor
Amy Lepore

Technical Editors
Jessica Speigel
Scott Balay
Jennifer Hall

Cover Production
Aren Howell

Designer
Paul Venaas

Compositors
Wil Cruz
Barb Kordesh

Proofreader
Teresa Hendey

Indexer
Lisa Stumpf

SECTION

01
Introduction

CONTENTS

c3 PG. 048

ACTIONSCRIPT BASICS

2.3.8   Content Plan
2.3.9   Shell Development
2.3.10   Database Development
2.3.11   Transition Implementation
2.3.12   Optimization
2.3.13   Experience Test
2.3.14   Alpha Phase
2.3.15   Beta Testing
2.3.16   Delivery
2.3.17   Documentation
2.3.18   Maintenance
2.4   Summary

Inspiration: James Baker

3.1   Movie Clip Architecture
3.1.1   Dissecting a Movie Clip
3.1.2   Loading External Movies
3.2   The Language of Variables
3.2.1   Variable Basics
3.2.2   About Variable Scope
3.3   Loops
3.4   Declaring Functions
3.4.1   Function Structure
3.4.2   Functions Summary
3.5   Arrays
3.5.1   Array Basics
3.5.2   Simple Arrays
3.5.3   Associative Arrays
3.5.4   Multi-Dimensional Arrays
3.5.5   Arrays Summary

Inspiration: Brendan Dawes

SECTION
02
JUXT Interactive Project Deconstructions

c4   PG. 076

JUXT INTERACTIVE
DEVELOPMENT PROCESS

Inspiration: Hillman Curtis

c5   PG. 104

JUXT INTERACTIVE.COM
ENVIRONMENT SCRIPTING

Inspiration: Glenn Thomas

SECTION

03

Deconstructing
Billabong-USA.com

SECTION
04
Creative Concept for nDecision

SECTION

05
Appendices

Inspiration: Matt Owens

JUXT INTERACTIVE TEAM
The people who make the work of Juxt happen.

1. Anthony Thompson

2. Brandy Lee

3. Brian Drake

4. Brian Dreiling

5. Brian Miller

6. Deborah Schultz

7. John Devine

8. Josh Mooney

9. Leanna Bush

10. Lisa Brabender

11. Luis Escorial

12. Matt Kipp

13. Paul Nguyen

14. Paul Venaas

15. Phil Scott

16. Scott Van Vliet

17. Steve Wages

18. Todd Purgason

(not pictured) Sue McDonald

ABOUT THE AUTHORS

Todd Purgason is the Creative Director for Juxt Interactive, a web-design studio based in southern California that specializes in Internet strategy and Flash-based interactive web sites. Todd has led Juxt in creating innovative work for clients such as Sketchers, Billabong, Macromedia, OmniSky, Nortel, MCY.com, Toshiba, Shorn, Fujitsu, and many others. This work has been highlighted in several publications and books around the world, including *PDN-PIX*, *I.D.* magazine, *Commarts*, *HOW Magazine*, *Print* magazine, *Cre@te Online*, and others. Juxt's work has earned a number of awards, including the Clio Award, *How Magazine*'s International Design Competition award, the *Print Magazine* Interactive award, Communication Arts Award, IPPA StudioONE and DesignONE awards, the *CommArts Magazine* Web Site of the Week, and the High Five Award. Under Purgason's creative direction, Juxt has been honored with 12 Macromedia "Site of the Day" awards and has been featured in several product galleries on Macromedia's web site. In addition, IPPA has selected Purgason as one of today's top 10 web designers in the world.

Purgason, an author and regular speaker on the subject of interactive web design, has contributed to a number of books, including Hillman Curtis's best-selling book *Flash Web Design* (New Riders), *New Masters of Flash* (Friends of Ed), *Flash Studio Secrets* (Hungry Minds), and *The Flash 5 Bible* (Hungry Minds).

Phil Scott is the Chief Technology Officer for Juxt Interactive, bringing his broad technology background to expand the horizons of the Internet through user experiences steeped in solid technology solutions. Delving into computer programming at age 10, Phil had a bit of an early career start. He grew up through a variety of M.I.S. and software development positions across a broad range of technologies. While actively developing business applications and expert systems, long-time interests in programming languages, telecommunications, and client/server business systems propelled this engineer and project manager into the growing frontier of the Internet in early 1995. Through the first few years of the web scene, he managed and assisted in developing several Internet-based, medical image analysis and diagnostics systems and became a web applications specialist, project manager, and business leader. Since joining Juxt in 1999, Phil has led the company to new levels of technical achievement, with efficient data-driven web sites and custom content management for Flash- and HTML-based solutions. Hidden beneath the stunning and strategic designs of Juxt Interactive, technology pumps through their veins, bringing them to life.

An author and speaker on the subject of interactive technology, Phil is contributing to two as-of-yet-untitled books on the subject of Flash and Generator. He has also contributed to Glenn Thomas's book *Flash Studio Secrets* and is preparing to speak on advanced ActionScripting.

Brian Drake has been working in the computer industry since 1992 and specifically in the Internet industry since 1996. Outside of work, Brian is a classically trained guitarist and a martial arts enthusiast. Aside from his capabilities as a developer, Brian is best known at Juxt for surviving two years of eating nothing but boiled chicken and rice, lightly salted.

Bonnie Blake, MFA, is an award-winning designer specializing in web design and multimedia. She is an Adjunct Assistant Professor of Digital Media at Ramapo College in New Jersey and has taught at the College of New Rochelle and Parsons School of Design, both in New York. Bonnie is the author *of How to Do Everything With Flash 5* and *The Premiere Virtual Classroom*. She is also the author of the best-selling online course *Flash 5 ActionScript*, located on ehandson.com.

ABOUT THE TECH EDITORS

Jessica Speigel, born and raised in Seattle, Washington, is cofounder of the We're Here Forums found at www.were-here.com. We're Here has existed as a haven for knowledge-seeking Flash designers since the release of Flash 4. We're Here is a sharing community where members have developed their creative and technical skills together, and many of them have become recognized professionals in the web industry. Her passion is building attractive user interfaces with ActionScript that integrate typography, dynamic content, and motion graphics into a fluid, user-friendly experience for visitors. In her spare time, Jessica shapes webstyles.net, her personal project and portfolio site.

Scott Balay is cofounder of NavWorks. He spends most of his time creating new interfaces for that, as well as other client work.

Jennifer S. Hall changed careers five years ago, from managing and programming in a scientific research environment to multimedia! For the past five years, Jennifer has worked with leading multimedia companies including Top Drawer (Human Code [Sapient]), Thought Interactive (Meritage Technologies), Cortex Interactive, and Eyeland Studios. Much of her work has focused on the development of educational materials for kids and adults. Some of her clients include Disney; Holt, RineHart and Winston; Prentice Hall; and the Austin Children's Museum. She also teaches Director and Flash and was one of the contributors to the *Flash 5 Magic* book. In her spare time, Jennifer eats, reads, runs, sits, rock climbs, dances, loves, and lives.

DEDICATIONS

Todd Purgason: *To the Lord God who, despite my inadequacies, has blessed me beyond measure with the family that is my foundation and reality. To my beautiful and endlessly supportive wife, Candice, and my two (soon to be three) children for the joy they bring to my life every day, even when I'm a thousand miles away. To my parents for making me a reality ;) and for their unfailing love and generosity. To my grandfather in heaven…this is what happens to a child who cannot sit still despite your adamant requests; all your frustration was worth it in the end, I hope. To my brothers and sister for closing the circle and being an integral part of who I am.*

Phil Scott: *To my beautiful and supportive wife, Katie, who listens to my late-night ranting and who has spent countless nights waiting up for me to get off the computer. To my hilarious and adoring son, Parker, whose brilliance and love inspire me to be a better person. To my mother for giving me life, having the patience to raise me, having the strength to put up with my crazed years, and being a wonderful friend, mother-in-law, and grandmother. To my stepfather for inspiring my intellect and giving me confidence as a free thinker, and for putting up with me. To my brothers for always being there to hang and for the memories of the unspeakable things we did together. To William Epp, whose humble genius as a programmer and brilliant techniques inspired me to be a better developer. To Hank Salerno for giving an unproven 17-year-old a chance. And to my immensely talented and wise executive partners at Juxt, for inviting me to the party.*

Bonnie Blake: *To my beautiful daughter, Kelly, and Matthew, who inspire me every step of the way; and to God, for supplying much abundance in my life.*

ACKNOWLEDGMENTS

Todd Purgason

First and foremost, I thank my partner, Steve Wages, for doing the many unglamorous and thankless tasks that made Juxt Interactive both possible and a reality. After that, I have to wholeheartedly thank the team at Juxt Interactive; you guys are the marrow of this book. Thanks Jeff, Mike, Lisa, Sue, Leanna, Brandy, JD, Luis, Matt, Paul, Brian Drake, Brian Drieling, Anthony, Scott, Deborah, and Chandler. Next, thanks to my coauthors: Phil for his genius and dedication and Bonnie for her warm personality, reliability, and most of all for making me sound halfway intelligent. Thanks to Paul and Wil for the amazing book design. Thanks to the whole New Riders team: Steve, Wil, Barbara, Robin, and Theresa. Thanks to all the featured designers for taking the time from their busy lives to help make this book a meaningful achievement for me personally. Thanks Hillman, Fred, Bren, Glen, Matt, Josh, Joshua, James, Jimmy, and Mike; you guys helped make Juxt what it is by doing what you do best and sharing your ideas with us all. Thanks to the whole Flash team at Macromedia, especially Eman and Schmitty. Special thanks to Billabong: Ian, Curly, and Graham, and also to Jeff Keyser and Jessica Spiegel. Finally, a very special thanks to Paul Venaas, the designer of the book; it was a great pleasure to work with Paul on this. His talent and dedication helped make this book happen. Thanks, Paul.

Phil Scott

Many people have contributed to the ideas and events that have made this book possible. Steve Wages (Juxt's CEO, cofounder, and hero) has done so much to make Juxt Interactive a successful business, and without his tireless and wise leadership, we would not have the opportunity to work on a project like this book. To my coauthor Todd, I owe thanks both for opening his world up to me and for cofounding a company that has made good on its vision. I thank my coauthor Bonnie for her extraordinary strength as an author and for pulling it all together. Without the collaborative learning from my fellow Juxtsters, I would not know what I know today about Flash; their intelligence, skill, and cunning inspire me…thanks. Thanks to the New Riders team and all of the featured designers. Thanks to Macromedia for bringing such an enabling technology as Flash to the party. Thanks to Fred, Phillip, Mike, Miko, Brian, Glenn, and Sam for sharing your ideas and being there for me learn from you. Finally, special thanks to K10k and Billabong for providing us with a reason to think, create, and innovate; without you, this book wouldn't have been half as fun as it was.

Brian Drake

Thanks to God, my friends and loved ones, my coworkers, and Jeff Keyser.

Bonnie Blake

I want to thank Todd for giving me the opportunity to work on this book. Your incredible wisdom, creativity, and spirit are a great inspiration. Thank you Phil for being such a pleasure to work with and for sharing your vast knowledge of Flash and related technologies in this book. Thank you, Brandy. I will miss connecting with everyone on Wednesdays. To Barbara, Theresa, Robin, Steve, and everyone at New Riders, thank you for your encouragement and support. Lastly, thank you Juxt, whose existence made this book possible in the first place.

A MESSAGE FROM NEW RIDERS

As the reader of this book, you are our most important critic and commentator. We value your opinion and want to know what we're doing right, what we could do better, in what areas you'd like to see us publish, and any other words of wisdom you're willing to pass our way.

As Executive Editor at New Riders, I welcome your comments. You can fax, email, or write me directly to let me know what you did or didn't like about this book—as well as what we can do to make our books better. When you write, please be sure to include this book's title, ISBN, and author, as well as your name and phone or fax number. I will carefully review your comments and share them with the authors and editors who worked on the book.

Please note that I cannot help you with technical problems related to the topic of this book, and that due to the high volume of email I receive, I might not be able to reply to every message. Thanks.

Email: steve.weiss@newriders.com

Mail: Steve Weiss
           Executive Editor
           New Riders Publishing
           201 West 103rd Street
           Indianapolis, IN 46290 USA

Visit Our Web Site: www.newriders.com

On our Web site, you'll find information about our other books, the authors we partner with, book updates and file downloads, promotions, discussion boards for online interaction with other users and with technology experts, and a calendar of trade shows and other professional events with which we'll be involved. We hope to see you around.

Email Us from Our Web Site

Go to www.newriders.com and click on the Contact Us link if you

- Have comments or questions about this book.
- Want to report errors that you have found in this book.
- Have a book proposal or are interested in writing for New Riders.
- Would like us to send you one of our author kits.
- Are an expert in a computer topic or technology and are interested in being a reviewer or technical editor.
- Want to find a distributor for our titles in your area.
- Are an educator/instructor who wants to preview New Riders books for classroom use. In the body/comments area, include your name, school, department, address, phone number, office days/hours, text currently in use, and enrollment in your department, along with your request for either desk/examination copies or additional information.

A FOREWORD TO A BOOK AND A NOTE TO A FRIEND

A few years ago, I got an email from someone named Todd Purgason. He was writing to inform me that he had come across a site that was exactly like mine. Someone had apparently downloaded my source, authored a couple of Flash movies to place where mine were, and posted. I checked out the site and felt strangely happy.

Then I went to Todd's company site, JUXTInteractive.com, and had a different reaction. His company's site was so different from mine, bright colors all over, serif fonts, flowing and lyrical. My first impression was that it was too busy, but after a couple of deep breaths—those breaths you have to take when something is slightly threatening to you—I saw the balance and the craft and pattern behind the design.

After that, I started to notice Todd's touch on other sites and in books and magazines. The style is really strong and unmistakable, and I quickly grew very fond of it. I remember writing a couple of emails back to him. The first thanked him for informing me of the copycat; the other was a comment on his design. It simply read, "Damn…"

We started to exchange more emails and talked a few times on the phone, Todd on the West Coast, me here in NYC. One day, I got the brilliant idea to ask Todd to design my first book, *Flash Web Design*. It turned out to be one of the best ideas I had that year and resulted in a wonderful book design and the start of a lasting friendship.

So when Todd asked me to write the foreword to his and Juxt Interactive's new book—the one you're holding—I didn't hesitate. Ever since I learned that Todd and company were writing a book, I've been excited to see it. When I learned that they would be sharing both their process as well as their ActionScripting knowledge, I got *very* excited to see it.

Juxt Interactive has one of the most airtight, thought-out, and tested processes for Flash design that I have ever had the pleasure to witness. It's really inspiring and manages to be both simple and extremely thorough at the same time.

As far as ActionScripting, Juxt Interactive has impressed me deeply with their ability to code stable, multibrowser, cross-platform, and incredibly complex—*thinking*—online Flash sites and applications.

Finally, I don't know too many people as passionate and committed to design as Todd is. He has a voice and a style that's unique.

Juxt Interactive is a leader both in their process and their design, and they're definitely a leader in the Flash community. It's my great pleasure to write this foreword for such an inspiring company… and to a wonderful friend.

Hillman Curtis
Summer 2001

01

deCONSTRUCTION

The Process, Design, and ActionScript of
Juxt Interactive

Section 01
Introduction

(a)

This book was written to share with you, the reader, how we do things at Juxt Interactive. Historically, Juxt has survived through many projects. Most of our projects have been very successful, and, admittedly, a few have met with less success. Nonetheless, our work has served as a great learning platform for us, both as individuals and as a group.

(b)

Over the last few years, Flash has grown from a simple animation tool to a full-featured programming environment that can be used for application development (something we previously did only in Java). Now that the application is maturing, Flash designers/developers are faced with a new set of hurdles to clear in order to produce work that is competitive with that of their peers.

(c)

This book shows you how we have learned to work with Flash in a team-based model on real world projects, geared toward the general public.

(d)

There are masses of personal sites in existence today that offer abstract trinkets of code for you to take and spin. The drawback with these sites is that you are left to fill in the gaps all by yourself. In this book and on our site, we cover subjects from A to Z regarding the process used on several of our projects. Our intention is to help you better define your role as a Flash developer and to give you a glimpse into the world of large-scale Flash project development within a team environment.

(e)

The body of this book is very literal. We deconstruct projects, design intent, and the code that is used to make the sites come alive. But before we dig into projects, there needs to be some discussion of how to use this book, our project process, and some basic ActionScript concepts that you need to know about for later in the book.

c1

CHAPTER
Flash deCONSTRUCTION
INTRODUCTION

Over the past two years, I've had the privilege of speaking across the country at various design conferences on the topic of Flash. Throughout this process, I've interacted with Flash designers and developers on many different levels. One of the observations I've made is that a lot of Flash users have not had the opportunity to use Flash on big-budget, complex projects. Rather, their experience has consisted of small-scale, single-process projects. These people are the sole authors of the project from start to finish and, as such, are limited in their capabilities. Because of their lack of experience, these users have a problem wrapping their minds around the process of developing large-scale, team-based Flash projects.

Not too long ago, I remember being the only designer in a small company of three, creating Flash sites for which I owned and controlled the design and the technical aspects of the project. Everything was easier back then.

As our company grew, along with our client base and project load, things started to get more complicated. With more intricate projects, deadlines, milestones, and all the other baggage that comes with large-scale projects, we needed to be able to work in a group environment. When Juxt was a newborn, we typically had one project running at a time with one person doing all the Flash design and development on that project. As Juxt grew, we started having to deal with several projects running concurrently. Several team members would then be involved on many projects at certain points in their life span.

What used to be done by one person over several months now had to be done by two to six people over several weeks' time. Working on a single Flash file and trusting that you, personally, had complete control over it was no longer a reality.

By working together in a collaborative team effort, the formula for a process took shape. This process, which is shared with you in this book, has become standard protocol for Juxt and has served us and our clients well for the past three years.

1.1 HOW THIS BOOK IS ORGANIZED

The purpose of this book is to share the following with you, the reader:

- Our project team structure
- Our development process
- A little bit of how we think about what we create
- ActionScripting techniques we've used to create four of our real-world projects

Plenty of books on the shelves today can show you how to do simple ActionScript techniques, including isolated actions that aren't connected to a real project. The goal of this book is to show you how we've used our process and ActionScript to create real projects. And, whether your projects are large or small, the information in this book is food for the creative process. We hope the book will spark new inspiration and the rethinking of old ideas.

In essence, the title of this book, *Flash deCONSTRUCTION*, reflects what the book is all about. It begins by deconstructing our process, walking through our team architecture and project process.

In Part I, "Introduction," we examine our design-development process using FreeHand, Flash, and optimization techniques. Then we get into some basics of ActionScript, including the fundamentals you'll need to know as we talk about some more intricate principles later in the book.

Then we deconstruct several projects. They were all built in Flash 5 to leverage ActionScript and to take advantage of the powerful features it offers for creating an online multimedia experience. Be aware that the user audience of Flash 5–enabled browsers is still growing. As of June 2001, 67% of U.S. browsers had installed the Flash 5 player. However, by the time this book is published, that percentage should be much higher.

NOTE

For the latest statistics of Flash player penetration, visit
www.macromedia.com/software/player_census/flashplayer/.

In Part II, "Juxt Interactive Project Deconstructions," we discuss our first project, the Juxt Interactive site, which was completed soon after the release of Flash 5. Remaking the Juxt site gave us an opportunity to explore some of the new features in Flash 5 and to learn about uncharted bugs, how to work around those bugs, as well as some of the elements that work well and those that don't. Our findings about Flash 5 bugs and workarounds are shared with you in Appendix A, "Flash 5 Hacks," at the back of the book.

Part III, "Deconstructing the Billabong Site," covers our second project: a dissection of the Billabong-USA.com site—the very engaging and complex project we built for the USA division of the international extreme sports apparel brand Billabong. We first look at some of the interesting elements that make up the site's unique interactive experience, and then we address content management involving Flash, Generator, and other technologies.

In Chapter 8, "Other Billabong Sites," we look further into Billabong by deconstructing elements of two other Billabong sites we created. The first site deconstructed in the chapter is Pickled.tv, a highly interactive micro site created to promote the surf film Pickled the Movie. Then we expose some effective e-commerce techniques in the www.billabong-usa.com/store site.

In Part IV, "Creative Concept for nDecision," we deconstruct our third project: an internal R&D assignment called nDecision, which we created for K10k (www.kaliber10000.net). In essence, this is a movie maker that enables you to mix movie clips and their properties to make your own movie. This project relies heavily on the new XML capabilities of Flash 5, talking directly to a server while saving data back and forth. This is very deep, heady stuff.

Because this book is a deconstruction of our company, Juxt, we feel it's important that it walk the same line we walk and follow the same philosophy we follow. That philosophy includes doing things a little bit differently—stretching and pushing beyond the mundane. Unlike a typical technology book, reading this book is meant to be a unique experience that's augmented by the book's web site. Because Juxt develops for the Internet and this book is about our work, we use the Internet to present and reinforce the information covered throughout this book. Visit www.JUXTinteractive.com/ deCONSTRUCTION. This site enables you to download and use the projects featured in the book, giving you a holistic perspective on the Juxt experience.

Finally, in combination with the technical data and our conceptual philosophies for each project, we have interlaced a layer of inspiration throughout the book. Juxt has participated in the Flash design community from its inception. We owe a lot to this global community of Flash developers for sharing their knowledge and fueling our energies. This has, in turn, pushed us to be more creative as well as give back to our community. Ten designers that have influenced us in many ways were invited to participate in our little book adventure. As you will soon discover, both the book and the web site are full of surprises and inspirations from our designers, making the whole experience very exciting and unique.

So we hope you enjoy this book and walk away with some nuggets of inspiration. Hopefully, you will learn from our experiences so you can avoid some of the pitfalls that may lie ahead. To share our years of experience working with Flash on real-world projects with you, we have developed the book, its accompanying web site, and inspirations from the Flash community.

Sharing in this book is only the beginning. You can, of course, read the book, learn, and move on, or you can join the others featured in this book and become a part of *Flash deCONSTRUCTION* through deCONSTRUCTION.com. You can think of this book as an ongoing forum of which we are all a part.

1.2   CONVENTIONS USED IN THIS BOOK

This book is chock full of code samples to help you better understand the relationship between programming and larger scale, interactive projects. Because the focus of the book is largely based on Flash technology, much of the code throughout the book demonstrates ActionScript techniques as they relate to our projects.

Because we do reference different programming languages, we've established a code convention to make it easier for you to distinguish between the two. ActionScript code is outlined in a blue block so that it stands out. The ActionScript is color-coded exactly as it is in the Flash interface. Actions are depicted in blue, comments are depicted in magenta, and properties are in green. The body of the script is depicted in black. For those of you who prefer to examine the actual source file, all examples are available on the book's site. The following is an example of how ActionScript is depicted in the book:

```
//
//--- Create a new array variable with people's names in it ---
var namesArray = new Array();
//
```

XML is depicted in solid black and is blocked out in magenta as in the following example:

```
<?xml version="1.0"?>
<Customer firstName="Sally" lastName="Booth" ID="424924">
   <ShoppingCart>
      <CartItem sku="AV-294" price="45.95" ID="9049"/>
      <CartItem sku="AV-313" price="12.95" ID="9134"/>
      <CartItem sku="SC-106" price="19.95" ID="10249"/>
   </ShoppingCart>
</Customer>
```

1.3   ABOUT THE BOOK'S SITE

Many of our readers have purchased other Internet design books from time to time. Many include accompanying web sites that offer downloadable source files and links to featured projects. If the site peaks your interest, there's an additional link to an online bookseller where you can actually purchase the book.

The book site for *Flash deCONSTRUCTION* attempts to go a little bit further than other books' web sites. We explore the transient bridge between print and web by appreciating each medium for its unique strength and using each effectively. In addition to the book and the source files available on the accompanying web site, the featured artists in this book have created their own unique Flash piece that is also posted on the web site. This art reflects their design, their workspace, and who they are. Adding to its uniqueness, the book's site includes audio files of the interviews with these inspirational designers, done via telephone conversation and recorded as actual, unedited interviews.

Building community is one of the things the web does best. What we have done is create an online forum so that our readers can come together and share experiences. You can also ask questions of us, the authors, and of your co-readers. You can rag on us; you can praise us; you can do what you will. We'll leave the online forum open to your interpretation. Whether you're using it as a resource or to interact with other Flash authors, it surely will grow and thrive with your support.

1.4 WHO SHOULD READ THIS BOOK

In today's world of Flash development, it's no longer a one-man show. In the early days, it was typical for a company to have a Flash developer (a guy who would do design, layout, motion graphics, and scripting) carrying out an entire Flash project. Today, the reality is that developing for Flash is very much akin to developing for other Internet technologies like HTML, DHTML, or XML. In Flash development, as in other technologies, specialists often work together in a team environment to execute the project as a whole.

There are rare individuals out there who are the true Renaissance men, doing design, motion graphics, good UI, and programming in XML. But for the average Joe like you and me, that's usually not the case. The constraints of being the master of all things inevitably become limiting. It is far more efficient to have specialists who can focus on and be masters of their own domain.

For most agencies, Flash development now consists of teams of designers, motion graphics artists, information architects, and programmers, all working together to create the project as a whole. It is our hope that this book has valuable information for all these people. If you are by choice (or by default) that Renaissance Flash person doing it all, this book should be great for you as well.

Although the primary focus of this book is ActionScripting, it also addresses process and design intent. We believe that Flash programmers bridge a gap between the typical code-minded programmer and the visual designer. Because a lot of Flash programmers evolve from positions as developers or designers doing UI and design, they have an affinity for things more visual in nature.

1.5 ABOUT JUXT INTERACTIVE

Because this book is a deconstruction of Juxt Interactive, both as a company and the projects we create, it seems appropriate at this point to provide you with a little bit of background on us as a company. The following gives you some perspective on our thinking and our processes.

The beginnings of Juxt Interactive go way back to 1990 when founders Steve Wages, Chief Executive Officer, and Todd Purgason, Creative Director, worked together for a small architectural firm in Newport Beach, California. The two worked on several projects and built a relationship based on creativity, a passion for the digital medium, and fun. Wages and Purgason worked hard as teammates in the office and on the volleyball court at lunch. Years passed and they separated paths, but they kept in touch as both developed a passion for design and the digital medium. In 1995, their passions found roots in a small Internet startup where they began to explore the web as a medium for design and communication. This exploration fueled a desire to seek out more relevant projects and clients with a vision to use the power of the Net to evolve their businesses. It was also here that Steve and Todd met Phil Scott, Juxt Interactive's CEO and co-author of this book.

In April of 1998, following their vision to create a company that would effectively juxtapose design and technology into engaging and rewarding Internet experiences, the two set out to find clients who were willing to embrace the Internet and who had the confidence to see their brand, and product, evolve for the new era of communication design. That was the foundation of Juxt Interactive and the guiding light that led them to where they are today (see Figures 1.1 and 1.2).

Figure 1.1 JuxtInteractive.com v1.0.

Wages and Purgason quickly found clients who shared their vision and created some solid projects that propelled this tiny new entity forward in its abilities and opportunities. Their first site, http://lundstromarch.com, was embraced with global recognition for its solid design and unique employment of technology in a seamless experience very rarely achieved on the Internet (see Figure 1.3).

Later that year, Phil Scott and Brian Drake joined the team, adding the depth that has been the foundation of Juxt ever since. Over the past several years, they have pulled together a team of very talented individuals who are ever pushing themselves in a daily exploration of where this medium is going and how it can best be used to help clients meet their business objectives.

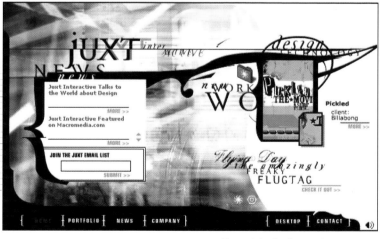

Figure 1.2 JuxtInteractive.com v2.0.

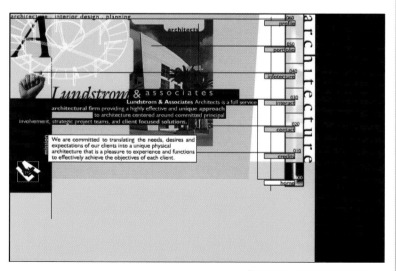

Figure 1.3 Lundstromarch.com.

Juxt continues to seek out projects in alignment with its vision and skills. This growth and innovation has resulted in many fruitful and rewarding relationships with clients. The affirmation of our passion and commitment to excellence has manifested itself in countless international awards and the publication of our work both on and off the Internet. Juxt has been cited by several sources around the world as one of the leading studios in the medium of online digital communications.

Because of the positive response to our work, the Juxt vision has been further fueled. We look forward to seeing the Internet and interactivity continue to mature as a medium. We also recognize that Flash technology is an important element in the growth of the medium. With its low bandwidth, ActionScript features, wide accessibility, and integration with other technologies (XML, Generator, QuickTime, and so on), Flash will undoubtedly continue to play a major part in the future of the Internet and interactivity.

Philosophically, at Juxt we believe in the medium we use for Internet development. It is a medium that steps beyond the boundaries present in most other forms of communication. It is not a design or technology medium; it is a communication and empowerment medium. It uses technology and design to communicate, and it empowers people young and old, male and female, with information. We believe the web is about content above all other things. It is up to us, as users of this medium, to deliver content in an interactive and engaging way that will motivate the viewer to respond. The challenge we face is ensuring that both the client and the viewer mutually benefit from the experience of visiting the client's site.

The relationship between the two becomes symbiotic because the viewers find what they need, and that is exactly what the client wants them to find. One of our goals at Juxt is to create an online experience so that the lines between design and technology are completely seamless.

We strive to create work that is engaging and appropriate for the audience. Our work employs technology in new and innovative ways, without compromising the user experience.

Flash has been a very important tool in helping us achieve this balance of experience and content. As a technology, it stepped in and solved many inherent flaws of HTML that were destructive to the experience for users. Through its streaming capabilities, we found a way to immediately reach users as soon as they enter a site.

Due to Flash's binary format, we were able to lay out our experience in a very fluid and controlled manner, allowing us to use color, typography, and motion in a way that effectively reaches the user.

The limitations of HTML and the differences in browser support force developers to design for the technology and not the user. Flash solves this problem. It also enables us to keep a continuous experience that is not fractured by the distracting breaks in loading HTML page after HTML page. This factor is just the beginning of the seamless interactivity that can be created in Flash, which can be both intuitive and powerful. With our years of experience using Flash, we have gone from creating simple web sites to creating extremely advanced online applications to now creating television commercials.

Throughout our history, we have found Flash to be the best technological solution available to match our vision for web-based communication and beyond.

1.6 THE EVOLUTION OF FLASH AS WE SEE IT

Because we got involved with the Internet early in our careers, we've seen Flash evolve from its beginnings, as a program called FutureSplash, to what it has become today. With each new version, we have witnessed the small and large steps in the Flash development process. We have had the fortunate experience of having Macromedia as a client. This has given us the opportunity to work together and help them make Flash a better tool for us all.

The introduction of Flash 4 was a large step forward, bringing Flash into the world of programming with ActionScript. Flash was a tool that was used for site design, rollovers, intro animations, and so on. The addition of ActionScript in Flash 4 expanded the program's capabilities and empowered us to do much more than what was previously possible.

Flash 4 also enabled us to do interesting applications—gaming, dynamic content—and introduced Macromedia's solution to dynamic database-driven content in Flash Generator (see Figure 1.4). It also opened the doors to interlacing some dynamically created content into Flash, which had been a big limitation in Flash's early days.

Flash 5 took the small steps made in Flash 4 and kicked the floodgates open. ActionScript in Flash 4 was considered a light scripting environment. In version 5, ActionScript has evolved into a robust scripting environment following the JavaScript syntax. In fact, ActionScript conforms to ECMA-262 specifications (the document that defines the rules and parameters of the JavaScript language). Version 5 ActionScript enables seasoned programmers to finally get into Flash and create powerful applications and projects (see Figures 1.5 and 1.6).

Figure 1.4   The Billabong-USA.com team rider section relies on Macromedia Generator for its dynamic content.

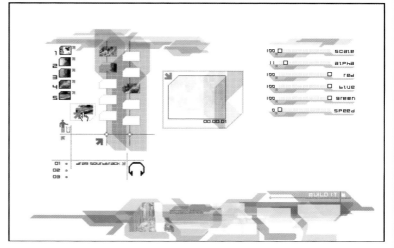

Figure 1.5   nDecision Movie Maker application.

Figure 1.6 Turd game from Pickled.tv.

1.7 SUMMARY

Despite our wealth of experience working with Flash as a medium on and off the Internet, we will always consider ourselves students of this medium. On an everyday basis, we learn new things, become engaged in new adventures, or see somebody do something that we didn't know was possible. In a world of constant evolution and advancement, we hope you can use this book and the concepts we've presented for your own advancement.

We are not saying that this is the definitive guide for the ideas presented in this book. With programming and design, there are several avenues you can take to achieve the same results. This book is merely a representation of our approach on these particular projects. We challenge you to find new and better ways to complete Flash projects. We hope you will use our experiences and ideas as a starting point and then go far beyond that to find your own way.

Our goal for the book's site (see Figure 1.7) is to open up the opportunity for individuals to share better ways to complete Flash projects. This is not an ego trip, and we're not here to say that we are the best in the world. We're trying to say, "Hey, this is what we have done. Take from it, learn if you can, improve upon it, and grow. Ultimately, please give back to the community, which has fed, nourished, and grown us to become the entity that we are today."

Figure 1.7   www.JUXTinteractive.com/deCONSTRUCTION.

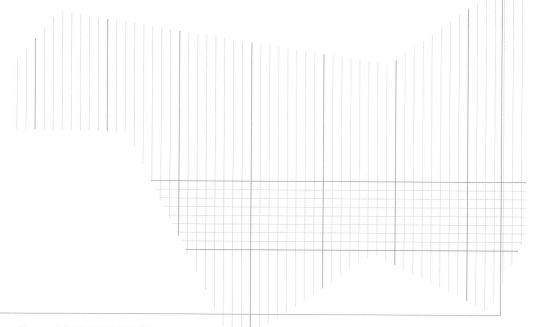

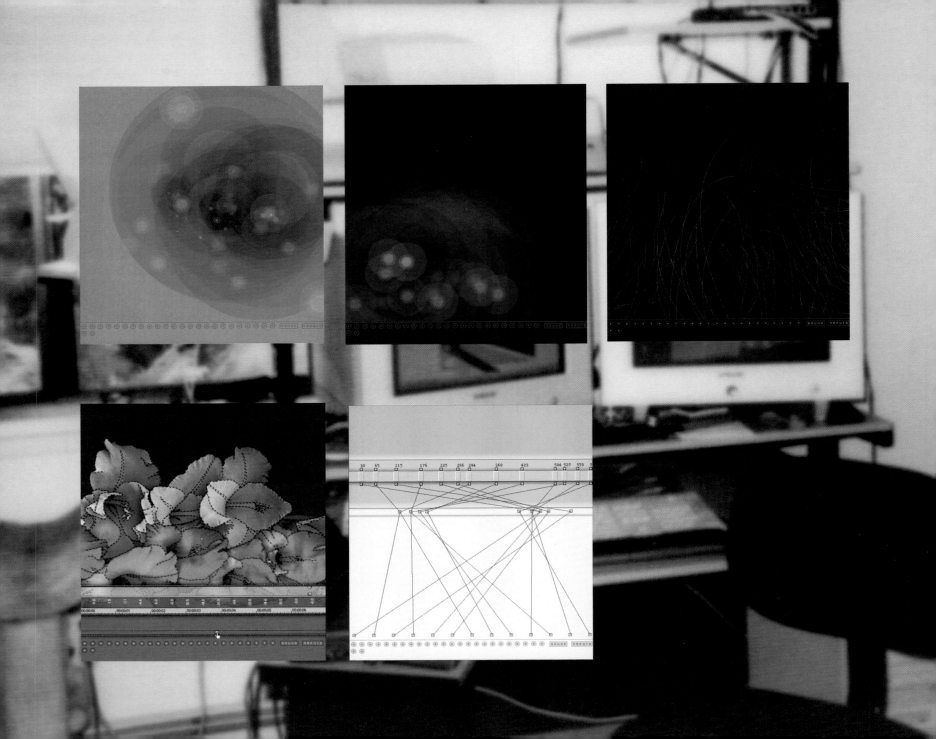

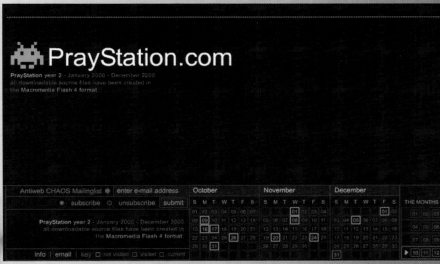

JOSHUA DAVIS

Joshua Davis Interview
by Todd Purgason

Introduction
www.praystation.com

I first met Joshua Davis online through a closed email list put together by a design community site named Uploading, which no longer exists. Josh has always been a very charismatic figure in the web design culture. His roots go way beyond the Praystation site that hundreds of thousands of Flash developers flock to almost religiously.

I met Josh face to face at the first FlashForward 2000 in San Francisco. Since then, I have had the good fortune to slum with him at many other conferences. Josh is one of the most unique people I have ever met. On the outside, he looks like he has a hard-core attitude from hell. But in reality, Josh is an extremely friendly and likable guy. His outside exterior is the product of his experimental and adventurous spirit that is the sum of all he has done on the web. It is this adventurous spirit, alongside a genuine creative nature, that has pushed Josh to tinker with Flash in so many beautiful ways.

I think one of the things that sets his work apart from other designers is that he often sets out on a path with no idea of what will be at the end. After conducting hundreds of experiments, he will wind up with an amazing result. Most people try to conceptualize first and then try to create. Neither method is wrong, but Josh's process is what makes his work unique. The bottom line is that his experiments and his source code have touched almost all of us out there in some way.

Teaser from the Interview

TP: Okay, so we're here with Joshua Davis from Praystation, á la Kioken, á la everything else about the web...the greatest designer on earth, is that what they wrote? (In reference to the cover of Shift magazine featuring Joshua Davis, entitled "The Best Web Designer on the Planet.")

JD: Oh, God...copy is not something I write.

TP: You know, we've a special little gallery on one of our walls of your images from Dreamless.

JD: Oh, are you serious?

TP: Yeah.

JD: Aren't they hysterical?

TP: Yeah, that was hilarious.

JD: If you can't make fun of yourself...I think it was kind of necessary to poke fun. Matt just kind of came out from Shift. We had dinner, we talked, and he went off and wrote his interview, and then I just saw the magazine.

I don't think these things. "I'm the best designer on the planet." That's just what they wrote.

Sure, I'll do an interview, but I need to proofread what you write. I don't want to be in a position to do that. But it was okay.

TP: It was great.

JD: Who is Joshua Davis if he's not the greatest designer on the planet? A lover of life. You know what I mean?

TP: Yeah.

JD: Anything and everything about life.

TP: So you're a lover of life, I can see that.

JD: Yeah you know, just an adventure. I'll try anything at least once. I tried onions once. Don't like 'em. Tried mushrooms once. Tried skydiving once.

TP: You tried red dye in your eye once.

JD: Yeah, well, a couple of times actually, more than just once.

TP: Once wasn't enough?

JD: Yeah, my wife, Melissa and I always joke that we're Mr. and Mrs. Livingston, you know, and that's sort of like just this embodiment of these two people who are just on permanent safari with life. You know?

TP: Yeah. That's great. You definitely see that in the work that you do. Just exploring it.

JD: Yeah, it's definitely like no boundaries, anything goes, you know? And that's certainly affected my work, but I think just as a person, you know, life certainly is an adventure.

TP: Well, I know that a lot of people like to live vicariously through you, so keep it up.

To hear the rest of Joshua's response to this question, as well as his answers to the following questions, please go to the Inspirations section of the book's site at www.JUXTinteractive.com/deCONSTRUCTION.

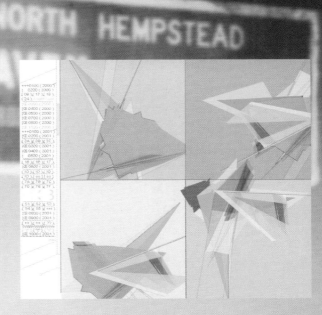

QUESTIONS

02. If your were a fish/sea creature, what would you be?

03. What CD or mp3 is in your player right now?

04. What is your definition of design?

05. What was your very first impression of Flash?

06. If you were walking down the street and came across John Gay and Jakob Nielsen engaged in a fistfight, what would you do?

07. You started out as an illustrator, and you say that you are not a designer. Do you consider "Once Upon a Forest" illustration?

08. Kioken has a philosophy about ignoring all limitations and designing for the future of the web. How do you explain this to clients, and why do you think this is appropriate for their projects?

09. You teach a class in New York on Flash. Do you find this rewarding? How so?

10. Do you ever sleep?

11. The first Praystation was a visual image experience. What motivated you to evolve it to what it is today?

12. Tell us about your CD!

13. Do you still skate?

14. What is it that happens in a typical day that gives you a feeling of satisfaction when you go home at night?

15. You have trotted the globe over the last year speaking about Flash. What has been the most memorable thing that has happened through that experience?

16. If you could do one last project before you had to hang up your designer's cap, what would you want that project to be?

c2 CHAPTER

Flash deCONSTRUCTION

THE JUXT INTERACTIVE PROCESS

c2

CHAPTER
Flash deCONSTRUCTION
THE JUXT INTERACTIVE PROCESS

2.1 PLANNING AND PROCESS

You've heard the cliché "One hour of planning saves three hours of work" a thousand times, but nonetheless it is true. The numbers can be argued, but the bottom line is that planning in advance does save work. The customer service and creative process has been evolving for the past five years at Juxt, and although it is not perfect, it has been successful for us and our clients. The Juxt process was formulated by myself and Juxt cofounder, Steve Wages. We brought much of it with us from our previous field of experience in traditional architecture, and it has evolved over time to suit the unique needs of Flash development.

Through the years, we have found that the basic principle of our process, or methodology, is to provide manageable steps in the development and maintenance of large and small projects. In this book, we explain how and why we use these processes. It is our hope that you can take the basic principles of our process and tailor aspects of them to fit your particular projects and team scenarios.

Our principles establish boundaries for the Juxt team and client, and this helps them set expectations and build an understanding of the scope and focus of the project and the directions the project might take. The scope of a project refers to the purpose of the project and what the production of this project will involve. The focus of the project determines the central concept behind the project.

Communicating small concepts to a group is hard enough, let alone trying to communicate large, very abstract, and often innovative concepts. We're talking about concepts that have to be pulled together and developed by several people at a hyper-rapid pace and actually work. They not only have to work, they also have to

work in the way the client wants and expects them to. At times, it might seem irrelevant and tedious. However, in the long run, it is the process and structure that enable us to foster and protect our creativity.

At its core, the Juxt process is a system of communication. Because the web is a new marvel of communication, our process relies heavily on using the web. In conjunction with all the thinking and experimentation that went into the process, we spent a lot of time and energy developing a project management extranet.

An extranet is actually an intranet that's partially accessible to clients and contractors, provided they are given a username and password. Extranets differ from intranets because intranets reside behind firewalls, which only allow access to individuals within that particular organization. Extranets are becoming an increasingly popular way for business associates to exchange information.

The Juxt extranet is an amazingly effective tool that facilitates the process and communication for our projects (see Figure 2.1).

Although I can't give you ours, I can tell you from experience that the inclusion of this element in the process is worth the cost to buy or build it. This extranet can help you pull together the work of remote team members and clients (see Figure 2.2). It saves time, keeps you on budget, and adds the security of knowing that all the project information is just keystrokes away from anywhere with Internet access. If you're going to take the time to develop a thorough process, it makes sense to create a much-needed tool that facilitates the process in the most efficient way possible.

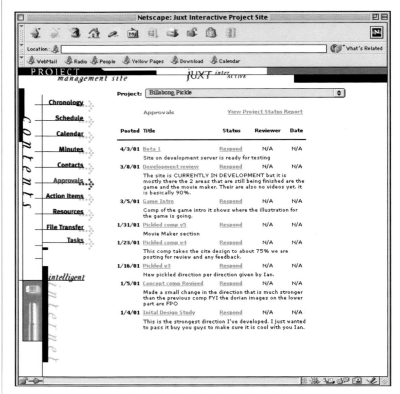

Figure 2.1   The Juxt interactive project management extranet.
Your extranet should be customized to your process.

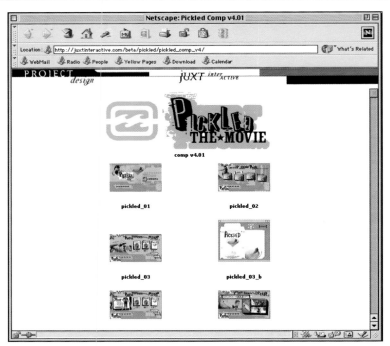

Figure 2.2   The remote project presentation interface. One of the key
features is being able to present work to the client remotely.

Here are some key features that your extranet should be capable of:

- Providing secure entry for the privacy of the client
- Logging all project-related communications, deliveries, and decisions
- Supplying important project development documents
- Providing all team members with contact information
- Documenting all deliverables and approvals
- Communicating critical path action items
- Providing a mechanism for presenting work

The extranet will become a key piece of your project, giving the internal team members, external consultants, and client access to up-to-the-minute information. It also gives each person the freedom to access project information at any time and from anywhere, provided the person has Internet access. The extranet also creates very accurate archive and project development documentation that is a great asset in the long run.

Some of you might be working for a small agency or an in-house team, and an extranet might seem a bit over the top for your needs. At Juxt, we developed the basic structure of our extranet when we were just a staff of three. This move was one of the smartest things we have ever done. It's not only an enormous time saver, it also helps out when we're confronted with one of those "he said, she said" incidents. Even for internal projects, you have to manage your work. The goal is to build a tool that does most of this for you in a consistent manner. Removing repetitive, redundant tasks from your life makes you more efficient and more effective.

In addition to the proper facilitation of a process, you will need to keep your eyes on the objectives and maintain flexibility in various situations that might arise. Each project and client is different. Does this mean we need a different process for every project? No, but we can modify an existing process for each project and client. As you carry out the project, you will need to decide if any of the steps are not necessary or don't make sense. Then communicate to the team that you are skipping these steps.

Communicating is very important; otherwise, chaos will soon ensue. I bring this point up for a very good reason. Many creative people fear or despise a highly structured work environment, so be sure to use good judgement and common sense, apply your creativity where it's called for, and keep it in check where it might create confusion or hinder the completion of the project.

2.2 THE JUXT INTERACTIVE TEAM STRUCTURE

In addition to the Juxt process, it's important to understand a little more about our team structure and how each player fits into the team.

Because Juxt is an interactive agency, Flash ActionScript has become an important tool that's frequently used in our project development. ActionScript, as you probably know, is the native programming language of Flash, and many designers feel compelled to master this language to remain competitive in their field. I interview a lot of people who are very stressed out over the fact that they are not ActionScript rocket scientists. They have strong design, UI, and motion graphics skills, but they can't talk to server-side scripts through XML from Flash. In today's world of Flash development, it is a very rare individual who possesses the skills of both an excellent designer and an ActionScript developer. These Flash-based developmental designers do exist, but they are rare. As a result, we have learned how to segment the process of design and development into several job functions. The lines between functions are often gray and blurred. Often, one person performs several functions. Although the function structure is not always adhered to, it provides us with a rough framework in which to work (see Figure 2.3).

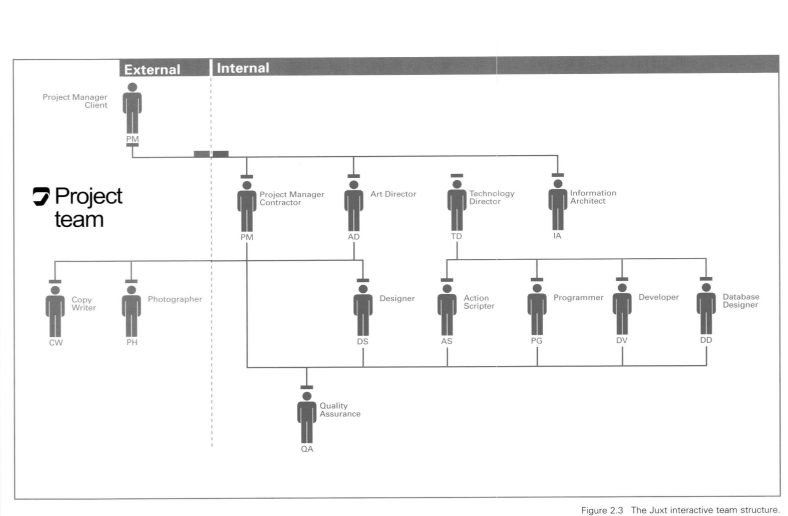

Figure 2.3   The Juxt interactive team structure.

2.2.1 JUXT INTERACTIVE TEAM BREAKDOWN AND FUNCTION

Before we can detail the Juxt process, we need to introduce you to the players who take part in that process. The following sections describe the various roles and responsibilities of Juxt Interactive team members.

2.2.1.1 PROJECT MANAGER—CONSULTANT

The project manager serves as the main catalyst between the project team and the client project manager. This project manager facilitates and directs the project team and the client to meet the end goal through communication and documentation. This person facilitates meetings, schedules, approvals, content development, asset acquisition, consultant management, and all other management aspects related to the project. He or she is also responsible for maintaining the project extranet.

2.2.1.2 PROJECT MANAGER—CLIENT

The project manager on the client side is the client liaison, who is responsible for giving approvals, delivering content, and ensuring that the client's needs and expectations are being met.

2.2.1.3 INFORMATION ARCHITECT

The information architect works with the creative project and technical leader, along with the client, to develop the architecture for the site's content. The architecture defines the information structure, content, and flow, along with the technology infrastructures of the site. Juxt's art director or technology director at times carries out this function.

2.2.1.4 CREATIVE DIRECTOR/ART DIRECTOR

The art director on the project is responsible for the creative design and the experience as a whole. The "experience" refers to the mood, feelings, and sensations, both visual and aural, impressed on the project's audience.

The creative director/art director develops the project vision and motivates, and communicates with the team to see that this vision is realized. The vision includes a balanced blend of the client's expectations and the designer's concepts. This vision results in a successful project conclusion. That is, a project that functions well, draws attention and excitement, and ultimately meets the clients needs. The art director/creative director starts off developing the creative strategy and storyboards and then works with the designers to lay out the entire project. Additionally, the creative director/art director is often involved in developing and creating motion graphics and sound design. It is a very hands-on role at Juxt.

2.2.1.5 TECHNOLOGY DIRECTOR/PROGRAMMING LEAD

The technology leader helps the art director conceptualize the interaction of the site and identifies the technology that needs to be developed. He often writes the technical and functional specifications and may also act as the programmer and database designer on the project.

2.2.1.6 DESIGNER

The designer works alongside the art director to develop the site's design. This individual often creates the Flash motion graphics and does light ActionScripting.

2.2.1.7 DEVELOPER

The developer extracts design layouts from FreeHand and converts them to Flash, optimizing and organizing the content, assets, symbols, and timeline. This individual is responsible for structuring the UI, while adding low-level ActionScript and developing the file structure for the project.

2.2.1.8 ACTIONSCRIPT PROGRAMMER

The ActionScript programmer is responsible for developing the interactivity for the user interface and dynamic content. Completing the high-level, hard-core ActionScripts and JavaScripts to interact with the HTML is part of this job function.

2.2.1.9 DATABASE DESIGNER

The database designer is responsible for developing the database structure, relationships, business rules, and stored procedures for the projects as needed.

2.2.1.10 PROGRAMMER

The programmer works with both the database designer and the ActionScript programmers to develop and integrate content management systems, XML, and/or dynamic applications. That is to say, the programmer develops web-based applications that enable content to be input into databases and that feed Flash with dynamic content.

2.2.1.11 QUALITY ASSURANCE ENGINEER/BETA TESTER

Beta tester(s) are external, objective, third-party people who go through the projects at the end with a fine-tooth comb and find the errors and bugs that need to be addressed. This individual or group is often overlooked but is very helpful for ensuring the quality of the experience and the work involved.

When all is said and done, the scope, budget, and available resources drastically affect the makeup of the team. For some sites, the team consists of three people who do all the listed functions. For other sites, one or more people are assigned to each function.

2.3 THE JUXT INTERACTIVE PROCESS

Okay, so now you know the players on the team, but how do we play the game? The Juxt process comes into the picture again. It is a framework to work from, but the process needs to be scaled according to the project and client (see Figures 2.4 and 2.5).

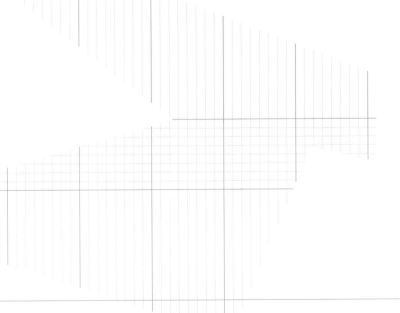

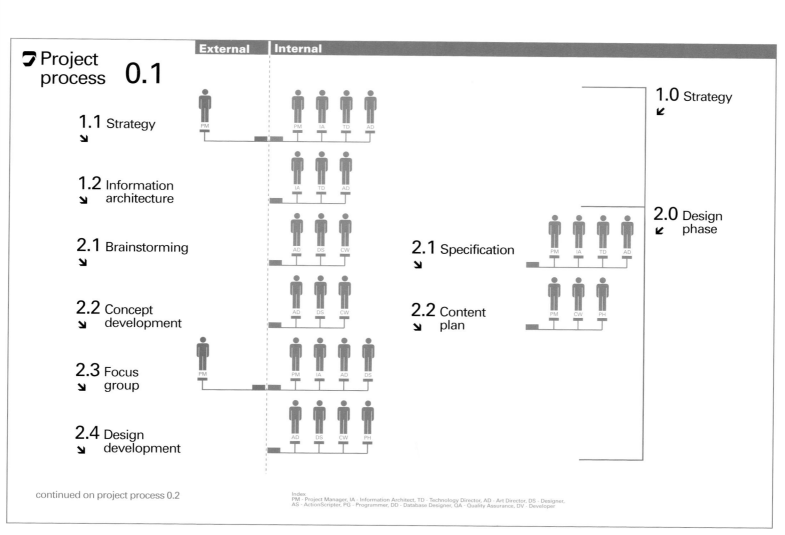

Project process 0.1

1.1 Strategy	**1.0** Strategy
1.2 Information architecture	**2.0** Design phase
2.1 Brainstorming	**2.1** Specification
2.2 Concept development	**2.2** Content plan
2.3 Focus group	
2.4 Design development	

External Internal

continued on project process 0.2

Index
PM - Project Manager, IA - Information Architect, TD - Technology Director, AD - Art Director, DS - Designer, AS - ActionScripter, PG - Programmer, DD - Database Designer, QA - Quality Assurance, DV - Developer

Figure 2.4 The Juxt interactive process.

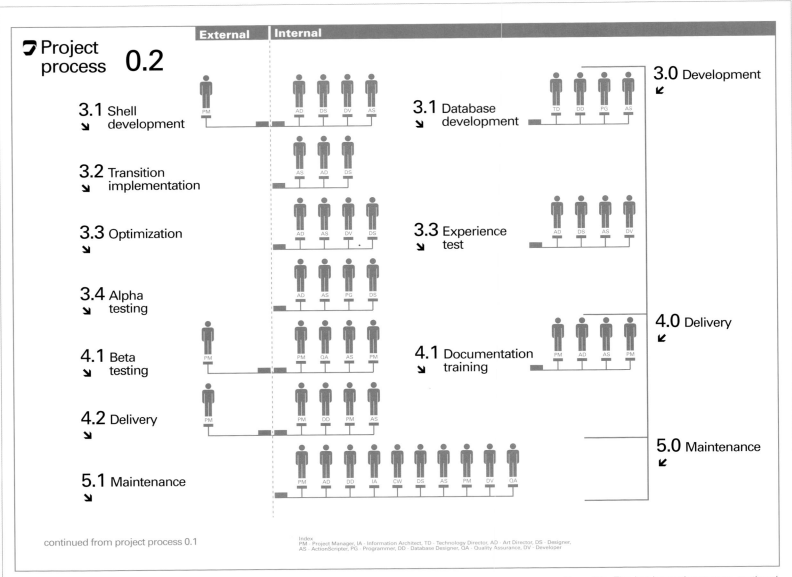

Project process **0.2**

3.0 Development

3.1 Shell development
PM   AD DS DV AS

3.1 Database development
TD DD PG AS

3.2 Transition implementation
AS AD DS

3.3 Optimization
AD AS DV DS

3.3 Experience test
AD DS AS DV

3.4 Alpha testing
AD AS PG DS

4.1 Beta testing
PM   PM QA AS PM

4.1 Documentation training
PM AD AS PM

4.0 Delivery

4.2 Delivery
PM   PM DD PM AS

5.1 Maintenance
PM AD DD IA CW DS AS PM DV QA

5.0 Maintenance

continued from project process 0.1

Index
PM - Project Manager, IA - Information Architect, TD - Technology Director, AD - Art Director, DS - Designer,
AS - ActionScripter, PG - Programmer, DD - Database Designer, QA - Quality Assurance, DV - Developer

Figure 2.5   The Juxt interactive process, continued.

2.3.1 STRATEGY

The process always begins with a strategy. *Strategy* is the step in which we analyze the client's needs, target market, assets, brand, competition, and objectives. The strategy process can vary from project to project and is based on the scale and scope of the project. A large strategy process can take up to a year and involves several key players such as the technology director, the creative director, and the information architect. Each team member is involved in the development of a series of documents that assist the team in building and executing the project. On the other end of the spectrum is the smaller project, which might just involve the creative director or the technology director sitting in a room with the client. These specialists review a number of strategic questions that are built to extract important pieces of information from the client. This enables us to build a project that meets our client's objectives.

2.3.2 INFORMATION ARCHITECTURE

The second step is information architecture. Here is where we define how the site's content will be broken down and look at primary navigation, flow, dynamic application interaction, content management, and site content. Flash technology enables non-destructive content transition, meaning that content can be loaded into a screen as needed, without ever leaving a particular screen. In other words, the original page content is not destroyed during the viewer's experience. It can remain visible while a new page loads. The Flash method of content transition is demonstrated in Chapter 3, "ActionScript Basics." This is a stark contrast to an HTML page, which relies on page reloads to change content. HTML pages are referred to as "destructive." Flash's nondestructive content transition augments the major difference between Flash movie clip architecture and traditional HTML page architecture.

After the architecture is in place, we start putting man hours down on paper and developing a time line or project schedule. This is the responsibility of the project manager, as is tracking progress against it.

Because Flash and HTML use different content transition models (as discussed previously), the content needs to be designed and communicated differently in Flash for clarity and scope. Because the Flash interaction model is far more flexible in terms of creativity, it also introduces a greater element of structural complexity into the project. Because of the technical complexities involved in developing a project, the information architecture stage becomes key to the successful outcome of any given project.

Figure 2.6 demonstrates a scheme for a typical HTML-based architecture. In the Andes Coffee Web Site storyboard, each page navigates from one page to the next, working within the restrictions of the HTML model. As you can see, it flows with balanced consistency from screen to screen, working within in the confines of HTML.

In contrast, the storyboard in Figure 2.7 demonstrates a project based on Flash architecture. In the web site project, screens open up with multilevel subcontent. The complexity of a project such as this involves a solid architectural plan up front to ensure that it flows correctly from all perspectives. The storyboard begins to bring the site architecture to life, depicting its content, navigation, dynamic application interaction, and how all of these elements will be managed.

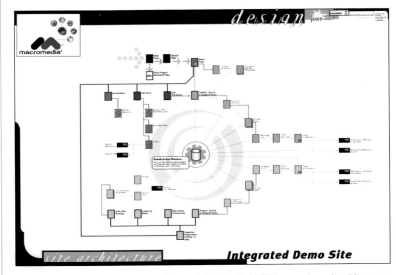

Figure 2.6 A typical HTML page–based architecture.

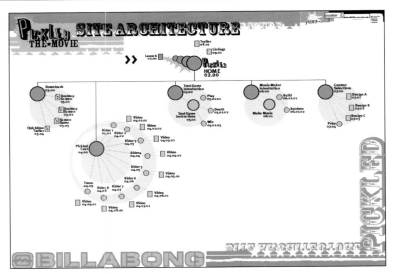

Figure 2.7 A Flash-based architecture created for the Pickled.tv project.

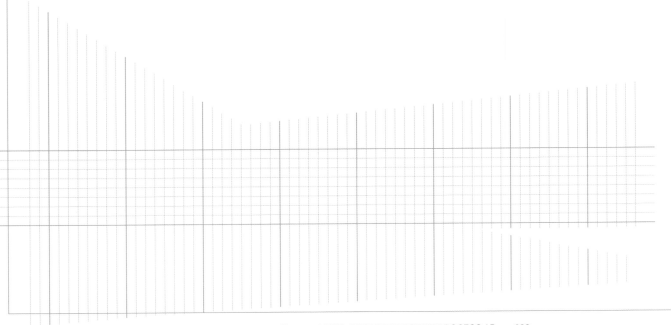

2.3.3 SPECIFICATION

From the information architecture phase, the Juxt process moves into the specification phase. Once the basic project architecture is defined, we need to hone in on a more detailed archetype of how things are going to work. This is where the specification stage becomes crucial. A specification is a document that outlines project components using wireframe diagrams and text, as shown in Figure 2.8. Three types of specifications may or may not be used, depending on the scope of the project. First, the most basic document is a content specification. A typical content specification documents a wireframe for each screen, laying out the navigation model and content alongside page objectives and simple interaction data.

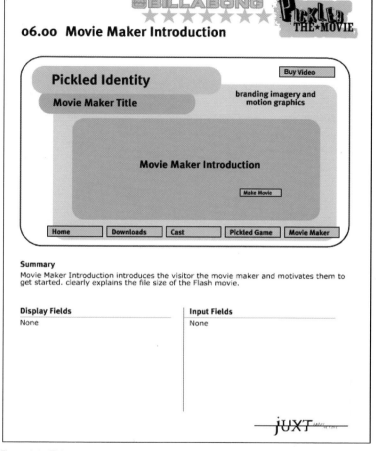

Figure 2.8   This content spec for Pickled.tv lays out content and navigation organization.

If the project is part of a more complex assignment, a functional specification is created instead of the content specification. The functional spec covers all the same bases as the content spec, in addition to all interactive behavior, fields, hidden fields, links, and expected behaviors of each screen. Interactive behavior includes any elements of the project that require user interaction to change the user experience. For example, a movie might load and play when a user mouses over a certain object. The user's experience is customized depending on how he reacts to the project. Figure 2.9 shows just the table of contents of such a spec. You can see from this that it is a much more involved document than the content spec.

The functional spec is much more complex and thoroughly explains the user experience that the site provides. If the project employs back-end database systems, a technology specification may be required. Because of its complexity, a technology spec is not for the weak of heart. This document covers the database structure, relationships, and business rules. A technology spec also communicates how the data coming from the front end is being processed on the back end, returned, and sent to the enterprise server. Specifications are key to the success of large and small projects. Obviously, they take time to develop and should be accounted for as part of the budget when bidding on a project. These specification documents work to ensure the quality of the project, and they can prove to be very helpful in keeping the team on track during development.

Throughout the strategy phase, extensive research is done regarding the client and its competition. This research is a crucial part of the concept development phase. This is carried out in two ways. First, we set up a series of meetings with key people in the client's organization to review their business and marketing plans. In addition, we draw as much information about their business and customers as we can through a series of structured interviews and debriefings.

1.1	**Background**	**5**
1.2	**Project Objectives**	**5**
2	**SCOPE & APPROACH**	**6**
2.1	**Scope**	**6**
2.2	**Approach**	**6**
3	**PAGE SPECIFICATIONS**	**7**
3.1	**Lot Map Page (Buyer's version)**	**7**
3.1.1	Objectives	7
3.1.2	Content	8
3.1.3	Navigation	8
3.1.4	Functional Behavior	8
3.1.5	Business Rules	8
3.1.6	Data	9
3.2	**Lot Map Selection Page (Customer Admin version)**	**10**
3.2.1	Objectives	10
3.2.2	Content	10
3.2.3	Navigation	11
3.2.4	Functional Behavior	11
3.2.5	Buttons	11
3.2.6		11
3.2.7	Business Rules	11
3.2.8	Lot Map Data	12
3.2.9	General Data	12
3.2.10	Lot Data	12
3.2.11	Customer Data	12
3.3	**Page Specification – Floor Plan Options**	**13**
3.3.1	Objectives	13
3.3.2	Content	14
3.3.3	Navigation	14
3.3.4	Functional Behavior	14
3.3.5	Buttons	14
3.3.6	Business Rules	14
3.3.7	Floor Plan Data	14
3.3.8	General Data	14
3.3.9	Floor Plan Data	14
3.3.10	Customer Data	15
4	**APPENDIX –**	**16**

Figure 2.9 The table of contents for a functional spec, done for one of our Shea Homes projects.

For the competition analysis, we have developed a web-based application that enables us to objectively rate the web sites of the company's competition. However, you don't need an application to do this; it can be done manually. It simply involves a process of assessing and reporting on the level of competence of the competitors' sites.

By conducting this research, you will get into the heads and hearts of your clients and learn who they are, what their brand is, what their brand values are, who they are talking to, how they've talked to them in the past, what kind of messaging is appropriate and inappropriate, and so on.

2.3.4 BRAINSTORMING
Once you know who your client is, you are ready for the brainstorming step. This involves getting together with the project design team to get the ideas flowing. Good brainstorming on a personal or corporate level is a key element of the creative design process. At least three or more people provide a good balance for generating and perfecting solid conceptual ideas. It is important for all the key players to have a solid understanding of the client's objectives and to be aware of the research results to keep the design focused. In this session, ideas are thrown out on the table for all to discuss. It's important to write the ideas down on paper or a white board. You want all ideas to flow because even bad ones might spark a good one around the corner.

When you've come up with some good ideas as a group, pick the best ones and start discussing them in depth to feel out their potential effectiveness. Usually the best ideas will rise to the top for the lead creative person to draw from. In the end, the leader should be empowered to make the final decision that all will stand behind, and he must do so respectfully. The respect issue is important. You don't want to carry resentment into a project because team members think that their ideas got railroaded.

2.3.5 CONCEPT DEVELOPMENT
The next step in conceptual development is visual studies, where we go in and develop physical design concepts and ideas that are developed and studied internally. We generally develop one to three directions, depending on the client. We prefer developing one concept because it allows us to focus and make one very strategic concept instead of several semistrategic concepts just for the sake of variety. This really depends on the nature of the project and the client. The concepts are generally rendered in FreeHand and Photoshop.

After ideas are perfected internally, they are pulled together to form a presentation to the client (see Figure 2.10).

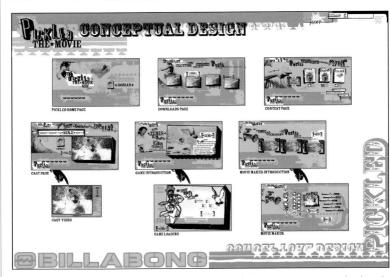

Figure 2.10   The Pickled web site design concept presentation board.

2.3.6   FOCUS GROUP

After the client has approved a concept, the next step is focus group feedback. It is always a good idea to take these early concepts and ideas out to the real world to test them. Bounce them off real people to get their feedback on whether you're successful or unsuccessful. You will often find that you hit the target with 80 to 90 percent of the concept, but that a small 10 to 20 percent of the details fail miserably. With a few small tweaks, you can develop a project that will achieve the client's objectives by having users respond appropriately.

There are marketing companies that specialize in testing focus groups. They give you the option to do a paper walkthrough, in which you print out your screens on presentation boards for the group to walk through (or navigate through). If the client can afford to do it right, you can build a prototype for the group to walk through on a computer. You supply a list of strategic questions and brief the moderator on how the prototype works and how it needs to be presented. This is crucial because the moderator can drastically affect the focus group if he or she misrepresents the project.

Then you sit behind a one-way mirror and eat nachos while watching the focus group. This experience is very good for designers because it gives them a much better understanding of the way users think.

If the client doesn't want to cough up the money for formal testing, do it informally. For example, show it to other people in the office who are not working on the project to get their valuable feedback.

Ultimately, it's all about ensuring that what you've developed is as close to being on target as possible.

2.3.7 DESIGN/DEVELOPMENT

Next comes design and development. Here, we take the conceptual design that's been approved by the client, add the feedback from the focus group, and then begin to lay out all the interfaces within the site. The actual pieces of the project begin to take shape at this point. We typically lay out the project in FreeHand as opposed to laying out these interfaces directly in Flash. Then, once the layout has been prepared and completed in FreeHand, it is brought into Flash, where the project begins to come to life with motion, interactivity, and other complex components. Working initially in FreeHand enables us to complete the layout more rapidly, get approval from the client, and then turn around and convert the FreeHand documents into Flash very quickly and efficiently. We examine this part of the process in depth in the next chapter.

During the design/development phase, the key members of the internal team come together to discuss interactive concepts and how they'll go about executing them. The meeting typically raises technological issues relating to the project that result in proof of concept prototyping. In a proof of concept prototype, we actually build small pieces of the project and check to make sure they will work or respond in the way we had envisioned.

2.3.8 CONTENT PLAN

Following the design and technical specification phases, we develop a *content plan*, which is a set of milestones and delivery dates for key elements of content, as necessary for development of the site (see Figure 2.11). These consist of photography, copy, illustrations, or any aspect that completes the site. It's very important to know how content will be generated and delivered so that the site can be developed and delivered on schedule.

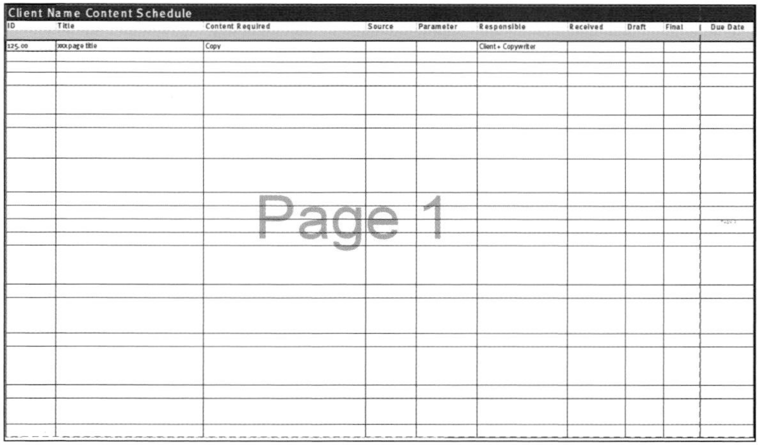

Client Name Content Schedule

ID	Title	Content Required	Source	Parameter	Responsible	Received	Draft	Final	Due Date
125.00	xxx page title	Copy			Client + Copywriter				

Page 1

Figure 2.11 The Juxt standard content plan is available for download on this book's site.

To manage content development and delivery, it is a good idea to develop your own tool that presents a clear picture of what is needed and when it is needed. It should be easy to update and, if something is late, should show what impact this will have on the schedule. If you prefer the keep-it-simple approach to life, Excel spreadsheets will do the trick. If your choice is to use the power of the computer and your information in a more complex way, you can use a tool like Microsoft Project or build your own database application. This is done by the project manager, who is responsible for communicating the ongoing needs to the client and getting the necessary assets to the team.

2.3.9 SHELL DEVELOPMENT

The next step is shell development. *Shell development* is taking our FreeHand layouts and converting them into Flash files. The designer or developer does this. The artwork in the FreeHand files is taken into Flash, turned into symbols, structured, and organized in layers and movie clips. In the next chapter, we will go into this in greater detail. Motion design, database development, and ActionScripting occur in tandem with the shell design. Motion design typically is done by the designer or art director, and heavier ActionScripting is done by the developers and programmers. Simultaneously, the database development is done on the back end by the lead programmer or database designer.

2.3.10 DATABASE DEVELOPMENT

Database development involves laying out the tables in the database and creating the relationships for the back end system if there is a content management system. This system must also be connected to a layer of middle-ware using JSP, ASP, ColdFusion, and often Generator. The middle-ware acts as a courier running between the database layer, where it gathers data, and the Flash layer, where it packages it up appropriately for Flash to display. We will cover how this works in Chapter 7, "Billabong-USA.com—Flash Content Management."

2.3.11 TRANSITION IMPLEMENTATION

The next step of the process is transition implementation. Often, in a large project, pieces are being developed abstractly and separately from one another. Several different people are working individually on their own piece of the pie. It is not until you are nearing the very end of developing a section, or sometimes the whole project, that you actually get to feel the whole experience. So, at this point, we develop the transitions, moving from one section to another section or one page to another page to determine how the motion of the transition works out. In other words, we need to make sure all components of the project move from one screen to another in a fluid manner. Some of this may be started in the motion graphic phase of development and then be finalized in transition implementation, until perfected.

Transition implementation involves setting up the .swf files to load into the project when the user clicks the buttons. There is a natural transition that needs to be developed as content is brought into view and taken away. We will cover much of this in later chapters.

2.3.12 OPTIMIZATION

Following transition implementation, we go through the optimization step. As the project takes full shape, the team takes a conscious look at the files being created while double-checking the actual file size against the required or desired file-size limits. Optimization should be addressed at the project's inception and throughout the entire process. Unfortunately, some optimization issues don't surface until pieces are fully integrated. This is the time to look for things that we can clean up or lighten up, or at the very least, the time to identify bloated elements that we overlooked in the development process. Optimization techniques are covered in Chapter 4, "Juxt Interactive Development Process."

2.3.13 EXPERIENCE TEST

The next and final piece in the actual creative development phase is the experience test. The art director typically sits down and walks through the experience that's been created, double-checking to ensure that it matches the intended vision. In the heat of development and deadlines, this step is often overlooked. This can result in missed opportunities or elements that weren't executed the way they should have been or as they were imagined. With a team of many people working hard to make their pieces solid while trying to meet deadlines, communication can be less than perfect. This means that things fall through cracks, small inconsistencies exist, or the "now" interactive system response is not good enough for an idea to work in the real world. When you try to push the envelope, from time to time it can burst open, and you need to account for this in your process. It is important to budget time to implement the final touches that make the difference between a good project and a great one.

2.3.14 ALPHA PHASE

The next step is the alpha phase. In this phase, we finally have a product that's built. Now we can go through our product internally—take a walk-through and check it. Everyone on the team goes through the project to check it internally, to feel it out and make sure it's working. This quickly leads into the beta stage. Whereas alpha typically deals with smoothing out some of the design edges, beta focuses on the heavy technology, getting in there and making sure the project works.

The alpha testing greatly depends on the complexity of the project. If you have been developing a project with several people over several months, you should plan a fair amount of time because nothing ever works the first time. Plan at least a week, maybe two, depending on complexity. If it is a one–person, one-week project, most likely alpha will be hours and beta may be a day. You want to try to pick up major, obvious bugs so that you don't look like an idiot when you release it out to beta.

2.3.15 BETA TESTING

The next phase is testing the front end, back end, and server environment. Outside the project team, coordinators need to bang on the site: checking that things aren't tripping over each other, uploading content, and evaluating how it uploads, serves, displays, and interacts. In beta two, which follows beta one after revisions have been created, the site or project needs to be tested again.

Beta is a tedious process, but it's the most crucial phase for you and your client to make sure what you deliver is actually going to work and work well. Web development is typically rapid-paced, allowing for missteps and errors/omissions in development; as a result, the timetable and budget are much smaller than in the world of application development. Another aspect that must be contended

with is the browser environment, which is very volatile and unpredictable. The project must be tested by our staff extensively on all browsers, including both old and new releases of these browsers and in multiplatform environments. Because Netscape and Explorer are the most popular browsers, particular emphasis is placed on them.

Microsoft frequently releases rebuilds of its browsers, often on a weekly basis. The result of this is that unavoidable and undetected bugs not found in the beta process can go out with the completed site. You should make sure to discuss this with your clients openly, before you launch the site, so that they are prepared for any glitches that might arise. The key to making these discussions work is to set the client's expectation level to the reality of working with the web and not the assumed reality that all work paid for is perfect. Should your client demand absolute perfection, they will have to budget for it, and you will need to bring in QA consultants who will beat the site to death in ways you never imagined possible.

Make sure your client knows that this can be a costly venture. Often it's a good idea to propose soft launches to your client. A soft launch is similar to a site going live, but you only announce it to a core group of trusted people. The feedback from this group helps you determine whether the site is solid at this point. Then you can move to hard launching with public relations and the other planned promotions.

2.3.16 DELIVERY

Delivery very much depends on the client's environment, how the server is set up, and whether you have a testing server in-house that matches the client's server environment. If you're working on a smaller project, it's just a matter of uploading files onto the FTP server. The absolute best-case scenario is to do beta testing in the client's final server environment or through a perfectly matched staging server. Delivery is a phase that shouldn't be overlooked. It should be thoroughly thought out, and you should have a process in place for delivering projects.

2.3.17 DOCUMENTATION

Documentation, prior to or immediately following delivery if the client is creating content for the actual delivery, defines the documentation phase. This involves the creation of documents used to communicate to the client how to develop and upload the content into the site for launch, as well as long-term site maintenance information. For Juxt, this documentation involves doing online style guides for the client to use in creating the visual assets that will be used throughout the site's lifecycle (see Figure 2.12).

Once you have completed the documentation, you need to bring in the content team and teach it how to use the assets you've created. Following the launch of the site, the content implementation for the future life of the site should be planned if it hasn't already been done. The content implementation for a developer is a key part of the process, making sure the vision of the site is carried out through future content inclusion, expansion, or evolutions.

No web site should remain idle and unattended. It should always grow and evolve. Content implementation might start out as standardized and evolve into a redesign of the site some 18 months later. It is very important that the tools for your client be built with a site update in mind from the beginning.

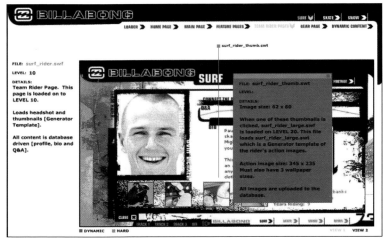

Figure 2.12   The Billabong-USA.com style guide micro site enables the client to generate the content so that it works perfectly with the content management system.

2.3.18 MAINTENANCE

The web is ever-evolving, and people want and need fresh content to make a web site useful. Part of the strategy phase involves determining just how the site will evolve and who will be responsible for that evolution.

We build content management systems that allow much of the content to be updated by the clients themselves. But we also define areas that will need to change over time, and we plan additional phases for the future. Business is a dynamic thing. It responds to the market and its customers to maximize profitability. Knowing this, you should be working in partnership with your clients for the long term, helping them to continually evolve and perfect their sites to help maximize marketing potential. These changes can range from the introduction of elaborate new features, to changes in products and promotions, to simply changing content on a site that was promoting something that was to come (to make it reflect on the last event and prepare visitors for the next such event). It all depends on what the client's objectives are. Rarely will you want to just walk away for good. Plan for this in the beginning so that the client is prepared to make the project a continued success.

2.4 SUMMARY

You now have an overview of our process. Again, this process is scalable to a particular project's needs, uniqueness, scope, and the client's expectations. For some projects, we'll go through all the tasks defined in this chapter. For other projects, we might go through half the tasks enumerated and described for you. It always depends on the particular project's needs.

It's always important to keep your mind focused on the ultimate objective. It's also important to realize that these things you're using—planning, design, technology—are just tools employed to develop a project that will meet the client's objectives. Sometimes you might find that the objective is more functionality based and requires deep technology, with lots of people having to work together. This, of course, requires very clear and concise communication, with planning as one of the most important tools. Other projects might be more on the loose side, design oriented and experimental. In these cases, too much planning up front might put an unnecessary box of constraints around the creative solutions that could be discovered in the process of development. It's important to recognize this fact and take it into each project with you so that you build a process that serves as an infrastructure and not a box. It's the series of paths available in your travel down the roads of the project that will help you make progress. It is not necessarily an isolated bridge, however; many options and avenues are made available to you. You can take the freeway, the highway, the road, or quite possibly go off the road completely.

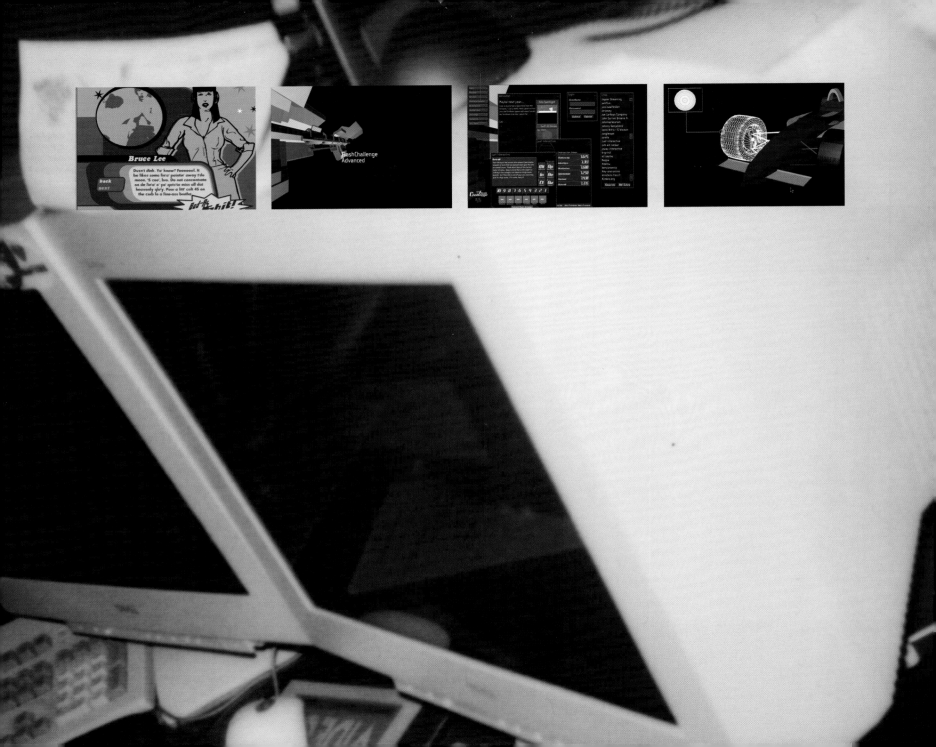

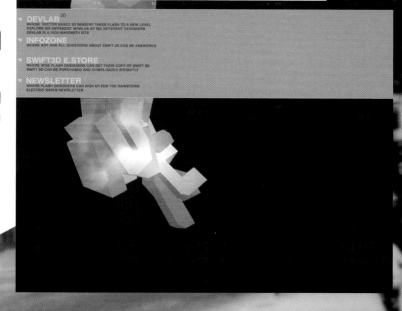

JAMES BAKER

James Baker Interview
by Todd Purgason

Introduction
www.wddg.com

I distinctly remember stumbling across the WDDG web site years ago. It was one of those times when, after working until midnight, I wanted to chill out with a surfing session. This site was very different from the Gabocorp mania (in reference to the cult classic gabocorp.com site) that was going on in Flash design at the time. There was a really odd mix of work on the site, and this was before personal sites became the force they are today.

I was intrigued by this site because I couldn't figure out if it was a company, an individual, or a teacher. Shortly after that, the WDDG began to produce some really solid client work, and as a result, I got it all figured out.

I first met James Baker at the first Flash Forward 2000 in San Francisco. Since then, I've been participating on lists and keeping in touch with him. The WDDG, in my book, has given the web some of the most solid commercial Flash work around. James's approach to design has always been to push the envelope and explore. This has been a driving force behind WDDG's many projects. We always know there are great things in the URLs he sends us to check out. This is a tribute to his commitment to doing it right and always working beyond the mundane for a more creative approach.

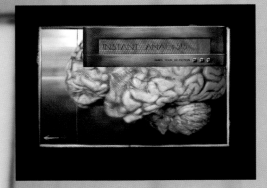

Teaser from the Interview

TP: So, we're here with James Baker from the WDDG. So, who is James Baker?

JB: I don't know. That's a really rough question to ask some-body. I like to think I'm just some guy who likes to make cool stuff and who appreciates, you know, likes design and likes technology, and that's about it. It's such a hard question to ask somebody.

TP: I'll buy that. I haven't asked myself that question, so I'm letting myself off easy.

JB: I'm not a very introspective person. I tend to do a lot, but I don't really think a lot about it.

To hear the rest of James's answer to this question, as well as his answers to the following questions, please go to the Inspirations section of the book's site at www.JUXTinteractive.com/deCONSTRUCTION.

QUESTIONS

02. If you were a fish/sea creature, what would you be?

03. What CD or mp3 is in your player right now?

04. What is your definition of design?

05. What was your very first impression of Flash?

06. If you were walking down the street and came across John Gay and Jakob Nielsen engaged in a fistfight, what would you do?

07. Were you serious when you came up with the WDDG name, or was it just a joke that stuck around?

08. You guys kicked out some great commercial work this year; previously most of your work was personal. Did you grow a lot?

09. You are a self-taught designer and programmer. Which do you enjoy more?

10. Okay, on the early WDDG, there was this very long, freaky movie made from animated still images. What was that thing about?

11. The new WDDG site is a portal scrool Flash site. What was your thinking and motivation on this?

12. What project in your history have you been the most proud of?

13. Most of your work is microsite stuff. Is this your niche, or are you working on some bigger, full-scale projects that we don't know about?

14. What is it that happens in a typical day that gives you a feeling of satisfaction when you go home at night?

15. What is your vision for the WDDG?

16. If you could do one last project before you had to hang up your designer's cap, what would you want that project to be?

c3

CHAPTER
Flash CONSTRUCTION
ACTIONSCRIPT BASICS

c3 CHAPTER
Flash deCONSTRUCTION
ACTIONSCRIPT BASICS

Before we start deconstructing our work, some of the fundamental basics of Flash ActionScript need to be covered. These basics include the movie clip structure, talking to movie clips, loading external movies, variables, functions, arrays, and loops.

3.1   MOVIE CLIP ARCHITECTURE

One of the fundamental components of Flash 5 interactivity is the movie clip structure. Similar in nature to other object-oriented programming techniques, movie clips are important because of their incredible power, flexibility, and scalability. If you think of movie clips as individual objects and ActionScript as a voice that talks to those objects with the main timeline as the placeholder for objects, you will better understand the nature of movie clip architecture. In the earlier days of Flash development, most work was done on the main timeline. If you wanted a new image to appear on screen, you would put an action or event on the main timeline that would jump to a frame further down on that main timeline. This, however, was a very limiting process. With myriad interactive options available, oftentimes you would find yourself building thousands of sets of frames that would need to be called in order to achieve your objective. To expand Flash's interactive capabilities in Flash 3, Macromedia introduced the movie clip. The movie clip is a symbol that has its own timeline and can be given an individual identifier or name, called an instance. This is a simple yet very powerful concept. Older versions of Flash would instruct a playhead to move down the main timeline to a labeled frame and play. Now you can move to a label inside any movie clip on the stage that can contain visuals, motion graphics, sound, or just ActionScript.

A primitive form of the movie clip has existed all along in the form of button technology. Buttons have their own timeline, which consists of four frames: the up frame, the over frame, the down frame, and the hit frame. Movie clips give you tremendous control of the direction your movie takes—so much control, in fact, that the whole Flash authoring model is now built around movie clips. In the button metaphor, you're rolling over a button and evoking an action. The power of interactivity can be exponentially increased when complex movie clips are created that have lots of frames and labels contained within them. Certain user events can call those movie clips, which can call other movie clips, go to certain frames, and carry out certain functions. It becomes much more complex and deep because a movie clip can have visual elements, sound, or only ActionScript. Movie clips with just ActionScript are referred to as engine scripts or sometimes action clips. They act like a function in which you're just sending variables and data to that movie clip, and all that exists in that movie clip is the script that runs.

In summary, movie clips are based on the following concept: Objects (movie clips) can be talked to individually and they can talk to each other. Movie clips free you from the boundaries of a timeline where everything must be fixed in stone.

3.1.1   DISSECTING A MOVIE CLIP

To further understand the movie clip's architecture, let's take a look at a movie called tunes_mc.fla (see Figure 3.1).

In this movie, there are two symbols on the main timeline. The first is a movie clip. Its instance name is set to tunes, and its symbol name is tunes_mc. The second symbol is the punch button. If the tunes movie clip is opened, we can study the movie clip's timeline.

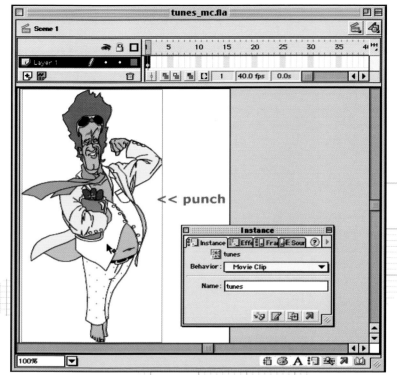

Figure 3.1 The tunes_mc movie.

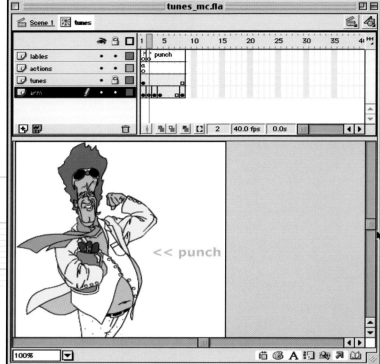

Figure 3.2 The tunes_mc movie clip-editing mode.

There are two labels on the timeline of the tunes_mc movie clip. The first label is set to "off" and has a stop. The second one, frame 2, is set to "punch" (see Figure 3.2). Now, if we look at the button script, we are talking to Tunes when the button is released. The script reads as follows (see Figure 3.3):

```
on (release) {
    tunes.gotoAndPlay ("punch");
}
```

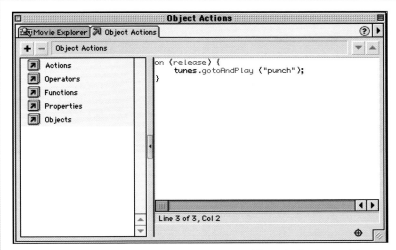

Figure 3.3 The script for the punch button.

specified SWF file and load it wherever you've indicated in the script without having to unload any movies. This enables you to develop very large, complicated sites without ever reloading the HTML page. This eliminates that destructive gap of experience traditionally associated with HTML development.

Let's open the Flash file called movieClip_tellTarget.fla (see Figure 3.4) to see how it works.

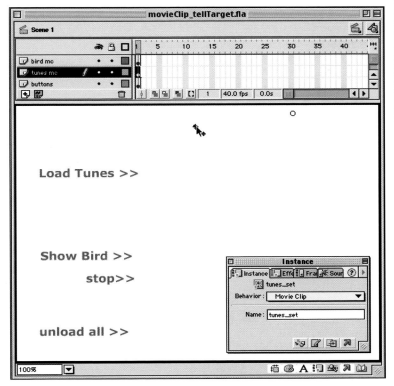

Figure 3.4 The movie called movieClip__tellTarget.fla.

When you click the punch button (on release), it tells the movie clip with the instance name of tunes to go to the label, punch, on its own timeline and play.

This concept is initially a bit confusing. Once you become comfortable with it, you'll discover that it's really very simple and provides a great method for organizing your interactive movie assets. The main timeline of an interactive project can become very cumbersome if it's packed with a lot of frames, instances, and labels. By organizing files into movie clips, you've created a logical order and structure that's easier to develop, update, and maintain.

3.1.2 LOADING EXTERNAL MOVIES

So, moving on, we advance a step further by taking these movie clips and putting them outside our Flash file. What do I mean by "outside our Flash file?" Well, it's kind of like calling an HTML page into a frameset without the limitations imposed on framesets. With Flash movies, you can click a button and hit a frame event, or any other event that can call an ActionScript. It can then grab the

This file has a main timeline that has one frame, which holds eight movie clips and four buttons. The movie clips are invisible (the first frame on the movie clips timeline is empty), and as such, all you see is the little white dot on the stage. Why they chose a white dot for this purpose, I have no idea.

The first movie clip placed to the upper left has an instance name of tunes_set. The movie clip to the right of that has an instance name of bird_set. If we look at the action set on the Load Tunes button, we see the following code (see Figure 3.5):

```
on (release) {
    loadMovie ("tunes_mc.swf", "_root.tunes_set");
}
```

This script is saying to load the movie named tunes_mc.swf into the tunes_set instance.

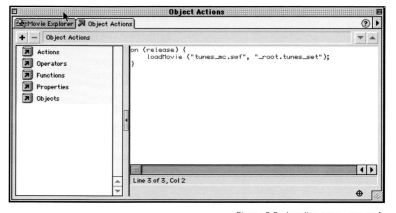

Figure 3.5   Loading tunes_mc.swf.

We address anything that's set on the root (basically the master timeline) by calling it _root. The dot is like a slash when you're calling a directory structure in HTML, except this dot is referring to the movie clip structure in the Flash file.

Looking at the Show Bird button, we see a script similar to the previous button, calling, on release (of the button), load movie, bird_mc.swf into the _root.bird_set (see Figure 3.6).

```
on (release) {
    loadMovie ("bird_mc.swf", "_root.bird_set");
}
```

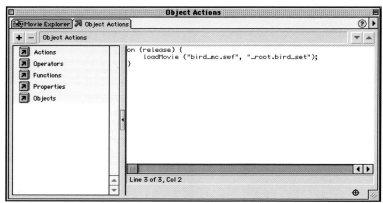

Figure 3.6   The script on the Show Bird button.

Now let's take a look at the file in action by opening movieClip_tellTarget.swf and clicking on the Load Tunes button. The tunes movie that we're working with, tunes_mc, loads into the target movie clip tunes_set. If I were to click the punch button (which lives inside the tunes movie clip, tunes_mc, external to the main timeline), I would still have control over the actions within that movie clip by talking to it internally.

Next click on the Show Bird button to see the seagull flying. Now let's click on the stop button to stop the bird's flying motion, as shown in Figure 3.7.

We're basically telling bird_mc (which is the file bird_mc.swf) to go to the label stopBird and stop (see Figure 3.8). Because this label is in a different timeline, we have to give the script the correct address to the movie clip to which we are talking, which is _root.bird_set.bird. In this script, we're talking to a movie clip that is loaded externally, outside of the movie clip. This is a good example of the ActionScript dot syntax structure used to address different movie clips at different levels; this is a very powerful feature in Flash.

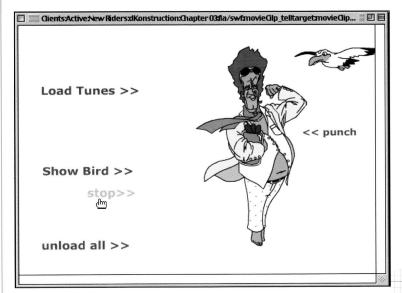

Figure 3.7 The stop button that stops the frames labeled stopBird.

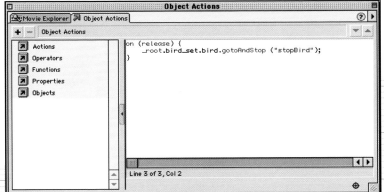

Figure 3.8 The script on the stop button.

The Show Bird button lives externally to tunes_mc, as opposed to the punch button, which lives externally to that movie clip and internally to the main timeline. So, from the main timeline, we can talk to the movie clips that are loaded from external files, or we can talk to those movie clips from within themselves. Let's look at the code:

```
on (release) {
    _root.bird_set.bird.gotoAndStop ("stopBird");
}
```

In addition, if you click the unload all button, all the movie clips disappear. Let's take a look at the code on this button, shown in Figure 3.9.

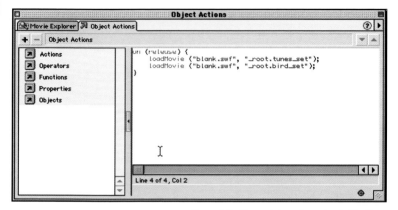

Figure 3.9   The script on the unload all button.

When the actions on the unload all button are examined, we see an on (release), loadMovie called .swift_root.tunes_set, and we see basically the same line of code for bird_set below that.

```
on (release) {
    loadMovie ("blank.swf", "_root.tunes_set");
    loadMovie ("blank.swf", "_root.bird_set");
}
```

When you examine these movies, you begin to see the simple but potentially powerful nature of the movie clip architecture. In addition, controlling movie clips can be a simple, straightforward process if your project is organized and well documented.

3.2   THE LANGUAGE OF VARIABLES

Variables are containers of information. They can hold many different kinds of data, such as the name of the user, an email address, or even a calculated value used to control a Flash movie. Variables can be stored in your movie and called on at your discretion. Variables can also exist simply as temporary containers that disappear from memory after their purpose in the movie is completed. And, just like their name implies, variables can change.

Variables are the key to creative and masterful ActionScript programming. If interactivity is an important element of your design, it's important to master all the variable basics. To further your knowledge, practice using them. You'll find endless uses for variables if you put your mind to it.

This section covers the basics of creating and controlling variables. In subsequent chapters, you will see many examples of variables in use.

3.2.1 VARIABLE BASICS

When using variables, there is a standard set of rules you need to keep in mind:

- Variables must always have a name.
- Names must begin with an alpha or an underscore character.
- Names can only contain alpha, numeric, and underscore characters (no spaces or punctuation).
- Variables live within something called a "scope." Variable scopes are explained in the next section.
- Variables are unaffected by frames. This means that once a variable is created in a timeline, it lives on into future frames. A variable can be called on other timelines in a movie by addressing its path within a script, using the Flash dot-syntax (_root.myClip.myData) or the Flash 4 syntax (/myClip/:myData).
- Variables contain several different types of data (check out the Flash typeof() function). A noteworthy feature of ActionScript is that you don't have to tell Flash which type of data to use. It figures it out all by itself. The following are the types of variables you can create:
    - string
    - number
    - boolean
    - object
    - movieclip

3.2.2 ABOUT VARIABLE SCOPE

In large and complex programs, keeping track of a multitude of variables is an awesome task. It's difficult for a programmer to ensure that variable names are unique throughout so that different parts of the program don't inadvertently overwrite the contents of some commonly named variable being used. It is for this very reason that *variable scope* exists. In ActionScript, variable scope addresses this problem so that each variable remains unique unto itself.

To better understand the concept of variable scope, consider the analogy of a city with an unusual town ordinance. Let's imagine that, in this city, there was a strange rule in which only one person that went by a certain name could live there. Anyone else living in this city with the same name would be forced to move out of the city limits or to change his or her name to ensure that each name was unique. Because everyone living in this city has a totally different name, there is never any confusion as to who's who. Such is the case with variables. Because we don't want to confuse which variable is which, we create little cities (scopes) that have a similar rule to the city in our analogy. The residents in these little cities (scopes) all have a unique set of names (variable names). If there is a JohnSmith in one city and a JohnSmith in another city, that's okay. These are two different people leading two different lives. Similarly, every scope has a different set of variable names.

Each movie (*.swf) has its own timeline. Additionally, each movie clip has its own timeline. We're in luck. Timelines, no matter where they reside, have their own scope. So you could have a variable called nTimeRunning in the main movie (_root) and another by the same name living in a movie clip called mcNavigator. In this scenario, our variables are residing in different "cities" (scopes), so it's okay that they have the same name. To reference these variables that live in different "cities" (scopes), the following syntax would be used: _root.nTimeRunning and _root.mcNavigator.nTimeRunning. Thus, their addresses are different, but their names are the same.

3.3 LOOPS

By its very nature, programming is full of repeating patterns. Writing repetitive chunks of commands over and over is bad form, is inefficient, and can cause problems in the form of bugs and increased difficulty in making changes later.

There are two ways to streamline repetitive blocks of code in Flash ActionScript. The first technique uses loops. The second uses functions. First let's focus on loops.

In ActionScript, a *loop* is a command that tells Flash to run a set of commands over and over. A loop can be set up to run a certain number of times, or it can loop until a certain event occurs.

There are four kinds of loops in Action Script: while, do...while, for, and for...in. Table 3.1 explains the differences between these loops.

Loop Type and Syntax	Most Common Usage
while (<condition>) {...}	Loops that keep running **so long as** the <condition> remains *true*. For example, keep looping as long as the _x property of a movie clip is less than 95.
do {...} while (<condition>)	Loops that keep running until the <condition> becomes *false*. For example, keep looping until the _x property of a movie clip is less than 95.
for (<init>;<condition>; <count>) {...}	Loops that **count** from a starting number to an ending number. For example, counting from 1 to 10.
for <item> in <object> {...}	Loops that step through the **contents of an object or an array**. (Arrays are covered later in this chapter. Objects are covered in Chapter 9, "Movie Maker.")

Table 3.1 *Loop commands in ActionScript.*

The following example shows how you might use a simple while loop. This script can be tested in the Flash authoring mode, viewing the results of the trace() command in the Flash Output window (see Figure 3.10).

```
var count = 0;
while (++count < 10) {
    trace("while loop: count=" + count);
}
```

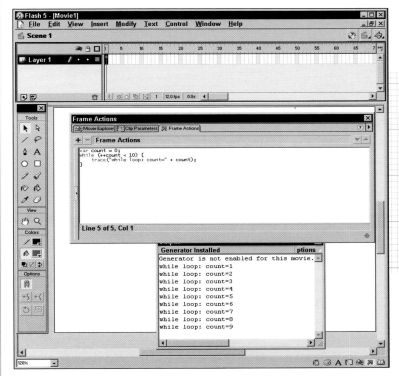

Figure 3.10   The trace results in the Output window of a simple while loop.

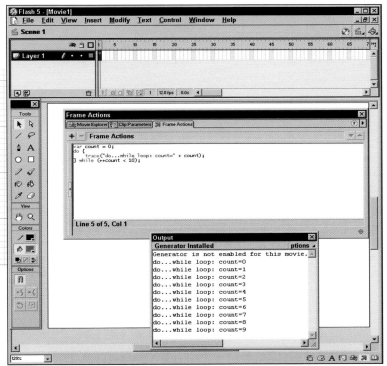

Figure 3.11   The trace results in the Output window of a simple do...while loop.

The same effect can be achieved with the do...while loop as follows (see Figure 3.11):

```
var count = 0;
do {
    trace("do...while loop: count=" + count);
} while (++count < 10);
```

The only difference between the while and do...while loops is that the while loop checks the condition in parenthesis before executing the commands in the curly braces, but the do...while loop checks the condition afterward. Notice the difference in output between the preceding examples. One shows a count of 1–9, while the other shows a count of 0–9.

Both loops do a fine job. However, since most modern programming languages have a while loop and only some have a do...while loop, most programmers prefer the basic while loop.

Also, if you haven't seen the ++ operator in use before, it is really handy for loops. This is the increment operator, meaning that it adds a 1 to the variable with which it's used. For example, it is much shorter to write count++ than to write the following line of script: count = count + 1.

The following for loop example does the same thing as the while loop example.

```
var count;
for (count = 1; count <= 10; ++count) {
    trace("for loop: count=" + count);
}
```

Inside the parentheses of the for loop are three sections separated by semicolons (;). From the left, these three sections perform the following functions:

- **Initialization.** This gets run once, just before the loop goes to work.
- **Condition.** This expression is checked every time, just before the loop runs the contents of the command block. If the loop finds that the condition is *true*, it will continue to execute the contents. Statements of truth (a.k.a. Boolean expressions) tend to come in the form of comparisons like $x > y$ or *yourName ==* "*joe cool.*"
- **Counter.** This gets run at the end of each loop iteration but before the condition is checked.

The for...in loop is used differently than any of the other loops previously mentioned. Its main purpose is to find every property in a movie clip, object, or array and loop through it. Here's an example:

```
var oImageFiles = new Object;
oImageFiles.thumbnail = "thumbnail_mugshot.jpg";
oImageFiles.small = "sm_mugshot.jpg";
oImageFiles.medium = "md_mugshot.jpg";
oImageFiles.large = "lg_mugshot.jpg";
for (sAttribute in oImageFiles) {
    trace( sAttribute + "=" + oImageFiles[sAttribute] );
}
```

As you can see, using loops can save a lot of time and can simplify scripting. Simplifying scripts always helps eliminate errors. Looping statements are particularly useful when you need to perform an action a specific number of times or until a condition changes.

3.4 DECLARING FUNCTIONS

Like loops, functions help reduce repetitive programming. Functions, however, serve a different purpose than loops do and are much more powerful in their capabilities. Functions are the key to flexible, maintainable, and understandable programming. Because the idea of functions can seem like a foreign concept the first time you learn about them, a familiar analogy will be used to help you understand what they are and how they're used.

When you order a cheeseburger at a fast-food restaurant, how do you place the order? Do you tell the clerk how to perform each step of the burger-making process in order to cook it and fetch it for you? Or do you just give him the bare essential information that he needs to accomplish the task? "Cheeseburger with extra cheese, hold the onions and pickles," is more likely what you might say. The restaurant employees know the procedure for making cheese-burgers, along with any exceptions to the rule of how to make a "normal" cheeseburger.

Jumping back to ActionScript, why would you want to repeat an entire procedure such as checking to see if a mouse is hovering over a movie clip in several different places throughout your movie? It's the same procedure each time. Just like the clerk at the fast-food restaurant, you can train Flash to do what you want it to, and when Flash takes the order, it knows how to complete the rest of the task.

This is exactly what functions do for you. They enable you to create a *named procedure*, define which pieces of information need to be fed into the procedure (extra cheese, hold the onions and pickles), and get the same type of outcome each time you want the procedure to be followed.

Here's a tongue-in-cheek example of a burger function:

```
function BurgerOrder ( sExtraItems, sItemsToRemove ) {
    var sFinalOrder = "Charbroiled all beef patty"
        + " on a toasted sesame bun"
        + " with special sauce"
        + ", pickles, lettuce, onions, and tomatoes"
        + ", with real American cheese";
    if (sExtraItems != null && sExtraItems != "") {
        sFinalOrder += ", and extra " + sExtraItems + ".";
    } else {
        sFinalOrder += ".";
    }
    if (sItemsToRemove != null && sItemsToRemove != "") {
        sFinalOrder += " Hold the " + sItemsToRemove + ".";
    }
    return sFinalOrder;
}
var myOrder = BurgerOrder("cheese", "pickles and onions");
trace(myOrder);
```

In the preceding example, there is a pattern of code that is repeated. See the if statement? It's checking for the same type of condition but with a different variable. This is an excellent example of how to seek out and destroy repetition. Here's an optimized version of the same script:

```
function notEmpty( strValue ) {
    return (strValue != null && strValue != "");
}
function BurgerOrder ( sExtraItems, sItemsToRemove ) {
    var sFinalOrder = "Charbroiled all beef patty"
        + " on a toasted sesame bun"
        + " with special sauce"
        + ", pickles, lettuce, onions, and tomatoes"
        + ", with real American cheese";
    if (notEmpty(sExtraItems)) {
        sFinalOrder += ", and extra " + sExtraItems + ".";
    } else {
        sFinalOrder += ".";
    }
    if (notEmpty(sItemsToRemove)) {
        sFinalOrder += "  Hold the " + sItemsToRemove + ".";
    }
    return sFinalOrder;
}
trace(BurgerOrder("cheese", "pickles and onions"));
```

The optimized version of the script isn't any shorter than the original version. It does, however, make it easier for the rest of your program to check for empty string values. In addition, it adds consistency to the way you check for empty strings. In fast food, as with program-ming, consistency is everything.

3.4.1 FUNCTION STRUCTURE

Functions are made up of several parts that contribute to their overall structure. First of all, there's the *function declaration*. This is where you train Flash on your custom procedure. After a function has been declared, it can be *called* at any time in the future.

Here is the breakdown of a function declaration:

```
function FunctionName ( Parameter1, Parameter2, ... ) {
    command1;
    command2;
    //...
}
```

The first word, function, tells Flash that you are declaring a function.

Next comes the *name* of your new function. Function names follow the same rules as variable names (and functions are, in fact, variables that reference your programming code).

Inside the parentheses, you define which parameters you want to be passed into the function. If the function does not have any parameters, you must still use an empty set of parentheses. Parameters allow the caller of the function to include additional information that the function can use as part of its procedure. Parameters are actually variables that have a special scope that pertains only to the inside of the function. So, in our previous script that contained the BurgerOrder function, the ExtraItems parameter is a variable that lives only within the BurgerOrder function and dies as soon as the function finishes running.

Braces (a.k.a. curly braces) are used in ActionScript to group commands together into what is called a *code block*. They are used by if statements, loops, and functions to group a series of commands together. With the function declaration, the code block (the contents of the curly braces) is what defines the procedure that will be run every time something *calls* this function.

If the function is going to produce some kind of output data value, then somewhere within the code block there should be a return command. Return does not necessarily have to be the last command in a function, but beware. When the return command is run, it exits the function, leaving the remaining commands unexecuted.

The caller of the function can get the *return value* either by saving it to a variable or by using it in an expression.

Consider the example of the following script:

```
var myOrder = BurgerOrder();
var hisOrder = BurgerOrder("pickles and onions", "cheese");
trace(BurgerOrder("special sauce"));
```

The first two calls to the BurgerOrder() function saved the return values to variables, while the third call just used the return value immediately in the trace function. Yes, you can pass the return values from functions into the parameters of other functions; this is a very powerful feature in ActionScript.

3.4.2 FUNCTIONS SUMMARY

Understanding functions is essential to programming in ActionScript. In long and complex scripting, functions offer a way to streamline the process and ensure accuracy. The power of functions is unlimited, and they give you the flexibility you need for truly creative programming.

3.5 ARRAYS

Arrays are groups of multiple containers of information. When dealing with lists of data values such as people's names and ages, it's more efficient to use arrays than simple variables.

In the following section, the basics of using arrays are covered. In Chapter 10, "Movie Maker XML," you will see examples of arrays in use.

3.5.1 ARRAY BASICS

There are nine basic principles to keep in mind when using arrays in a script:

- Arrays follow the same naming and scoping rules as variables.
- Arrays contain data values, called *elements*.
- Elements are organized by an index (like a location name).
- Element indexes can be whole numbers or strings.
- Arrays can have one or more "dimensions" (called multidimensional arrays).
- There are two types of arrays: simple arrays and associative arrays.
- Simple arrays are indexed by whole numbers.
- Associative arrays are indexed by string values.
- Simple arrays have a .length property, while associative arrays do not.

3.5.2 SIMPLE ARRAYS

Imagine that you are working on a Flash project, and the purpose of this project is to keep track of the names of multiple people. You could accomplish this by using a variable. The program could store the names into a variable, but then there would be the problem of keeping the names separate and finding individual names one by one. That would involve a bit of programming. It would be much simpler to maintain such a list of names using an array (see Figure 3.12). The following code is an example of just such a list:

```
//

//— Create a new array variable —

var namesArray = new Array();

//

//— Add some people's names to the array —

namesArray[0] = "Joe Smith";

namesArray[1] = "Mary Richardson";

namesArray[2] = "Joanne Rodriguez";

//

//— Examine the array in the Output window —

trace("array length=" + namesArray.length);

for (var index = 0; index<namesArray.length; index++) {

    trace (namesArray[index]);

}
```

In this code, several points regarding arrays are noteworthy:

- An array must be created using the Array() object.
- Individual values can be assigned to an array directly using the equals (=) sign.
- The index numbers 0, 1, 2 are used to give each data value a unique location in the array.
- The index numbers start at 0.
- All arrays automatically have a length property.
- Although the array elements range from 0 to 2, the array length is 3.
- Even though the array elements were initially assigned with the numbers 0, 1, and 2, the array index can be accessed using a variable that contains the index value (see the for loop's variable "index").

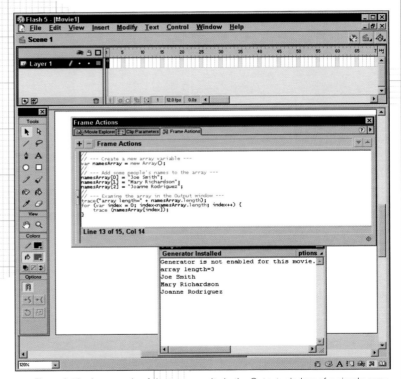

Figure 3.12   An example of the trace results in the Output window of a simple array.

Another way to create the same array and assign values can be seen in the following code. You will notice that the outcome is the same as in the previous example.

```
//
//— Create a new array variable with people's names in it —
var namesArray = ["Joe Smith", "Mary Richardson",
    Joanne Rodriguez"];
//
//— Examine the array in the Output window —
trace("array length=" + namesArray.length);
for (var index = 0; index<namesArray.length; index++) {
    trace (namesArray[index]);
}
```

The simple array is the most commonly used form of array. With it's numerical order, numeric indexing, and convenient .length property, the simple array is easy to use and works very well within loops.

3.5.3 ASSOCIATIVE ARRAYS

In the preceding names example used for simple arrays, the ActionScript kept an array only of people's names, and the elements were indexed by a number.

Associative arrays differ from simple arrays in that they use string values instead of numbers to index the array elements. So rather than numbering the elements in the array 0 through 2 (for a three-item array), an associative array assigns a unique "name" to each element. Because an array element is *associated* with the array by a descriptive name (rather than being numerically indexed into the array), these types of arrays are called *associative arrays* (see Figure 3.13).

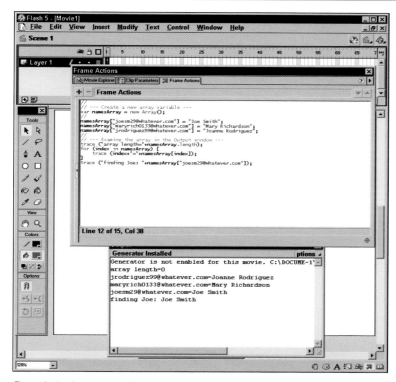

Figure 3.13   An example of the trace results in the Output window of an associative array.

Examine the following code for a better understanding of how associative arrays can be used and how they differ from a simple array:

```
//
//— Create a new array variable with people's names in it —
var namesArray = new Array();
//
namesArray["joesm29@whatever.com"] = "Joe Smith";
namesArray["maryrich0133@whatever.com"] = "Mary Richardson";
namesArray["jrodriguez99@whatever.com"] = "Joanne Rodriguez";
//
// — Examine the array in the Output window —
trace ("array length="+namesArray.length);
for (var index in namesArray) {
    trace (index + "=" + namesArray[index]);
}
trace("finding Joe: " + namesArray["joesm29@whatever.com"]);
```

This code uses the value joesm29@whatever.com as the index for the Joe Smith element instead of a numeric index (as seen in the last trace command).

Notice that, in the output window for the preceding code, the array length is 0. Associative arrays are not indexed numerically. They are more like a table of contents in a book. The program must access the elements by index name rather than index number. When looping through the contents of an associative array, the for...in loop is really the only loop that will work.

Remember, the for...in loop accesses every element of an associative array, object, or movie clip. Well, guess what? Movie clips and objects are treated by Flash like associative arrays. You can also access elements of a movie clip with this syntax: myClip["_framesLoaded"].

3.5.4 MULTIDIMENSIONAL ARRAYS

The preceding examples for simple and associative arrays have all been one-dimensional. This means there is only one index that points to the elements in the array.

A multidimensional array is an array that has more than one index for the array. So if you need to store additional information, you would use this type of array. See the following two code samples for a better understanding of how arrays can be used with multiple dimensions (see Figures 3.14 and 3.15).

```
//
//— Create a new array variable —
var namesArray = new Array();
//
namesArray[0] = new Array();
namesArray[0][0] = "Joe Smith";
namesArray[0][1] = "joesm29@whatever.com";
//
namesArray[1] = [];
namesArray[1][0] = "Mary Richardson";
namesArray[1][1] = "maryrich0133@whatever.com";
//
// — Now let's use the short form of array creation —
namesArray[namesArray.length] = ["Joanne Rodriguez",
    "jrodriguez99@whatever.com"];
//
// — Examine the array in the Output window —
trace ("array length="+namesArray.length);
for (var index_a = 0; index_a<namesArray.length; index_a++) {
    for(var index_b = 0; index_b<namesArray[index_a].length;
      index_b++){
        trace("["+index_a+"]["+index_b+"]="
            + namesArray[index_a][index_b]);
    }
    trace("");
}
```

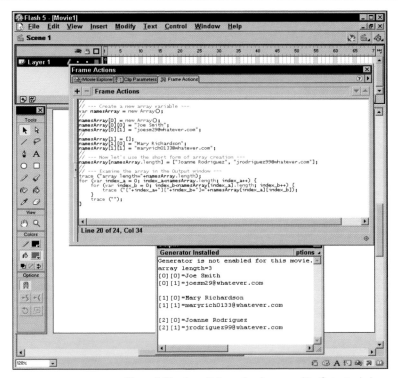

Figure 3.14.   A multidimensional array and its Output window.

```
//
//— Create a new array —
var namesArray = new Array();
//
namesArray[0] = [];
namesArray[0]["name"] = "Joe Smith";
namesArray[0]["email"] = "joesm29@whatever.com";
//
namesArray[1] = [];
namesArray[1]["name"] = "Mary Richardson";
namesArray[1]["email"] = "maryrich0133@whatever.com";
//
// — Now let's use the short form of associative array creation —
namesArray[2] = {name:"Joanne Rodriguez",
          email:"jrodriguez99@whatever.com"};
//
// — Examine the array in the Output window —
trace ("array length="+namesArray.length);
for (var index_a = 0; index_a<namesArray.length; index_a++) {
   for (var index_b in namesArray[index_a]) {
      trace("["+index_a+"]['"+index_b+"']="
         + namesArray[index_a][index_b]);
   }
   trace("");
}
```

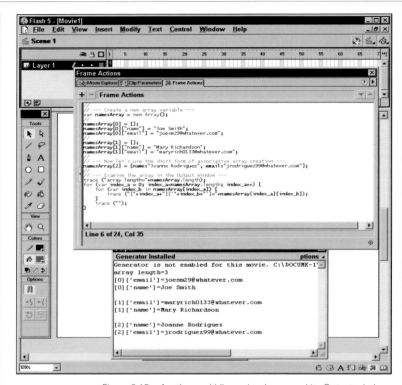

Figure 3.15.   Another multidimensional array and its Output window.

In this first piece of code, notice that both indexes (index_a and index_b) use numbers. That is to say, both index_a and index_b are variables that contain numbers. So the first dimension of the array (index_a) is a simple array. Also, the second array dimension (index_b) is a simple array. However, in the second code sample, the second array dimension (index_b) is a string rather than a number. In this latter case, the first array dimension is a simple array, while the second array dimension is an associative array. These two code samples show that you can mix and match the types of arrays at each dimension of a multidimensional array.

Another important point is that there's a short way and a long way to create arrays.

A simple array (indexed by numbers) can be created using the following:

```
var myArray = new Array();
myArray[0] = "zero";
myArray[1] = "one";
```

or

```
var myArray = ["zero","one"];
```

Here, the square brackets indicate a simple array, and the comma-separated item inside the square brackets is placed in sequence into the array, starting with an index of 0.

An associative array (indexed by strings) can be created using the following:

```
var myArray = new Array();
myArray["zero"] = 0;
myArray["one"] = 1;
```

or

```
var myArray = {zero:0, one:1}
```

In this example, we use curly braces instead of square brackets to indicate the shortcut for an associative array. The comma-separated items inside the curly braces are placed into the associative array. Each comma-separated item in the list has two parts: an index name and a value. The index name appears before the colon (:) and the value appears after.

The following are a few samples of the shorthand notation for you to practice with:

```
var aryNames = ["jim", "tammy"];
var aryAges = [22, 27];
var aryPeople = [{name:"jim",age:22}, {name:"tammy",age:27}];
var aryDemographics = {names:["jim","tammy"], ages:[22,27]};
```

3.5.5 ARRAYS SUMMARY

Arrays make it possible to organize a number of data values into a single variable and to access those values in a structured and organized manner. When combined with loops, arrays can make your ActionScript more flexible and easier to maintain. Although simple arrays are more commonly used, associative arrays can be quite powerful as a useful alternative to simple arrays. In Flash, arrays are not *the* most important topic to master, but having a full understanding of arrays will open the door to a number of new opportunities and features in your projects.

what? | can't see anything? | email | desktop | mac screensaver

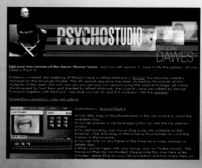

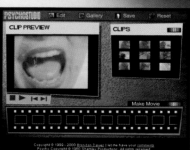

BRENDAN DAWES

Brendan Dawes Interview
by Todd Purgason

Introduction
www.brendandawes.com

I was first introduced to Brendan by Hillman Curtis at Macromedia Web World 2000. I liked Brendan immediately, with his British, off-the-wall humor and his totally down-to-earth attitude. At Web World 2000, Brendan did a 10-minute segment on his psycho studio, which blew me away. He started out at an interactive shop in Manchester called Subnet. During this time, he worked on several very successful and award-winning kids' sites for clients like Kellogg's and Disney.

He is currently the creative director for a new agency in the UK called Magnetic North, working for clients like Benetton and Kellogg's. He is a definite leader in using Flash to create unique and useable applications. Brendan has inspired many people with his work and creativity. Since our first meeting, we have spent a lot of time slumming at various conferences together, and I am honored to call Brendan one of my good friends.

Teaser from the Interview

TP: Alright, here with Brendan Dawes. So, Brendan…

BD: Todd.

TP: Explain to me, man, who is Brendan Dawes?

BD: I thought this was one of the toughest questions you'd ask me because it's pretty hard to answer this one. I think, right now, I feel like one of the luckiest people on the planet. Lucky to be doing the job I'm doing. After working in the factory for like eight years, I saw things on the other side of just doing a nine-to-five job to pay the bills, and now I just am thankful every day when I get up. I look forward to going to work, and I know some really great people, and right now it's still really lucky, and I'm lucky to be doing what I'm doing and having a good laugh doing it. I think most of what I do is about having to laugh every day, actually.

TP: So Brendan Dawes is a happy guy.

BD: Yeah, basically. Wish I could complain of something, but right now, no, I can't really complain about a lot, to be honest.

TP: I'll give you some stuff. Just email me.

BD: I'm sure you will.

TP: Yeah, okay.

BD: I mean, I've complained about writing the book (*Drag, Slide, Fade* by New Riders).

TP: Yeah, that's true.

BD: It's a bit of a bind, but like, you know, it's gonna be worth it in the end. So that's about the only thing I could probably complain about at the moment. But other than that, I'd have to say life's pretty cool. You know, I'm heading where I want to head. Really, I just want to push things and that's all. I think the last two years have been phenomenal for me anyway. So, yeah, it's all going well.

To hear the rest of Brendan's answer to this question, as well as his answers to the following questions, please go to the Inspirations section of the book's site at www.JUXTinteractive.com/deCONSTRUCTION.

QUESTIONS

02. If you were a fish/sea creature, what would you be?

03. What CD or mp3 is in your player right now?

04. What is your definition of design?

05. What was your very first impression of Flash?

06. If you were walking down the street and came across John Gay and Jakob Nielsen engaged in a fistfight, what would you do?

07. You started out as a sound engineer mixing for raves, and you actually produced some CDs. Has this had any influence on you as a designer and programmer?

08. You have worked on some very successful kids' branding projects. What, in your opinion, is effective branding on the Internet?

09. Why did you do the Saul Bass site?

10. Living and working in Britain sets you apart from the others featured in this book. Do you see any differences in the design that

comes out of Britain and the States?

11. You are a creative director, yet you do a ton of ActionScripting. How does that work?

12. What aspect of design for you is the sugar on your cereal?

13. So what is up with the whole copyrights of the Psycho Studio thing?

14. What is it that happens in a typical day that gives you a feeling of satisfaction when you go home at night?

15. Last time we were hanging out, you told me that you're now involved with broadcast and print. Are you enjoying these aspects of your work, or do you prefer to do interactive?

16. If you could do one last project before you had to hang up your designer's cap, what would you want that project to be?

02

deCONSTRUCTION

The Process, Design, and ActionScript of
Juxt Interactive

Section 02
Juxt Interactive Project Deconstructions

(a)
The Juxt Interactive site was created to promote the Juxt brand to potential and existing clients, new hires, and the press. As a company, we are dedicated to quality and are focused on the creative application of design and technology. We wanted our site to communicate a sense of who Juxt is to the world. Instead of working for every client in the world, our goal is to work for clients who will allow us to do projects that are interesting and intelligent on the whole. We are also challenged by projects that involve a little risk-taking. Although we focus on our client's needs and objectives, our essence as a company is creativity, in strategy, design, and technology. We wish to attract clients who appreciate us for these reasons, not just because we can do the job.

(b)
The Juxt site design, which is the backbone of our brand, was developed as an extension of our thought process. Our brand is based on the metaphor of the flower, which represents the organic nature and beauty of design. The metaphor of the bolt represents technology: effective, yet not overstated technology, used creatively to achieve amazing things. To us, creativity seems an organic force that spreads itself throughout all aspects of what we do. You get two or three people together throwing ideas around and the boundaries of one person's creativity collide with the boundaries of another's. As a result, the ideas take on a life of their own. When an idea is spawned, grown, and nurtured, it's hard to wrap your mind around this idea and define its boundaries succinctly.

(c)
We visually interpreted this creative force throughout the Juxt site and content by developing black organic branching forms we affectionately refer to as "fringies." They are black typographical forms that are given life using an ActionScript that responds to user interaction. They seem to evolve and spread in numerous directions. As you roll over buttons, they grow out, contract, become part of the interface, as well as each section. They're always taking on different shapes, forms, spreading themselves around, reaching around corners and crevices, and becoming entwined with all existing elements.

(d)
On the site interaction, we used ActionScript to create a very solid, focused presentation. The branding represents our company, and our information is center-focused. If you dig through the site, there are all sorts of little nooks and crannies that reward the user with a fresh uniqueness, built around the content and its functionality.

(e)
We're a diverse group of people with our own strengths and weaknesses. By working together as a whole, we're Juxt Interactive. As unique individuals, each of us brings a lot to the company and each other. We wanted to illustrate this individual quality in the site. When people visit the site, they get a sense of who Juxt is as a company, its brand, and also a glimpse into each of us as individuals.

(f)
The further you dig into the site, the more personal the content becomes. We share source code and things like that on some levels, on other levels we share the thoughts and opinions of our staff and management.
Our site represents Juxt in concept, design, structure, and content.

CHAPTER

c4

Flash deCONSTRUCTION

JUXT INTERACTIVE DEVELOPMENT PROCESS

c4 CHAPTER
Flash deCONSTRUCTION
JUXT INTERACTIVE DEVELOPMENT PROCESS

In most technical books and manuals, you'll find a lot of information on how to use specific tools, what the menu options are, and what functionality you can expect from the application. Often lacking in these books is information that's vital for you to know to fully grasp what the application does and how it relates to what you want to do. For example, it's essential for the serious user to know how to utilize a specific tool in a process and how to start from step A, go to step B, and so on, all the way to step Z. *Flash deCONSTRUCTION* fills in many of the empty holes left in these technical books by addressing the tools in relation to the designer's process.

Before jumping into the deeper levels of deconstruction projects, let's step back and look at the development process of a project.

4.1 FREEHAND AND FLASH

In Chapter 2, "The Juxt Interactive Process," we looked at our meta project process. Chapter 2 is a granular, step-by-step walkthrough of the Juxt process, where our designs are laid out in FreeHand, assembled in Flash, and made ready for ActionScript.

To that end, it must be noted that we love Flash very much, but we thoroughly and wholeheartedly believe in using the right tool for the right job. Although this might come as a shock to you, there's a lot more out there in the world than just Flash. Flash is excellent for motion graphics and interactivity on the Web. However, we use many other tools that take us from the beginning to the end of a fully developed project. For example, we use sound software to generate sound, 3D software to generate 3D, image-editing software for images, and so on. For our graphic design and layout, we use Macromedia FreeHand and Adobe Photoshop. We rely heavily on FreeHand because it provides a vector-based environment and works very well with Flash. In fact, over the last several years, we've been fortunate to work with Macromedia to help them develop a synergy between FreeHand and Flash and create a better authoring environment between the two.

4.1.1 FREEHAND IN THE FLASH DEVELOPMENT PROCESS

Over the years, we've seen FreeHand, primarily a print and graphic design tool, adopt new functionality that enables the Flash development process to begin in FreeHand. The new features of FreeHand enable you to design graphic elements, symbols, and links in FreeHand, which can be seamlessly integrated into the Flash authoring environment.

In Flash 5 and FreeHand 10 (which as of this writing are the latest releases), it is quite evident that Macromedia has worked very hard to create a consistent UI that's carried across applications. This is extremely helpful when you need to work between these two applications. Once you become familiar with one set of standards, it carries over into the other application, resulting in a much more efficient workflow (see Figures 4.1 and 4.2).

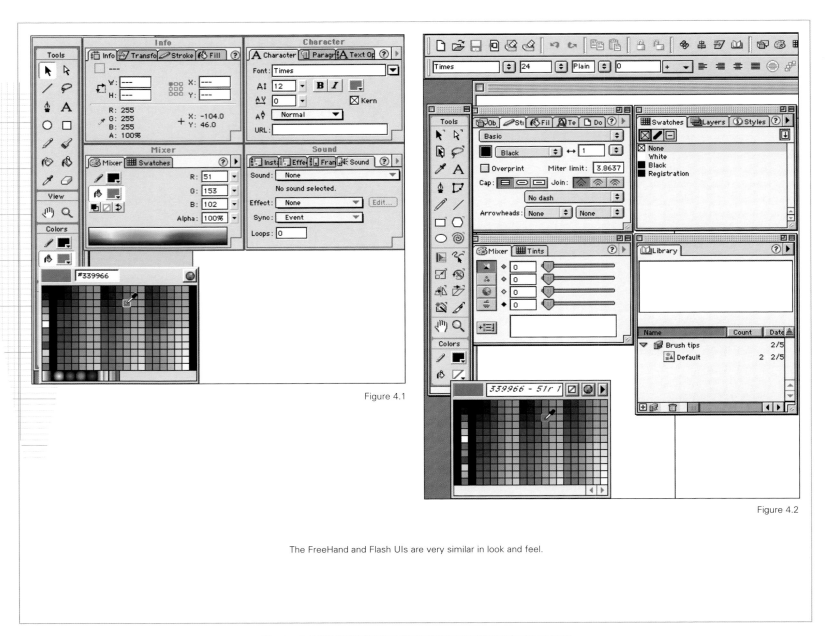

Figure 4.1

Figure 4.2

The FreeHand and Flash UIs are very similar in look and feel.

4.1.2 STREAMLINING THE INTEGRATION OF FREEHAND AND FLASH

Whether you are using Flash or HTML in a project, it's a good idea to develop a standard set of naming conventions with which all the developers on the staff are familiar. This enables a project team to successfully work alongside one another and predict and react to the development process. Naming conventions can often be difficult to enforce because the individual team members' personalities and work habits differ. However, if everybody keeps the final project objective in mind, they'll typically fall in line, work with the program requirements, and develop the project, working under the required conventions.

The naming convention style you use for your projects is a matter of personal preference. It's up to you, the individual, to define what names work for you and your group. There are a few guidelines we use at Juxt for naming conventions:

- First, the team must be consistent with the conventions used in a project.
- Second, the convention standards should be flexible to keep pace with technological evolution. Because technology is always changing, the name should be adaptable for future change.

At Juxt, we recently developed such a cross-project, office-wide naming convention. This convention is available on the book's site for further scrutiny.

4.2 THE FLASH DEVELOPMENT PROCESS

The development process works best with a plan. At Juxt, we begin by working with the functional spec, a document created by the information architect or technology director. The purpose of a functional spec is to explain how the project functions, including navigation models, content, and interactivity for each page in the site.

At Juxt, we often build our functional specs in FreeHand. The functional spec can easily be developed in the FreeHand workspace. Figure 4.3 is an example of a functional spec done in FreeHand with notations around the layout and on layers that are turned off in the view mode.

The FreeHand documents are printed out by the developer and are reviewed by the project team. Then a plan of action is devised for the project. The developer decides how to break up the project into movie clips and, as such, develops the movie clip architecture. It's very important to document this architecture so that the rest of the team understands how the structure works. This document also serves as an important reference tool for future updates on the project.

After the movie clip architecture is thought out and documented, certain technological concepts that are more complicated than others will be revealed. In fact, a large portion of the site might hinge on technological elements. Because of this, it's wise to go through a "proof of concept" phase. In this phase, we dissect little pieces of the project, down to their nuts and bolts, to try to prove that this technology actually works the way we envisioned. We explore the functionality itself without wasting time implementing the visual nature of the functionality. This is especially important when we're working on a project that involves repetition of a piece. If the first piece is correct, the others will follow suit. This is a more efficient way of working and eliminates the frustrating task of revising the piece numerous times.

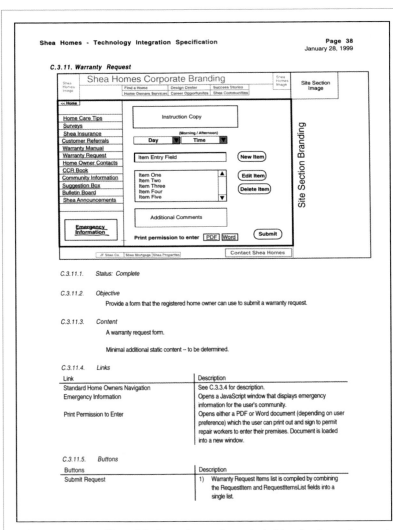

Figure 4.3   A sample page from a typical functional spec document.

4.2.1   PROTOTYPE DEVELOPMENT

Another aspect that requires consideration is a model for development, or "prototype" development. It's more efficient to break a project up into small, manageable segments and then develop each piece as far as it can go. In other words, we develop a segment of a project first and then logically move on to subsequent segments. By developing in prototypes, we are alerted to potential problems that could occur in other parts of the development phase. Solutions can then be developed that carry over into other areas of the prototype.

Through experience, we have discovered that the most efficient way to approach a project is to break up the sum of the whole into a series of manageable accomplishments. This enables us to complete one task (or piece of a project), learn from the experience, move on to the next chunk, and apply the knowledge gained from our previous experience. The prototype development stage of the project largely defines the way these tasks, or pieces, are to be broken up and executed and by which team members.

4.3   MOVING WORK FROM FREEHAND TO FLASH

For study and presentation, our artwork is laid out in FreeHand (as mentioned earlier in this chapter) and then travels on to Flash for development. In this section, we reference layouts from the Juxt Interactive site so you can see how our files are moved from FreeHand into Flash.

> **NOTE**
>
> Most of the FreeHand art in this book was created in a late beta version of FreeHand 10. FreeHand elements might appear slightly different from the way they would look in the final version of FreeHand 10.

Now we'll take the layout of the Juxt Interactive home page and move it from FreeHand to Flash. With the introduction of FreeHand 9 and Flash 5, the authoring environment of the two applications became seamless. FreeHand 9 introduced the symbol library, which looks and works very much like Flash's symbol library. One major drawback in FreeHand 9 was the inability to edit a symbol. The artwork went from FreeHand to Flash via the SWF export. FreeHand 10, however, solved this problem and allows the editing of symbols. This gives us the flexibility we need to incorporate symbols into our FreeHand layout process. Layouts can be created in FreeHand 10 and above using symbols, layers, text, and guides, which will be completely retained when brought into Flash.

To further clarify, let's walk through the process of how a page from the Juxt web site was created:

1. Open the file Juxt_home.fh9 in FreeHand 9 or above (see Figure 4.4).

2. In the FreeHand file, notice that there are a number of symbols and a handful of layers. It's easy to create a symbol in FreeHand. First, open the Symbols palette. In FreeHand 9, select Menu Window > Panels > Symbols. In FreeHand 10, go to the Menu Window > Library.

3. Next, select an object or group and drag it to the lower portion of the Library palette. A symbol will be created, and the existing object will now be a symbol instance. Just double-click on the default name that FreeHand gave the symbol, name it what you like, and you're done. If you want to be organized, you can create folders and move symbols into the folders by dragging and dropping just like you do in Flash.

4. Now let's move this file to Flash. First, close the FreeHand 9 file. Launch Flash if you do not have it running. Now let's set up the movie to match the page in FreeHand. In the Movie Properties dialog box, set the Frame Rate to 30, set the Dimensions to 640 wide by 400 tall, and then click OK (see Figure 4.5).

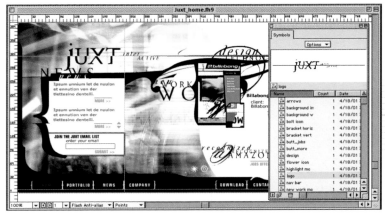

Figure 4.4   The Juxt site began in FreeHand, including the construction of symbols and layers.

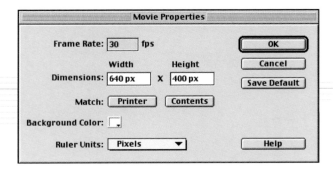

Figure 4.5   The Movie Properties dialog box in Flash.

5. Now go to File > Import and select the FreeHand file Juxt_home.fh9, as shown in Figure 4.6.

6. Click OK. Flash presents you with the FreeHand Import dialog box (see Figure 4.7).

You have many options for mapping different content to keyframes, layers, or scenes. FreeHand layers that are invisible can also be ignored. This can be very helpful if you structure your files well. Click OK and—voila!—Flash imports the FreeHand file intact while retaining symbols with names, layers with names, guides, and images. It also converts objects in clipping paths (pasted inside FreeHand objects) to symbols with a mask in place for you (see Figure 4.8).

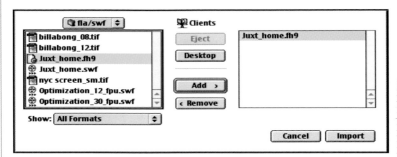

Figure 4.6   Navigating to a file in the Import dialog box in Flash.

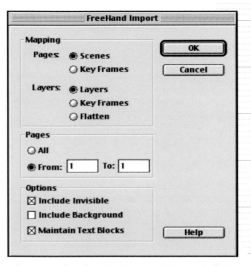

Figure 4.7   The FreeHand Import dialog box in Flash.

Figure 4.8   The FreeHand file has been imported completely intact to Flash, retaining the named symbols, named layers, guides, and images.

4.3.1 ORGANIZING ARTWORK IN FLASH

Now that the file (or artwork) is in Flash, it needs to be further organized. The symbols are moved to levels, and the movie clip structure is ready to be built. It's much easier to break apart a symbol than to make a group into a symbol after it has already been tweened several times.

FreeHand, as a drawing tool, deals with objects. In contrast, Flash deals with more *wet, or editable*, elements. We use the term "wet" because these objects are like wet paint on a canvas that can be painted on and rubbed off. FreeHand objects come into Flash as groups of wet elements. The groups might deceivingly feel like a symbol, but they aren't. They lack the small crosshairs that indicate the center point of a symbol. It is important for you to get used to this to avoid creating unnecessarily heavy files.

NOTE

On export of an SWF, Flash makes every frame in a tween a keyframe. This makes tweening a group very destructive to a file's size. In this situation, you would be forced to download the group on every frame in the tween.

It's good to get into the habit of creating symbols out of everything and moving elements to their appropriate layers for animation once the FreeHand file has been imported to Flash.

4.3.2 FLASH TEXT

In Flash, text imports as a grouped object. Because we're making symbols out of all the imported elements, we go through and ungroup the groups containing text blocks so that we're dealing with only raw data. You want to be careful that you only break apart the group and not break apart the text characters. This way, the text block remains intact.

4.3.3 SHARED LIBRARIES

In Flash 5, the shared library was introduced. After symbols are collected into a shared library, they might need to be distributed across movie clips. In our development plan, elements heading for the shared library always need to be accounted for. So, at this point in the development, we have an understanding of what we do and don't need in our shared library.

NOTE

When the Flash Player reaches a shared symbol, it has to load the entire shared library that contains that symbol before the movie can proceed. This being the case, you want to manage your shared libraries and have several small libraries as opposed to one very large one.

Even in the early stages of a project, it's never too early to start optimization. The whole project needs to be examined to determine how best to keep the file size down without compromising quality. To accomplish this, we take a look at our file, see what elements are redundant, test the movie, and look at the bandwidth profiler to make certain there aren't any corrupt elements weighing the file size down. We start optimizing in the beginning of a project and do so frequently throughout development. Remember the prototyping concept we discussed earlier? The purpose of prototyping is to make sure that the piece being created is solid enough to move forward and is devoid of time-consuming mistakes. Optimization is also discussed in more detail later in this chapter.

Once we have all of our movie elements symbolized and on their own layers, it's easy for us to begin creating the motion graphics and the ActionScript. The most efficient way to approach a project at this stage is to logically break it up into different pieces so that the designers and programmers can start building it simultaneously and in a way that enables them to tie all the pieces together later.

The way a project is broken up and distributed among the different players largely depends on the scope and nature of the project. By using externally loading movie clips as a consistent standard, you are free to distribute almost the entire project into small, manageable files that can be developed by many people simultaneously, as opposed to one massive file that can be developed by only one person at a time.

At the same time, the database is constructed along with the middleware applications built in whatever technology you might be using. At Juxt, we like to use Cold Fusion, PHP, and JSP. We also do ASP, but we prefer the other applications for most situations. It's very important to have tight communication between the middleware programmers and the ActionScripters who are tying their Flash and Generator files to the middleware applications.

Once the dynamic content generation programming and motion graphics are complete, the transition development begins. In this part of the development, the movie clips are tied together, as explained in Chapter 3, "ActionScript Basics." There is a base movie that loads into the external movie clips as needed, based on the project structure and user interaction. This creates a consistent pattern of opening, closing, and loading/unloading to help you get that fluid flow experience.

4.3.4 SOUND DEVELOPMENT PROCESS

The last step in the development process is the sound integration phase. We always like to do sound as the last step. The only exception is when sound is synched to motion graphics. When this is the case, the sound needs to be brought into the movie earlier so that the sound and the motion graphic can be tied together.

NOTE
The projects displayed in this book don't have sound synched to motion graphics.

The sound design is done last for two reasons. The first reason is to maintain our sanity. The second and most important reason is that the MP3 encoder, used for Flash files with sound, takes a lot of time to encode. This encoding dramatically slows down the development process. So to work efficiently, we leave the sound design until the very end, or we implement the sound and strip it out for the duration of the development. This way, the sound can be reintegrated at the end of the movie.

4.3.5 EXPERIENCE TEST

After the sound is integrated, we go into the experience test, where we touch and feel the project to make sure it flows the way we had envisioned it would. Remember that we have only seen bits and pieces of the project up to this point. Now we get to experience the real touch test. This is also a big checkpoint for optimization because there are often many people involved in the development of a project, all working on fast connections and building the site over a local network. It's easy to lose sight of the realities of bandwidth, so this is a good time to take inventory of the project as a whole. The experience test examines the overall experience of a project and fine-tunes the rough edges, resulting in a solid flowing and optimized site for visitors. Things often need tweaking or revising after we see the site working in context.

4.4 OPTIMIZATION

Because Juxt is concerned about creating a positive user experience for the general Internet audience, we take optimization very seriously. Many of us at Juxt started working with the web back in 1995. Back then, you would break out into a nervous sweat over even the smallest amount of file size added to each and every element that was put on a web page. Because of this file-size issue, we were "web" raised in an environment in which optimization became the most important element of the job.

Design was nice, but if the files were too slow, they were useless. We were really restricted in what we could do in the early days because the typical user had a 14.4 modem, and that was considered smokin'. Now, in the realm of broadband, DSL, and dial-ups reducing at the same rate as the rain forest, people are less concerned about optimization. It is always an issue that should be taken seriously, however. As of this writing, the average web user is still on a 56K modem. Seemingly a lot faster than its predecessors, a 56K modem can still suffer from slow connections down to 33K or 28.8K levels. Because of this, optimization has to be considered very seriously.

The first key to optimization is *designing* for optimization. This means making design decisions that will give you a small file size from the very beginning of a project. It's always painful when you blindly develop a great concept with lots of beautiful visuals. You then bring it into Flash, animate it, and give it life, only to discover your file size is twice the size of the required specs. Always start smart and set a file limit for yourself from the beginning; you can always justify things later as you add elements to your design file. Take images into Flash and test the compression to see how much they add to the file size as you're laying out in FreeHand.

The following are some design tips that can help the optimization process work in your favor:

- **Movie Size.** Whether the movie is in a pop-up window or built into a standard HTML page, the actual size of the movie will impact performance. We have found that the larger the movie is, the more Flash has to deal with, and the slower it runs. A large, slow movie that is scaled down will often give better performance. Consider limiting the size of your Flash movie for better and lighter results.
- **JavaScript window**. If you use this technique, keep in mind that the smaller the window size, the faster the movie will play. Also, you eliminate the Back button, which causes problems in many Flash projects. HTML visitors are accustomed to pressing a back button, so as they proceed in a Flash project, they press the back button and wind up on the launch page. Finally, JavaScript windows provide a smaller space in which to work, forcing you to design for less screen real estate. This often means less content, which logically results in smaller file sizes. Ultimately, the file size depends on content. But by limiting the space you have to fill, you can often reduce the content amount.
- **File streaming**. If you're designing a project with some larger elements, graphics, and sounds, it's best to start the file with lighter elements, such as fonts or vector artwork, that build up to the larger bitmap graphics and sound. Use the Bandwidth Profiler as the movie develops to track how the design is streaming.

4.4.1 FRAME RATES

One of the little-known secrets of Flash optimization is the frame rate issue. For each frame in Flash, there's a small price to pay that keeps adding up as the file is being created. This is due to the fact that when an SWF is exported, every frame in all the tweens is converted to a keyframe. So the more complicated the file, the greater the price you pay in the end. In other words, a file running at 12 frames per second as opposed to 30 frames per second, with the same content, will ultimately be smaller in file size.

To illustrate this, take a look at the file Optimization_12_fpu.fla from the book's site (see Figure 4.9). This is a simple movie containing a movie clip sliding across the screen, running at 12 frames per second with a total duration of 30 frames. In Figure 4.10, you'll see the Bandwidth Profiler report for that file, showing the file size as 7,014 bytes.

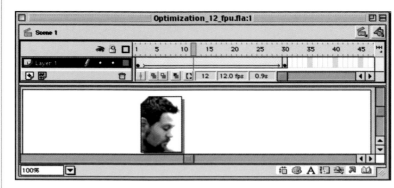

Figure 4.9   A simple 12fps movie created in Flash.

Figure 4.11   A simple 30fps movie created in Flash.

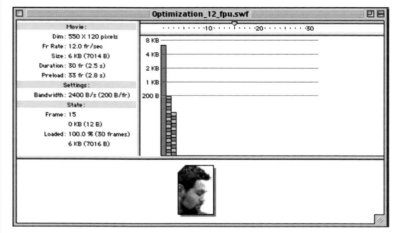

Figure 4.10   The size of this 12fps movie is indicated
in the Bandwidth Profiler as being 7,014 bytes.

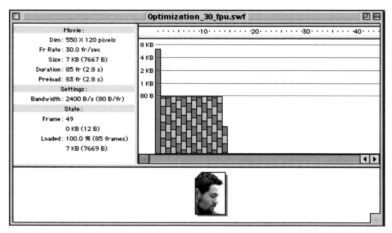

Figure 4.12   The same movie as in the previous figure, except the
Bandwidth Profiler indicates a file size of 7,667 bytes.

Now compare that with the file Optimization_30_fpu.fla from the book's site (see Figure 4.11). This file is of the same makeup as the previous example. It's a movie clip running across the screen at about the same motion pace, but in this version of the movie, there are many more frames (30fps) so the movie runs much smoother.

In essence, it's the same motion if you export that file. When you look at the Bandwidth Profiler in Figure 4.12, you'll notice that the file is 7,667 bytes, a difference of roughly 650 bytes.

We know the size difference between the 12fps movie and the 30fps movie seems insignificant, but keep in mind that this example is a 30-frame movie with one element in it. In a movie that contained a lot of animation among numerous movie clips, the size of the file would add up. I'm not saying to always make your movies at 12 frames per second. The point is that you need to justify your fps. If you know the site is heavy from the get go, you might pick a frame rate that's slower, perhaps something along the lines of 12 or 18 frames per second. If you know your site is going to be relatively light and you want a quick, snappy animation effect, don't be afraid to push it all the way up to 50 or 60 frames per second. Always keep in mind that there's a cost with regard to size that has to be figured into the equation.

NOTE

Although you can adjust the frame speed in Flash to a higher number than the default, a percentage of users with low bandwidth and/or slower computers will not be able to experience your anticipated results. Also, version 4 of the Flash Player on Netscape browsers will only play back a maximum of 24fps.

4.4.2 FONT OPTIMIZATION

The next issue we need to address is font optimization. At Juxt, we tend to use a lot of fonts because typography is one of our favored design tools. We're not suggesting you should always conform to the Macromedia white paper on Flash design that tells you to use one sans serif font, but always consider fonts as an important optimization issue.

There are basically two types of fonts: serif and sans serif. In Figure 4.13, there is a serif font in the top left. A serif font can be identified by the following trademark: It has the little feet that protrude off the ends, little marks on the s, the r, the i, and the f. These are called serifs or, in some cases, spurs. A sans serif font has hard edges, straight lines, and no serifs.

Figure 4.13   An example of serif and sans serif fonts.

Vectors are descriptions between points that work with a point in line to the next point with curvature of the mathematics that make up that curvature. Therefore, the fewer number of points, the fewer number of curves, and the less file size it takes to describe that font. So if you look at the serif *f* character and count the runs on the face, there are about 21 to 22 runs on that *f*. If you look at the sans serif *f* character, there are roughly 14 runs on that character. Consequently, the serif font is about 25 to 30 percent larger in file size than the sans serif font.

Again, I'm not advocating just using sans serif fonts. However, if you're dealing with a banner ad campaign that has a very tight file-size limitation, sans serif fonts are probably the best way to go.

The other font issue to consider is stroking fonts. If you look at Figure 4.14, you'll see the word "text" with a red stroke.

serif
sans serif
text

fonts

Figure 4.14   In this figure, the word "text" was given a stroke of red.

Less-experienced designers, who might want a heavier weight font that doesn't exist, might try to make a regular font heavier by stroking the font. I'm not suggesting you should never use this technique. However, it's important to know that Flash makes up an object in a different way than FreeHand or Illustrator. In these programs, the object has a line and a fill, and the fill is contained within the line space. Flash has to describe the same outline of each letter twice. You can see how this would increase the size of a file.

When you're working with masks (layers used to mask out portions of objects on lower layers) and making invisible buttons (buttons with only hit states defined) in square shapes (or any shape for that matter), if you don't need the line, turn it off. If you keep the line on, you're basically using it twice for each object and thus increasing the file size.

4.4.3   IMAGE COMPRESSION

Next on the optimization agenda is image compression. In Flash, there are basically three types of images you can create. You can have a photographic image, which is typically JPEG in nature. You can also have a bitmap image, which is typically a PNG or GIF type of image, or you can have a PNG image with an alpha channel, which is usually a 32-bit PNG allowing you to carry an alpha channel.

In Figure 4.15, these three types of images are depicted. In this file, the PNG file is first (from the left). In the middle, there is a typical JPEG. On the right, there is a bitmap PNG.

image compression

Figure 4.15   From the left: sample PNG, JPEG, and bitmap PNG files.

4.4.3.1   JPEG COMPRESSION

Many people have questions about JPEG images in Flash and the default export. This is the way it works: If you import a JPEG into Flash, by default, Flash will adhere to the JPEG compression settings you applied to that image before you brought it into Flash. This can cause problems for some people if they make the JPEG file as high quality as they possibly can. So keep in mind that if you set your compression within Flash, but fail to set it on the image in the symbol properties in Flash, you'll wind up with fat files.

NOTE

Because the JPEG format is lossy compression and Flash recompresses JPEG images, you need to test the quality of the JPEG after the recompressing occurs in Flash. For best quality in images, use a nonlossy format like PNG, PCT, or BMP.

Figure 4.16 indicates the bitmap properties for rub1.jpg, our first image in the previous figure. Notice that there is a checkbox for use with imported JPEG data. If it is deselected, the image quality can be set manually. So if we set this image to a Quality of 20 and click the Test button, Flash conveniently comes back and indicates that our original image was 45.4 kilobytes, now compressed at 1.5 kilobytes. The new size is 3 percent of the original. This is a very handy tool for setting your compression.

Some people prefer to set their compression in Fireworks, which has one of the best CODECs for compression in the industry.

If you prefer to use Fireworks, just leave the box checked next to Use imported JPEG data. Don't use the manual setting. At Juxt, we often use the manual setting for bitmaps we're using in motion sequences. This enables us to go in and study each image individually and use the settings of 20, 30, 50, 80, or as low as we can go to obtain the best balance of compression and visual quality. With moving images, compression often adds a motion blur that can sometimes work well as an effect. We can also get the files much smaller in size. This can only be done in Flash because smoothing is applied to the images along with the compression.

4.4.3.2 PNG COMPRESSION

Now let's look at the next image, shorn_32.png. This image (see Figure 4.17) is a 32-bit PNG. Most PNGs are 24 bit, but this one happens to have another 8 bits, which is the alpha channel. This channel describes the opacity of the image.

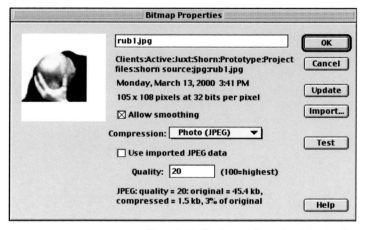

Figure 4.16   The Bitmap Properties dialog box for the graphic named rub1.jpg.

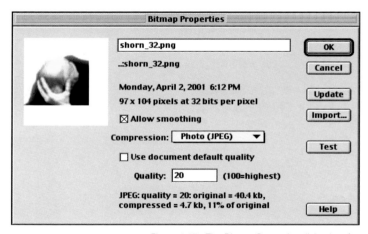

Figure 4.17   The Bitmap Properties dialog box for the graphic named shorn_32.png.

NOTE
A CODEC is a compression algorithm, and it differs from application to application.

If you look in the main window of this file, you see that it kind of fades off. It's particularly evident in the portion of the image over the amber bar. If the JPEG compression is set to be the same as in Figure 4.17, which had a compression Quality of 20, the file size changes from 40.04 kilobytes to 4.7 kilobytes, which is not nearly as efficient as the previous JPEG image. This happens because we have added another 8 bits of transparency to this file, and if you examine the image, it's very nasty looking at this setting. So, for this type of image, we typically want to stick with *lossless* compression, which is going to be much larger in file size, as evidenced in Figure 4.18. Here, the file size is 19.1 kilobytes. In file formats with lossless compression, no data is lost when the file is saved. The quality of the file remains the same throughout multiple generations, as opposed to what happens with lossy compression. Remember, with lossy compression information is stripped out of the file each time it's saved, resulting in image degradation.

PNG images can also be very effective for placing a transparent image over other elements in your Flash movie. However, they're very heavy, and this needs to be considered in a Flash site design.

4.4.3.3 BITMAP IMAGE COMPRESSION

Looking at the same file, the third and final image is a cupid. It represents the last type of image: the bitmap. This could be another PNG or a GIF image. At Juxt, we typically make bitmaps into 2-bit TIFFs, or 2-bit images. Then, in Fireworks, we make them into PNGs, or we use FreeHand import, which retains the transparency set on 2-bit TIFFs.

These images are interesting in nature. If you look at the cupid in Figure 4.19, you'll see that if we crank the JPEG compression all the way down to 10, the smallest it gets is 1.5 kilobytes. If you take it up to 30, it still is only 1.5 kilobytes.

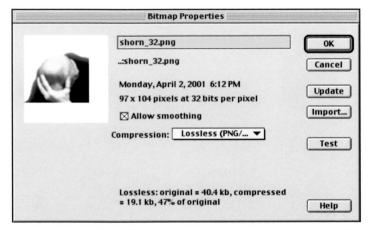

Figure 4.18 Lossless compression was selected for this PNG image to achieve a better quality image.

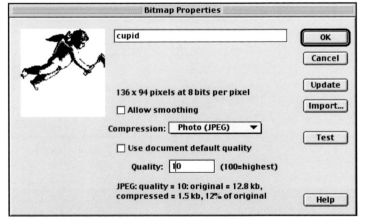

Figure 4.19 In this graphic, the JPEG compression was brought all the way down to 10, yielding a size of 1.5KB.

This is the lowest JPEG compression we can use on this image due to the nature of JPEG compression. However, if we set it to Lossless PNG/GIF, it goes down to half the size, which is 0.7 kilobytes, as shown in Figure 4.20. Compared to the previous example, we can see that PNG doesn't always mean heavy; it just depends on the content in the image. To work efficiently in Flash, a thorough knowledge of image compression is needed.

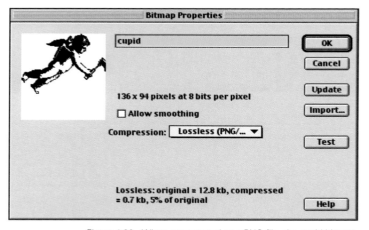

Figure 4.20   When compressed as a PNG file, the cupid bitmap, with an original size of 12.8KB, becomes 0.7KB in size.

Basically, PNG and GIF compression work well in runs. With GIF formats, it's all horizontal; with PNG, it's horizontal, vertical, or both. So it starts and then stops. Then it's white to this point, black from this point to this point, then white again from this point to this point, then black again from this point to this point, and so on. JPEG compression creates averages in areas within the image; then it goes through and sucks out the extreme chromas (the extreme highs and lows of an image) and averages them out. That's why, when you overcompress a JPEG, the image appears muddy. The whites are kind of grayish, and the high-saturated colors are muted. Overcompressing a JPEG literally sucks the color out of the image.

Understanding compression guidelines and knowing what type of images to use in certain applications can help tremendously in the design process. For instance, if you have a very large background image, it might be in your best interest to choose an image that's going to be subtle, blurry, and muted in tone, such as a grayscale image having only 20 to 60 shades of gray. This way, you can really compress the image, and it won't be very obvious to the viewer. If you have a very crisp, fine, highly saturated, very detailed image in the background, you won't be able to compress the image very much. The image, therefore, will be very large in file size. And if you're choosing PNG compression for the transparency, be judicious. Use it in certain situations and try to make the images you apply as small as you possibly can. Our experience has shown that if you create a large background image that has another 8-bit transparency on it, it's going to be very heavy.

4.4.4   NESTED SYMBOLS AND OPTIMIZING

Another good optimizing practice (which is also a good production practice) is nesting symbols. When you place symbols inside other symbols, a common way of organizing in a Flash movie, it's known as *nesting*. If you go to the scene nested symbol in the movie called optimize_examples.fla, you will see four buttons to the right (see Figure 4.21). Now, zoom in on these buttons to examine them.

Figure 4.21   Buttons from the movie called optimize_examples.

These buttons are identical, with the exception of the text label in each button. If you roll over a button, the background turns green; on clicking, the background turns white. In addition, the label and the dot-dash line turn black.

Let's analyze the makeup of one of the buttons (see Figure 4.22). Each button consists of the background shape, a dash line symbol, and the label symbol. Notice that each one of these elements is a symbol.

Figure 4.22   The button called butt_home in editing mode.

Experience dictates that nesting symbols is an efficient way of working for the sake of file size, optimization, consistency, and production. Also, it's best to create a graphic unit as a whole and migrate from that unit to make it a well-formed element. Many people believe that since text is essentially a symbol (referring to the font), it makes no sense to symbolize that text. On the contrary, it makes absolute sense for better and more efficient production. In Figure 4.21, all four buttons were made by simply creating the first

button, indicating the label, and then duplicating the button three additional times. We were able to go in, duplicate the label symbol as another symbol, and change the properties of the text within that label, thereby giving us a new button. And if for any reason we had made a mistake in the label (and we all know that designers rarely make spelling errors), we could simply go back and correct that spelling error in one instance, and all subsequent instances would be corrected. This was possible because all the labels for all the states of that button were referencing one symbol.

4.4.5 THE BANDWIDTH PROFILER AND THE FILE SIZE REPORT

The next optimization issue is the Bandwidth Profiler. The Bandwidth Profiler is like the Hutch of optimization (of Starsky and Hutch, that is; now I just severely dated myself). The Bandwidth Profiler is always your best buddy in that it helps you break down and analyze your file. Flash provides you with two tools for this purpose. The first tool is the Bandwidth Profiler. This is a very visual and interactive method of examining your file optimization. The other tool is the File Size Report that you get if you select Generate Size Report from the Export Flash Player dialog box. This is also a very good and useful feature.

The File Size Report generates information on the file size for each element in a movie. It breaks down symbols and text characters and provides all the details of a movie. You'll appreciate this feature if you're very anal. The Bandwidth Profiler is much more visual and interactive and is a good way to assess a file, to look at it to see how efficiently it's streaming and/or loading data. It also helps determine whether a preloading scheme is needed. This way, you'll know when enough frames have loaded so you can let the user into the site without having to make him or her wait for all frames in the movie to load.

Figure 4.23 shows the Bandwidth Profiler and the Juxt Interactive base movie.

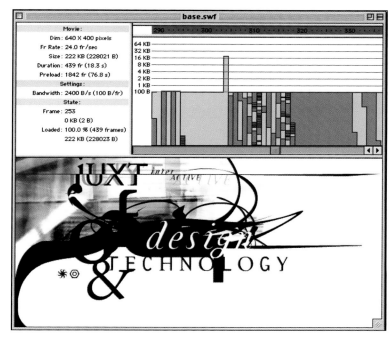

Figure 4.23   The Bandwidth Profiler displayed above the Juxt Interactive base movie.

The Bandwidth Profiler is basically a chunk-to-chunk representation of the file size. If you click on the blocks to the lower right of the profiler, above where your files display in playback, you're highlighting frames within the movie. The left side of the profiler indicates exactly what that frame consists of. So if you analyze the information on the left, the Movie information indicates the movie's dimensions (640×400), the frame rate (24fps), the file size (222KB), the duration (439 frames), and the preload (as set to 1,842 frames). The Bandwidth setting in this movie is 28.8Kbps, or 2,400 bits per second. Below this, the State displays information about the frames.

There's a summary of the information on the right that relates to the currently highlighted frame. It also indicates how much information is on that frame, including the number of bytes. It tells you what the percentage of the load is and what the total percentage of the load is. The last two elements are basically a reflection of the streaming in the movie.

Figure 4.24 displays the pop-up menu under View. If Show Streaming is selected, a modem connection is emulated (that is set within Flash) to show you how a file will play back over different connection speeds. The bottom two fields in the Bandwidth Profiler (Frame and Loaded) represent two variables that are being displayed: the loaded percentage and the actual file size that's loaded. So this is a very handy tool that previews how the real world sees a file.

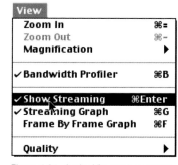

Figure 4.24   In the View pop-up menu, you can turn Show Streaming on and off.

The Show Streaming tool can also be customized. In the Debug menu (see Figure 4.25), you can choose from 14.4, 28.8, 56K, or user settings. You can even set it for ISDN, DSL, or T3 if you're really excitable.

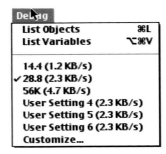

Figure 4.25 In the Debug menu, you can customize Show Streaming.

It's a good idea to watch the Bandwidth Profiler while developing your movie. On several occasions at Juxt, when we've imported artwork from other applications, that artwork has somehow been corrupted. It can be very frustrating when, at the end of a project, you're looking at a file that you know should be 100K, but it's 200K. At this point, it's so late in the game that you have to pick your way through everything to analyze what the problem is. If you're watching the Bandwidth Profiler as you're developing, you can, at a moment's notice, see if your file just jumped from 40K to 140K. You can also pinpoint exactly where it happened. Was it when I imported that word, that font, or that element? If there's something wrong with that element, you can go in and dissect it to figure out what the problem is. It's a lot easier to catch a problem during the project's development than at the end of the file. There's nothing more frustrating than getting to the end of a project and realizing that you're two or three hundred K over budget in file size. You then have to go

in, trim the fat off, and hack content out of your Flash movie just to meet the spec. So by keeping the Bandwidth Profiler as your close ally, you can define and address problems as they arise and know exactly where you stand at a moment's notice.

4.4.6 OPTIMIZING SOUND IN FLASH

Another significant issue that needs to be discussed in relation to optimization is sound. The two elements that impact file size more than anything else in Flash are bitmap images and sound.

The quality of sound in a typical Flash movie is akin to AM radio, which is not a good thing. We live by the standard of degradation, meaning this is all we can afford, so this is all we can get. The release of Flash 4 gave us access to MP3, which is roughly twice the quality of sound for half the file size. Inclusion of sound is still pretty limiting. If you're not careful, just adding a handful of simple sounds can double a file size.

There are basically two types of sounds in Flash: a synch sound and an event sound. An event sound can be set to start on an event. Event sound and synch sound are in essence the same, with the exception of Start. This checks to see if a particular sound is already playing. If it's already playing, it won't play. Event just plays whenever you call the action to play that sound. In Flash 5, there's now the action attached to a sound, also known as a sound object. This is, in effect, a new form of a sound. Once you define the sound object, you can attach actions to the sound to control it. This is similar to an event sound in that it's called with an ActionScript. It's not a synch sound; it merely calls on an event, which is a call from an ActionScript. Action sounds, however, have a kind of cache. Any action sound used in a file will be forced to load at the very beginning, before anything on frame 1 displays. Therefore, you have to be judicious with organizing movie clips that incorporate action sounds. It is a good idea to load a base movie with no action sounds first. Then action sounds are called in other movies that are layered on top, later on in the movie experience.

The synch sound is basically the only type of sound that is synched up to the motion on the screen. Therefore, when you scrub (or drag the playhead) along the timeline, you can hear the sound playing to the motion. This is great for creating animations that are tied to the sound for voiceovers, cartoons, or soundtracks. The downside to synch is that it takes up a chunk of your bandwidth, so you're automatically just giving away your bandwidth to the synch sound. It doesn't cache and just keeps loading continuously. So if you need to loop it again, you're still giving up that bandwidth.

Another drawback to synch sound on slower computers is that the computer will drop frames from the animation to keep up with the sound. The sound is basically like God in the playback, and therefore your animation might appear choppy. In fact, if your sound buffering runs out and your playback catches up with the level of what you've downloaded, your synch sound will stop, and it will buffer again. This is kind of like breaking the file experience. Because of this, it's important for you to set your buffering or your preloading to a generous level to accommodate any slow connections.

We tend not to use synched sound too much at Juxt. This is because we're very visual in what we create, and we usually don't want to give up the bandwidth to synched sound. This is especially true because event sounds can be cached. We often default to the event sounds, which, if done effectively, can create a very solid sound experience in a relatively small file size.

Typically, the strategy we use is to develop one prominent base loop, sometimes (depending on the project) a few base loops. But primarily we try to break it down to one base loop that is somewhat monotone in quality, which doesn't have too many highs or too many lows, so that it doesn't wear out your senses in the loop. Rather, it gives a sense of passively looping in the background. Along with that, we might develop a handful of other accent sounds. We use the Flash timeline to score the project, adding in these accent sounds to reinforce visual dynamics that are happening within the motion graphics or the interaction of the site. This results in a more robust sound experience. Although there are limitations to what can be done, we use the sound files that we've already downloaded over and over again to create a very dynamic sound experience. The drawback to looping sound is that, inevitably, it does become annoying. So it's very important that, when you do create or select your looping sound, you do so with great care so as not to annoy your user. Also, it's a good idea to create a Sound Off button to give the user the option of turning off the sound. In some cases, it doesn't matter what kind of sound is used; some people will hate it. Always use sound judiciously.

Like images in the library, sound compression should be set individually. In the library, if you select the properties for the sound symbol, a dialog box pops up. This enables you to manually set the compression at the bottom of the box. To date, MP3 is the best compression option. Depending on the desired quality, you can set your bit rates and quality accordingly. Figure 4.26 represents the main background loop for the Juxt Interactive site.

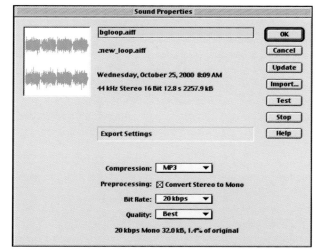

Figure 4.26   The Sound Properties dialog box for a sound called bgloop.aiff used in the Juxt Interactive site.

This is a big, thick, long sound file. Actually, it's 32 kilobytes with a bit rate of 20KBps (kilobytes per second), which can go all the way down to 8KBps or all the way up to 160KBps. Although 20KBps is pretty low, people don't expect as much quality in sound format on the web. Therefore, it's better to give users lower quality sound and lighter files than higher quality sound and fatter files. After all, most people don't own speakers for the pure enjoyment of sound on your site. It's also best to convert stereo to mono because it makes the file size much smaller.

There's an issue to be aware of when importing in MP3 format. At the very end of the MP3, there's a small gap due to its compression method, so there's no way to create effective or continuous looping of sound from an imported MP3. This gap creates a nasty glitch when the sound loops. So, if you want to loop a base loop or a background sound, I advise you to leave the raw sources in AIF or WAV file format.

We could write many chapters on the subject of sound in Flash. However, this is not our primary focus in the book. If you want more information on sound, pick up *The New Masters of Flash* by Friends of ED. We did a whole chapter on sound, and it will answer any questions you might have. We also encourage you to participate in discussions on our book's site. For those of you who know more about sound, please share your knowledge with others on our site. For those of you who know less, sound has its own culture, with a vast amount of information and experience throughout the community.

4.5 SUMMARY

This wraps up our discussion of the development process and optimization. We felt it was crucial to include this information in the book and to provide you with a lot of the secrets we've learned over the years developing Flash content.

The next chapter jumps straight into ActionScript and explores the magic behind the Juxt Interactive site.

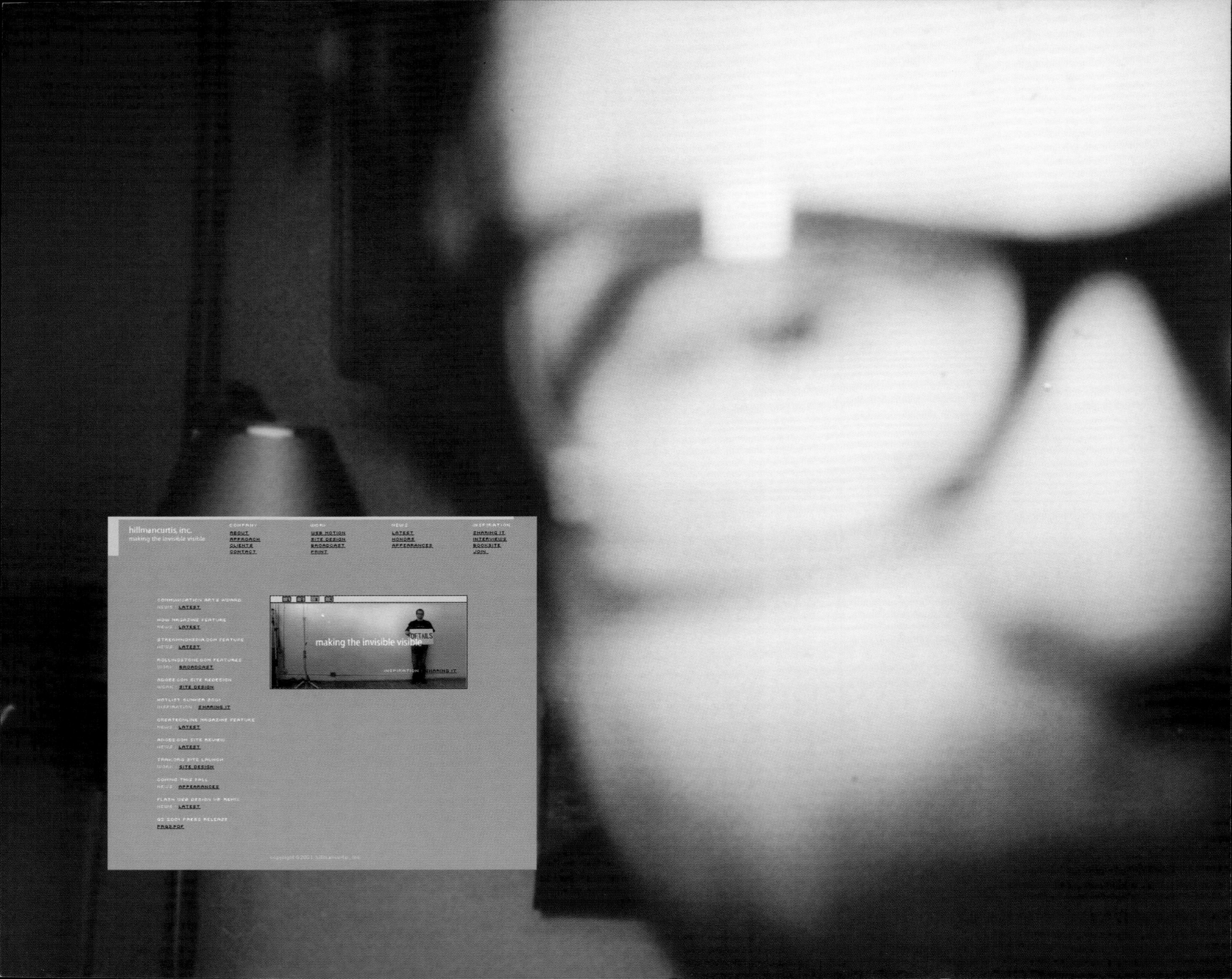
hillmancurtis, inc.
making the invisible visible
COMPANY
ABOUT
APPROACH
CLIENTS
CONTACT
WORK
WEB MOTION
SITE DESIGN
BROADCAST
PRINT
NEWS
LATEST
HONORS
APPEARANCES
INSPIRATION
SHARING IT
INTERVIEWS
BOOKSITE
JOIN
COMMUNICATION ARTS AWARD
NEWS : LATEST
HOW MAGAZINE FEATURE
NEWS : LATEST
STREAMINGMEDIA.COM FEATURE
NEWS : LATEST
ROLLINGSTONE.COM FEATURES
WORK : BROADCAST
ADOBE.COM SITE REDESIGN
WORK : SITE DESIGN
HOTLIST SUMMER 2001
INSPIRATION : SHARING IT
CREATEONLINE MAGAZINE FEATURE
NEWS : LATEST
ADOBE.COM SITE REVIEW
NEWS : LATEST
TRAK.ORG SITE LAUNCH
WORK : SITE DESIGN
COMING THIS FALL
NEWS : APPEARANCES
FLASH WEB DESIGN V2 REMIX
NEWS : LATEST
Q2 2001 PRESS RELEASE
PRQ2.PDF
DETAILS
making the invisible visible
INSPIRATION : SHARING IT

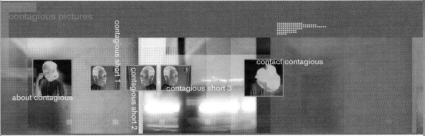

Contagious Pictures 212.343.2233

HILLMAN CURTIS

Hillman Curtis Interview
by Todd Purgason

Introduction
www.hillmancurtis.com

I first met Hillman at Macromedia UCON 99. Macromedia had
paired us up on a Flash session together even though we had
never met. We talked via phone and email, planning out the session prior to the event. We also planned to meet the day before.
We hit it off and ended up spending hours talking about everything other than the session, which in the end we just winged.
Since then, we have developed a friendship that has taken us
through client projects and book projects together. I have always
felt it an honor to call Hillman my friend, and I have the utmost
respect for him personally and professionally.

Cysive.

Reliable.

Scalable.

Valuable.

Teaser from the Interview

TP: Alright, we're here with Hillman Curtis. So Hillman, tell me, who is Hillman Curtis?

HC: Todd, that's the most ridiculous question I've ever heard.

TP: I should expect that from you.

HC: Yeah, but I'll pay you back later.

TP: I know it's cheesy.

HC: Yeah all right. Well, my name's Hillman Curtis. I'm a graphic designer. I run a small, five-person shop in the Soho district of New York City and do mostly new media design and a little bit of print. But new media design is something that I describe as anything that's done digitally that plays on a screen. That screen could be a movie screen, or it could be a computer screen, or it could be a TV screen. And so that's what we do. And we've been at it for a little while now and had some real fortunate jobs come our way, amongst them, well, we can get into that later, but that's it.

TP: That's who you are.

HC: Yeah, as a designer. You know, we don't want to get into the other stuff.

TP: Please don't.

HC: Whole other chapter.

TP: Spare us that.

HC: Yeah.

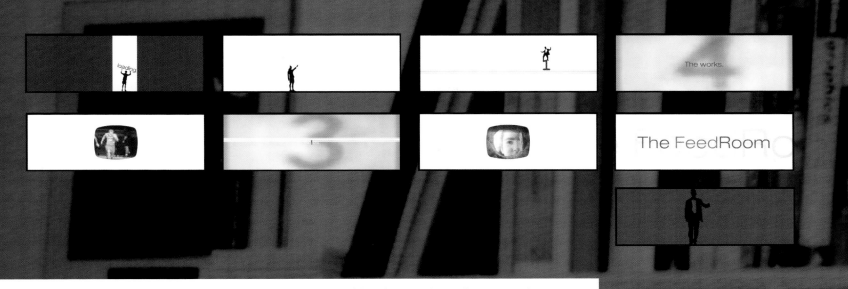

To hear the rest of Hillman's response and his answers to the following questions, please go to the Inspirations section of the book's site at www.JUXTinteractive.com/deCONSTRUCTION.

QUESTIONS

02. If your were a fish/sea creature, what would you be?

03. What CD or mp3 is in your player right now?

04. What is your definition of design?

05. What was your very first impression of Flash?

06. If you were walking down the street and came across John Gay and Jakob Nielsen engaged in a fistfight, what would you do?

07. Your history is in rock and roll. How has that influenced you as a designer?

08. You recently redesigned your site using very little Flash content. What was the reason behind this decision?

09. You have been doing some video work recently. Is that the direction you're heading as a company?

10. You live in New York City. Do you feel that the environment in New York affects your work? If so, in what way?

11. What do you mean when you say "eat the audience?"

12. How do you continue to grow yourself as a designer?

13. At some point last year, when we were hanging out at some conference, you told me that you were starting to get obsessed with simplicity and that you were tired of all the clutter around us. I can see how that has impacted the design of your new site. What is your opinion of the chaos theory of design?

14. What is it that happens in a typical day that gives you a feeling of satisfaction when you go home at night?

15. You have created a lot of award-winning work and have gotten a lot of PR these past few years. What project that you have created has given you the most personal satisfaction and why?

16. If you could do one last project before you had to hang up your designer's cap, what would you want that project to be?

c5 CHAPTER
Flash deCONSTRUCTION
JUXT INTERACTIVE.COM
ENVIRONMENT SCRIPTING

c5 CHAPTER

Flash deCONSTRUCTION

JUXT INTERACTIVE.COM
ENVIRONMENT SCRIPTING

When Flash first made its debut in the web design arena, web sites quickly became a soapbox forum for long, animated motion graphics and embellished rollovers. We were all enamored of the application's unique capabilities because our once-static designs could now have movement, tempo, and timeline-based content.

With the introduction of Flash 4, designers discovered interactivity, which served as a new venue for creative expression. For the past few years, Flash interactivity has been explored by designers world-wide. These designers have been preoccupied with mastering Flash ActionScript, driven purely by the challenge to create the next cool ActionScript effect.

This collective ActionScript frenzy has contributed to new explorations in interactivity. At Juxt, it has pushed and inspired us to approach multimedia content in new and creative ways that ultimately enhance the visitor's experience.

Today, web designers have the freedom to present content in unique ways that can make or break the visitor's experience. Readers, fear not. I'm not going to venture into the realm of usability dogma. I'm sure we've all had enough of that subject to last a lifetime. My point is that we are now designing and creating experiences that are multi-dimensional, thanks to Flash 5 ActionScript.

Flash 5 was a very large step for ActionScript, offering many new features and providing much simpler ways to achieve an interactive vision. This chapter examines the way that Juxt uses ActionScript as a creative expression behind the JuxtInteractive.com web site. In this site, we've created an environment that not only reinforces content, it also enhances the user's experience. At Juxt, we call this environment "scripting" because it is, in effect, an interactive presentation environment. The primary goal of the Juxt site is to build a unique and engaging experience in which the user becomes more of a participant in our content, and less of an observer.

5.1 CLIP EVENTS

In Chapter 3, "ActionScript Basics," we discussed the movie clip model. Movie clips are one of the great features in the Flash ActionScript arsenal. And with Flash 5 came the clip event.

In the past, we relied on a few very basic ActionScript events, related to the mouse and specific frames. However, the clip event enables us to develop more complex interaction with greater ease. Clip events are an important building block in the Juxt site. Therefore, we'll cover clip events thoroughly before diving into specific code deconstructions.

5.1.1 WHAT IS A CLIP EVENT?

A *clip event* is an ActionScript technique used to assign unique actions to individual instances of the same movie clip symbol. They also add more functionality to the movie clip symbol (see Figure 5.1).

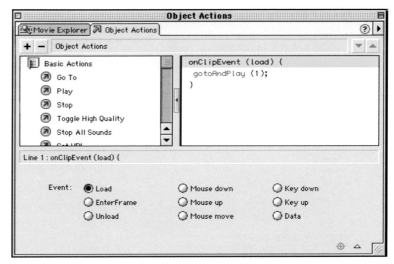

Figure 5.1   The clip events available in Flash 5 are listed in the Object Actions palette when a movie clip is selected.

The clip events available in Flash 5 are as follows:

- Load
- EnterFrame
- Unload
- Mouse down
- Mouse up
- Mouse move
- Key down
- Key up
- Data

Clip events are used by selecting a movie clip, opening the Action palette, and adding the following ActionScript:

```
onClipEvent(movieEvent) {
    //ACTIONS
}
```

One useful way to use a clip event is to replace the old, two-frame, looping clip technique used in Flash 4.

For a quick demonstration of how a clip event handles a looping technique, create a new movie clip and name it clipEvents. Drag it to the stage and give it a unique instance name. Enter the following script into the Actions palette:

```
onClipEvent (enterFrame) {
    _root.increasingNumber += 1;
}
```

On the main stage, add a dynamic text field called increasingNumber. Now, run the movie and watch the number in the text field increase due to the constant loop of the clipEvents movie. Refer to the file clip_event.fla as an example of this script.

Clip events are used throughout the Juxt site to loop actions that track the mouse, control the sound volume, draw dynamic lines, scroll text fields, and do other actions that require looping feedback.

5.2 ORGANIC MOTION

One of most visually interesting features of the Juxt Interactive site is the organic forms (the "fringies," as we affectionately call them) that appear to grow out of the main navigation as you roll over the section buttons (see Figure 5.2). The fringies feel organic for two reasons. First, the form grows out of the navigation buttons and then retracts again on rollout. Believe it or not, creating this effect sounds complicated but is actually very simple.

Figure 5.2 The organic rollover effect in the main navigation.

Certainly, it's easy to create a button that tells a movie clip to go to and play on rollover and rollout events. What makes the fringies unique is the natural manner in which they appear to grow. For example, if you roll over a button and the form only grows halfway out, and then you roll off, it retracts from that point. If your were to simply tell the movie clip to go to a preassigned starting point for the retraction and retract, the element would snap out to the fully revealed state and then retract. In contrast to our organic forms, the latter effect would feel mechanical and unnatural and would work against the effect we are trying to create.

5.3 MOVIE CLIP FRAME TRACKING

To create a rollover like the fringie effect, you'll need to structure your rollover movie clip so that the animation is mirrored around the center frame. For example, in the file named randomize, the rollover clip News Movie is 10 frames long, and the center on frame is frame 5 (see Figure 5.3). All of the animation is mirrored around frame 5 so that the rollover animation builds up to frame 5 and the rollout animation is after frame 5.

The following action is on frame 1 (see Figure 5.4):

```
stop ();
function outRoll () {
    gotoAndPlay(_totalframes-_currentframe);
}
```

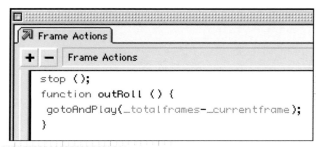

Figure 5.4 The frame tracking script on frame 10 in the News Movie movie clip.

We'll be calling this function from the rollover button on the main timeline. This button has the following actions:

```
on (rollOver) {
    news.gotoAndPlay("in");
}
on (rollOut) {
    news.outRoll();
}
```

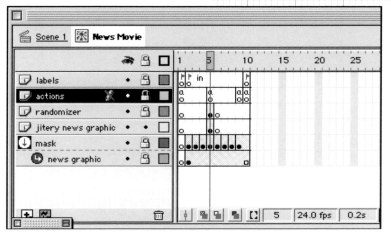

Figure 5.3 The fringie movie clip growth retraction timeline.

On rollout, the button calls the action that we placed on the frame "rollout." This action will take the current frame and find its mirror frame. For example, if we're in the middle of the rollon animation at frame 3, the corresponding rollout frame is frame 7.

NOTE

Math.round(Math.Random()) is new syntax that supercedes the old method of Random(). The older method is much simpler and still works, so it is your call which you choose to use.

5.4 RANDOMIZING

The other aspect about the fringies that makes them feel organic and alive is the random nature of the jitter that occurs as you hold the mouse over the button. Four elements make up this effect:

1. The first element is a movie clip with 10 frames. If you are re-creating a similar effect, you can use as many frames as you like. We chose 10 frames for our movie clip because we felt this was sufficient. Also, each frame has the fringie symbol placed in a slightly different position and opacity.

2. The second element is a script that tells the movie clip to go to a random frame within the 10 frames of our clip.

3. The next element is a script that picks a random amount of time to wait before executing the go-to-random-frame script.

4. The final element is a script that tells the movie clip's playhead to go back to the random script.

Let's take a deeper look at how all these elements work together to create the organic forms in the Juxt site.

5.4.1 GENERATING RANDOM NUMBERS

Generating random numbers is fairly straightforward. To generate a random number, you simply write the following:

```
Math.round(Math.Random()*range)
```

The *range* is a number, or a variable, that evaluates to a numeric value. It represents the range of numbers that the randomize function will choose from, starting with 0. Here's an example:

```
Math.round(Math.Random()*1)
```

The preceding line will return a random number of either 0 or 1.

We used random number generation to set the time delay and to pick the frame to go to. Open the file named randomize.fla and we'll demonstrate, step by step, how to create this effect:

- First, edit the News Movie movie clip. This clip contains an animation of a graphic being unmasked and then masked again. We'll concentrate on frame 5 of this movie clip. The actions on frame 5 are the following:

```
stop ();
maxTime = Math.round(Math.Random()*5) ;
```

The maxTime variable is a random number between 0 and 4 that defines the amount of time that the jittering animation will play.

- Now, edit the movie clip called Random Timer. The first frame, init, is the initialization frame. This is where the following parameters are set up (see Figure 5.5):

```
timeStart = getTimer();
timeCurrent = getTimer();
maxTime = _parent.maxTime*100;
```

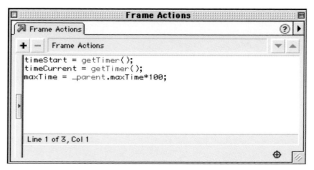

Figure 5.5   Random time generator script.

Figure 5.6   Time generator with frame randomizer.

- The variable timestart is set to the current time using the getTimer() method. The getTimer() method returns the time elapsed since the start of the Flash movie in milliseconds. We'll set the variable timeCurrent to the same value. Finally, we set a local variable, maxTime, to the previously set maxTime in the parent timeline. By multiplying the value by 100, we've set the maximum animation time between 0 and .4 seconds. Calculated by our movie frame rate, 24 fps, this maximum time evaluates to between 0 and 10 frames.

- Frame 2 has the following script (see Figure 5.6):

```
timeCurrent = getTimer();

timeDiff = timeCurrent-timeStart;

if (timeDiff>maxTime) {

  _root.news.jitter.gotoAndPlay(Math.round(Math.Random()*9)+1 );

}
```

- The variable timeCurrent is updated with the current time. Then the start time (timeStart) is subtracted from the timeCurrent variable to return the variable timeDiff. This represents the number of milliseconds since the movie clip was initialized. The if statement determines whether the time passed since the initialization of the movie clip (timeDiff) is greater than the maxTime. If it is, it sends the movie clip, jitter, to a random frame between 1 and 10.

If you look at the news_jitter movie clip, you'll see that each frame is keyframed. If the movie clip were to play all the way through without the randomizer, the jitter effect would still happen. However, after a few loops, the user would detect a visual loop in the motion. The randomizer breaks up this loop so that the user will never see the same animation twice, resulting in an organic, natural effect.

5.5 CONTENT FLOATERS

Screen real estate always challenges interactive designers. They grapple with this issue on every screen of a project. It's not just the art and science of getting all the necessary content on a particular screen. It's also the balancing of that content to draw the eye and effectively guide people to content. By default, there's often too much content to balance. The more content you add, the harder it is for users to find the content they need.

In the Desktop section of the Juxt site, we wanted to abstractly emulate the visual and interactive nature of a computer OS. However, this emulation limited our communication with the user. We needed a way to visually hint at content that wouldn't eat up a lot of real estate and destroy the simplicity of the section. The solution was to create a content floater, similar to the tool tip metaphor. This is a common feature of many applications running in computer OS environments, so it was a perfect fit for our design.

5.6 BUILDING TOOL TIPS

The tool tip is the basis for our content floaters, so we'll start by showing how to create one. The text in a tool tip generally describes the tool's name or function. This aids the user in deciphering what the visual icon is about. Because the subject of tool tips is at hand, we'll discuss how to create a simple tool tip. This example creates a text label that appears when a user lingers over a tool or navigation option (see Figure 5.7).

There are many ways to create this tool tip technique. The following is only one example:

- Create a movie clip with an instance name of tooltip that has two frames. Label the first frame off and the second frame on. Put a stop action on each frame. On the on frame, place a dynamic text field and name it tiptext.

- The tool tip clip is now set up. To use it, place the following actions on your tools, icons, or whatever you want the tool tip to hover over:

```
on (rollOver) {
    _root.tooltip.tiptext = "This tool is called";
    startDrag ("_root.tooltip", true);
    _root.tooltip.gotoAndStop("on");
}
on (rollOut) {
    _root.tooltip.gotoAndStop("off");
    stopDrag ();
}
```

Check out the file named tooltip.fla on the book's site to see this technique in action.

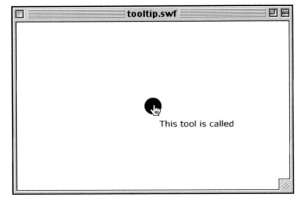

Figure 5.7   A simple text-based tool tip.

The Juxt site uses a variation of this technique for the Desktops section (see Figure 5.8).

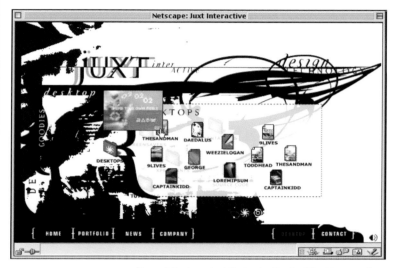

Figure 5.8 A content floater for the Juxt Desktops section.

Let's look at another variation of the tool tip. In the movie named tooltip2 on the book's site, there's a script on a movie clip with an instance name of tooltip that contains a frame for each tool tip state. On each icon, there's a script that tells the tooltip clip to gotoAndStop to the correct frame, startDrag on rollover, gotoAndStop, and stopDrag on rollout (see Figure 5.9).

```
Object Actions

+ —   Object Actions

on (rollOver) {
  _root.tooltip.gotoAndStop( _name );
  startDrag ("_root.tooltip", true);
}
on (rollOut) {
  stopDrag ();
  _root.tooltip.gotoAndStop("off" );
}
```

Figure 5.9 Action script for the desktop content floater.

In the file tooltip2.fla, you can examine the setup of these clips. The download thumbnails have corresponding instance names of download1 and download2. The download clips have a hotspot that tells the clip tooltip, on rollover, to gotoAndStop to the frame with the same label as the instance name of the thumbnail.

The tooltip clip is set up with three frames that consist of an off-frame label and a frame label for each of the two downloads. Each frame label in this clip corresponds to the instance name of the thumbnails.

5.7 DRAG-AND-DROP NAVIGATION

It seems ironic that with all the long hours of work we put in, at the end of the day, a complex project just gets packaged up into a little screen icon. We wanted to play on this irony in the project section of the Juxt site by wrapping the projects into icons and forcing the user to drag and drop that icon onto a directory to reveal its contents (see Figure 5.10).

Figure 5.10 Draggable project icons in the Juxt Projects section.

5.7.1 DRAGGABLE OBJECTS

Dragging a movie clip is as simple as invoking the startDrag action. To make a movie clip with a drag-and-drop action, just include a hotspot (blank button) in the movie clip with the following actions:

```
on (press) {
  startDrag ("");
}
on (release, releaseOutside, dragOut) {
  stopDrag ();
}
```

Having the additional event in there to trigger the stopDrag() function acts as a safety net against dragging difficulties.

Keep in mind that you can only drag one movie clip at a time. Any previous clip being dragged will be dropped once you start to drag another clip.

You can lock the drag of the movie clip to the mouse by adding the following:

```
startDrag("", true)
```

The area where the movie clip can be dragged can be constrained by adding the following:

```
startDrag("", true,  left, top, right, bottom)
```

The left, top, right, and bottom in the preceding line represent either numeric values or variables that evaluate to numeric values. These are the boundaries of the draggable area.

The Juxt site uses many draggable movie clips. The volume control (see the file volume.fla on the book's site) is an example of a constrained, draggable movie clip. The Portfolio section is an example of an unconstrained drag.

5.7.2 DRAG-AND-DROP COLLISION DETECTION

The file named dragdrop.fla is a stripped down version of the Portfolio section of the Juxt Interactive site. This file demonstrates how to do a simple drag-and-drop operation with a drop target.

The name of the clip we'll be dragging is projectthumb, with an instance name of juxt02. juxt02 was the project code for this item in our portfolio. Let's examine the actions on the hotspot in this symbol:

```
on (press) {
    // Establish X and Y of slot
    xpos = _x;
    ypos = _y;
    // Start Drag
    startDrag ("", true);
}
on (release) {
    // Stop Drag
    stopDrag ();
    // Determine if clip has hit drop spot
    if (_dropTarget == _root.folder._target) {
        _root.project = _name;
    } else {
        _root.project = "";
    }
    _x = xpos;
    _y = ypos;
}
```

The first set of actions is activated with the on (press) action. Because we want the clip to snap back to its original position once dropped, two variables, xpos and ypos, are set to the current X and Y coordinates. Then the startDrag method is used with the clip locked to the mouse center (see Figure 5.11).

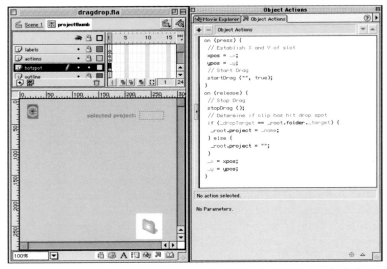

Figure 5.11   File dragdrop.fla and the drag ActionScript.

Once we've started dragging the clip, the next set of actions is activated when the clip is released.

The first action is to drop the clip using the stopDrag method. Then it's determined whether the clip was dropped on the folder icon. The folder icon is a movie clip with an instance name of folder. We can check to see if the clip was dropped on the folder by using an if statement. The if statement compares the dropTarget with the target of the folder. The dropTarget is a property of a movie clip that has been dropped. It represents the path of any other movie clip that the clip was dropped on. If the dropTarget is the folder, we'll set a display variable called project on the main timeline to the name property of the dropped clip. If the folder isn't dropped on, the display variable is blank. Finally, the drag clip is repositioned to its original coordinates.

5.8 DYNAMIC LINE GENERATION

There is an art and science to creating diagrams that communicate ideas. At Juxt, we use diagrams to create all kinds of communication documents. We use these diagrams to visually communicate structure, order, organization, navigation, interaction, content relationships, and many other ideas. We find that our concepts can often be communicated more effectively with pictures than with words.

For the process section of our site, we wanted to play with this aspect of our company. Because our process includes diagramming skills, it seemed appropriate to make that section a diagram. We created an abstract, interactive diagram that coalesced with the abstract nature of the site. We also wanted it to feel dynamic and responsive to the user in an unexpected way. One of the methods used to achieve this was to dynamically draw connection lines between a step in the process and its supporting copy, based on user interaction.

5.8.1 LINE GENERATION

The concept behind scripting a line drawn between two points is to position the end of the line at one point and then scale it so that the end of the line is at the second point. This technique only works with hairline-weight lines because the scaling of lines with a heavier weight would scale the line weight along with the dimensions.

The following represents the steps involved in creating such a line (refer to the file called dynamicline.fla on the book's site and see Figure 5.12):

1. First, create a square that's 100×100 pixels.

2. Using the square as a guide, draw a hairline-weight line that connects from the top-left corner of the square to the bottom-right corner. When you're done, delete the square so that you're left with a line slanted down to the right at exactly 45 degrees. Make this line a movie clip.

Figure 5.12   Diagonal line movie clip.

3. In the library, right-click (for Windows) or Ctrl+click (for Mac) on the new symbol and select Linkage. Give the symbol an identifier name of line. In the Symbol Linkage Properties dialog box, select Export this symbol (see Figure 5.13). Click OK.

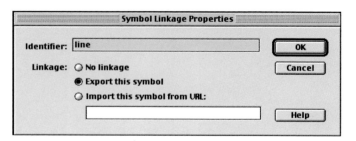

Figure 5.13   The Symbol Linkage Properties dialog box.

4. Edit this symbol and make sure the top-left corner of the line is at the center point of the symbol.

5. Pick two points that will be the endpoints of the line. These points can be X and Y coordinates that you provide or the X and Y coordinates of two movie clips you want to track. In this example, two movie clips are used. These movie clips are just circles with hotspots to make each clip draggable. The instance names of these clips are point1 and point2. With this setup, we'll be able to interactively drag the endpoints of our line.

   We should now have two draggable endpoints called point1 and point2 and a 100×100, 45-degree, hairline-weight line movie clip called line with an identifier name of line, too.

6. Now we'll create an action clip that will draw and control the line. We could use either of the "points," but to keep things separate and simple, we'll create a blank movie clip. Drag the blank clip to the stage and give it a clip event set to enterFrame.

   The first action that's added to the script is root.attachMovie. This will attach the line clip to the root timeline (see the following script).

7. Set the X and Y position of the new line instance to the X and Y position of point1.

8. Set the x and y scale of the new line instance to the difference between the X and Y positions of point2 and point1. Your finished code on the action clip should look like this (see Figure 5.14):

```
onClipEvent (enterFrame) {
    _root.attachMovie ("line", "line1", 1);
    _parent.line1._x = _parent.point1._x;
    _parent.line1._y = _parent.point1._y;
    _parent.line1._xscale = _parent.point2._x - _parent.point1._x;
    _parent.line1._yscale = _parent.point2._y - _parent.point1._y;
}
```

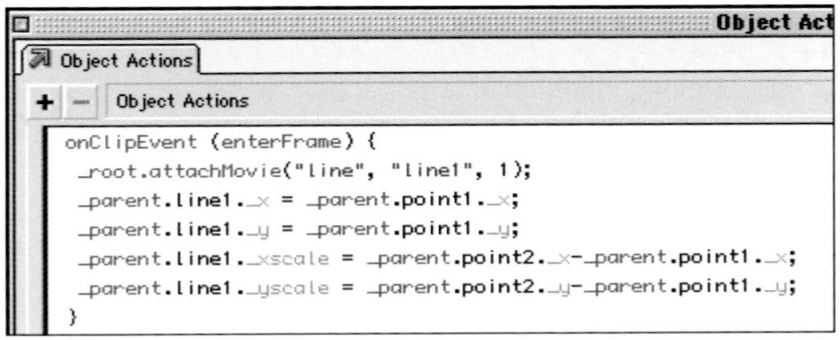

Figure 5.14   Dynamic line generation ActionScript.

Your action clip will now attach the line and position/scale it so that it connects the two points. If you don't attach the line to each loop, the line will flip every frame. On runtime, you should now be able to drag the two points around, and the line will connect them.

5.8.2 DYNAMIC LINE GENERATION IN THE PROCESS PRESENTATION

On the Juxt Interactive site, we used dynamically drawn lines in the Company section to create dynamic highlights for the Process presentation. Rather than allow the user to drag the endpoints of the lines, we scripted the movement of the endpoints to predefined X and Y coordinates that were set based on the section on which the user clicked.

If you examine the file named dynamicline2.fla, you'll notice that on the layer named dots, there are four empty movie clips called anchor1, anchor2, dot1, and dot2. These movie clips are the end-points of our dynamic lines. The anchors don't move, but the dots do. Notice that, in the Object Actions window, the clips start by setting two variables each to their current position.

Notice that the dot clips are positioned where they would be for the Strategy section. The next step was to move the dots around to the position they'll be to when the user clicks on the section hotspots and then jot down the X and Y coordinates of each spot.

Next, you'll see on the nav layer that we've set up hotspots for each section. The script on the strategy hotspot is the following:

```
on (release) {
    _root.dot1x = 150.5;
    _root.dot1y = 225.7;
    _root.dot2x = 150.5;
    _root.dot2y = 245.6;
}
```

These numbers came from the numbers just jotted down. If the script is examined on the other hotspots, you'll see different numbers based on the spot to which we want the lines to move.

The action clip is on the linemaker layer in the upper-left corner. Click on it to see the clip events:

```
onClipEvent (enterFrame) {
    // Move Dots
    _root.dot1._x = _root.dot1._x-((_root.dot1._x-_root.dot1x)/5);
    _root.dot1._y = _root.dot1._y-((_root.dot1._y-_root.dot1y)/5);
    _root.dot2._x = _root.dot2._x-((_root.dot2._x-_root.dot2x)/5);
    _root.dot2._y = _root.dot2._y-((_root.dot2._y-_root.dot2y)/5);
    // Draw Lines 1 and 2
    for (a=1; a<=2; ++a) {
        _root.attachMovie("line", "line"+a, a);
        _root["line"+a]._x = _root["dot"+a]._x;
        _root["line"+a]._y = _root["dot"+a]._y;
        _root["line"+a]._xscale = _root["anchor"+a]._x-_root["dot"+a]._x;
        _root["line"+a]._yscale = _root["anchor"+a]._y-_root["dot"+a]._y;
    }
    // Draw Line 3
    _root.attachMovie("line", "line3", 3);
    _root.line3._x = _root.dot1._x;
    _root.line3._y = _root.dot1._y;
    _root.line3._xscale = _root.dot2._x-_parent.dot1._x;
    _root.line3._yscale = _root.dot2._y-_parent.dot1._y;
}
```

The next step is to move the dots to the correct position. We do this by taking the current position of the dots, comparing it to the target position variable set by the hotspots, and then moving the dot the difference divided by five to smooth out the motion. Once we've moved the dots, we do a for loop to connect lines 1 and 2 between the anchors and the dots. Finally, we draw line 3 between dots 1 and 2 (see Figure 5.15).

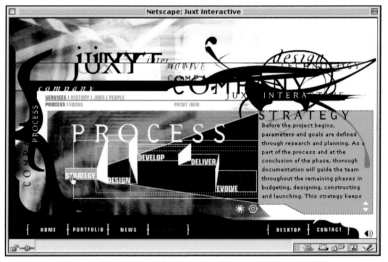

Figure 5.15 The JuxtInteractive.com process diagram.

5.9 GLOBAL SOUND CONTROL

One of the long-awaited features of Flash 5 was the capability to control sound with ActionScript. Due to the limitations of the player, the control that we have is very subtle. It's not nearly as robust as it could be if it were done in Director. But the control we do have is a positive addition to the application.

In Flash 5, we now have the capability to dynamically adjust both pan and volume of any sound. We took advantage of this technique on the Juxt site to enable users to control the volume of the background sound and the transition sounds (see Figure 5.16).

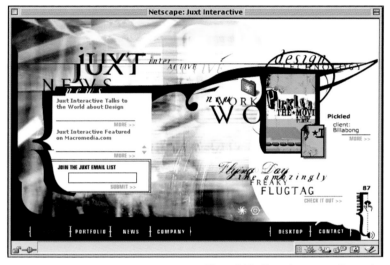

Figure 5.16 The volume controller on the JuxtInteractive.com site.

5.9.1 DYNAMIC VOLUME CONTROLLER

The first step in controlling the properties of sound in Flash is to give the sound a linkage name in the library. Open the file volume.fla. In the library, there is a sound file called sound. Right-click (for Windows) or Ctrl+click (for Mac) on this sound and select Linkage. In the Symbol Linkage Properties dialog box, we've given the sound an identifier name of sound and have set the linkage to Export this symbol (see Figure 5.17).

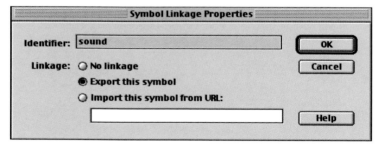

Figure 5.17 The Symbol Linkage Properties dialog box.

Take a look at the actions on the first frame of the main timeline. The script reads as follows:

```
sound = new Sound();
sound.attachSound("sound");
sound.start(0, 200);
soundbutton.volume = "100";
```

The script creates a sound object referred to by the variable sound. The next step is to attach the sound to the object through the attachSound method and pass the identifier of our exported sound, named sound. We start the sound playing by invoking the start

method. The "0" is the offset of the sound (the time into the sound where we begin playing), and the "200" is the number of loops we want the sound to play. The number 200 is just a large number, randomly picked so that the sound will keep looping. The final action sets the variable volume to 100. This is full volume. The movie clip soundbutton is the volume controller we'll work with next. At this point, we have attached a sound and started it playing.

Next, the movie clip volume controller is edited. The actual functionality of this clip is in a clip event on the sliderbutton movie clip.

Select the sliderbutton clip on the layer named volume slider in the volume controller clip. Open the Object Actions window and view the ActionScript attached to that clip (see Figure 5.18). The script reads as follows:

```
onClipEvent (load) {
    dragTop = -60;
    dragBottom = -6;
    valueMax = 100;
    valueBase = 0;
    valueRange = valueMax - valueBase;
}
onClipEvent (enterFrame) {
    _parent.volume = -((_y-dragBottom)/-((dragTop-
        dragBottom)/valueRange)) +valueBase;
    _parent.volumedisplay = Math.round(_parent.volume);
    if (_parent.volume ne "") {
        _root.sound.setVolume(_parent.volume);
    }
}
```

```
onClipEvent (load) {
    dragTop = -60;
    dragBottom = -6;
    valueMax = 100;
    valueBase = 0;
    valueRange = valueMax - valueBase;
}
onClipEvent (enterFrame) {
    _parent.volume = -((_y-dragBottom)/-((dragTop-dragBottom)/valueRange))+valueBase;
    _parent.volumedisplay = Math.round(_parent.volume);
    if (_parent.volume ne "") {
     _root.sound.setVolume(_parent.volume);
    }
}
```

Figure 5.18   The volume control ActionScript.

All of the actions in the onClipEvent(load) are the initial conditions for the slider. The dragTop and dragBottom variables are the Y positions at the top and bottom of the draggable area for the slider. These numbers were determined by positioning the slider at the visible top and bottom of the draggable area and noting the Y positions. The valueRange variable is the range of values controlled by the slider and is determined by subtracting valueBase from valueMax. The values 100 and 0 are predetermined because full volume is 100 and sound off is 0.

Once the initial conditions are set, the looping actions in the onClipEvent(enterFrame) are dealt with. The volume is determined with basic math, using the variables we initialized in the onClipEvent(load) and the current Y position of the scroller.

Once the volume has been calculated, the volumedisplay variable is set to the volume converted to an integer (which will get rid of unsightly decimal values). The setVolume method is invoked with the newly calculated volume.

Lastly, edit the sliderbutton movie clip and view the actions of the button (see Figure 5.19). You'll see the following ActionScript:

```
on (press) {
    startDrag ("", false, _x, dragTop, _x, dragBottom);
}
on (release) {
    stopDrag ();
}
```

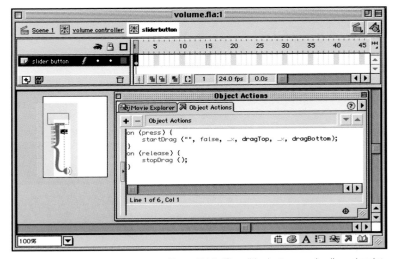

Figure 5.19   The slider button movie clip and script.

This script creates a simple drag-and-drop setup. It uses the variables dragTop and dragBottom to constrain the vertical drag and the X coordinate to constrain the horizontal drag.

5.10 BUILDING A SMART CLIP

Smart Clips are a feature of Flash 5 that virtually "idiot proof" ActionScript and/or content editing in Flash. The apparent benefit of Smart Clips is that they can be edited by a client or a fellow employee who has little or no Flash or ActionScript experience. In other words, it provides a means for the inexperienced user to edit scripts or content in their Flash movies.

At Juxt Interactive, we don't use Smart Clips too often. If a project requires dynamic content and updates provided by the client, we provide a back-end administration tool that utilizes database storage and retrieval of content. However, there are always those occasions when we need some idiot-proof development done.

On the initial launch of the Juxt site, we had limited resources for doing the database and content management work. As a result, we built some pieces manually for the first launch. These were eventually replaced with database-driven pieces. One of these pieces was the project description section. For this section, we chose to build a simple Smart Clip. This way, we could throw anybody and everybody on this project and not worry about human error, which could potentially cause unwanted bugs (see Figure 5.20).

In the file named smartclip.fla, you'll notice that the library contains a movie clip called smartclip. You can tell in the library that the movie clip is a Smart Clip because the icon is different from the standard movie clip icon (see Figure 5.21).

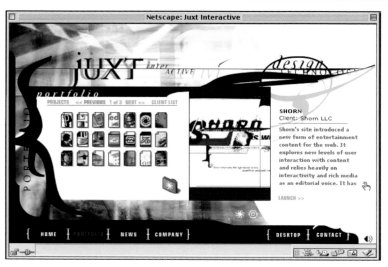

Figure 5.20   The Juxt Projects description movie clip in context.

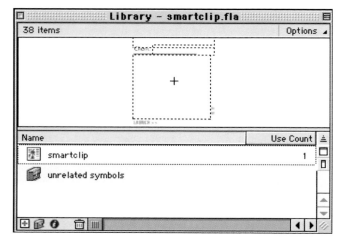

Figure 5.21   The smartclip symbol contains just the text-based content for each project.

Edit this symbol to see how the clip is structured. Essentially, the clip contains three dynamic text fields and a button to launch an HTML page. The text fields are info, client, and copy. The button is set to getUrl using the variable url.

Once the clip is set up, it can be converted to a Smart Clip. Do this by clicking on the symbol in the library and selecting Define Clip Parameters from the pop-up library menu (right-click for Windows; Ctrl+click for Mac). This opens the Define Clip Parameters dialog box. This is where you define the editable parameters of the Smart Clip. Add a parameter by clicking the + icon.

Edit the Name column and give the parameter the same name as the variable you want to edit. For a variable value of a string or number, leave the Value column as defaultValue and the Type column as Default. The Smart Clip in this file is already set up with the correct parameter/variable names (see Figure 5.22).

To use this Smart Clip, drag it to the stage. In the Clip Parameters palette (Window > Palettes > Clip Parameters), notice the parameter/variable names next to an editable Value column (see Figure 5.23).

Figure 5.23   Enter the data for the clip instances in the Clip Parameters palette.

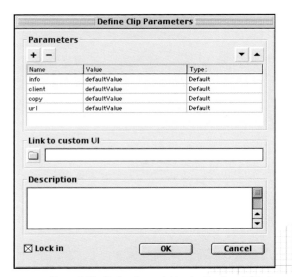

Figure 5.22   Define the variables for the Smart Clip in the Define Clip Parameters dialog box.

By changing the parameter values, when you run the Flash file, you'll see that the values have been transmitted to the movie clip's dynamic text fields.

NOTE

Clip parameters are passed to the clip before any actions on that clip have been run.

5.11 SUMMARY

This chapter represents a selective group of ActionScript techniques used in the Juxt site. In its totality, the Juxt site is far more complex and rich in ActionScript than the few methods discussed here. However, this chapter will provide you with a glimpse of how some of the techniques used in our site evolved. We hope you can take the simple pieces we have shown in this chapter and use them as building blocks in your own projects.

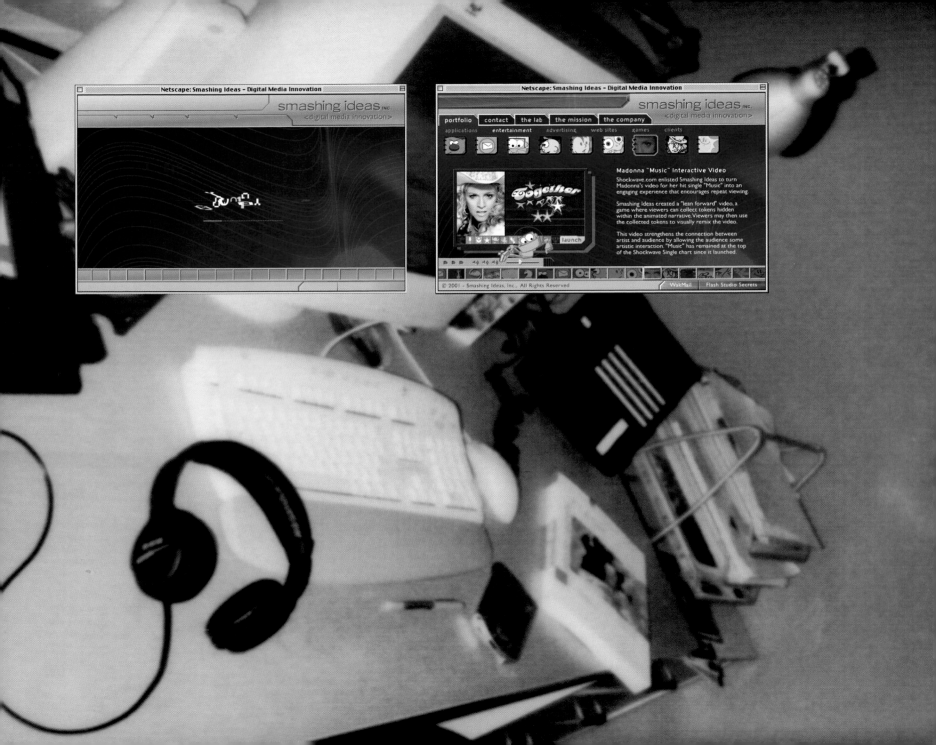

GLENN THOMAS

Glenn Thomas Interview
by Todd Purgason

Introduction
www.smashingideas.com

Flash and Smashing Ideas have been synonymous to me since
the very beginnings of Flash content on the web. Every time I
talk to friends at Macromedia, they say, "Have you seen the
latest thing from Smashing Ideas?" Well, after way too long, I
finally got the chance to meet one of the main minds behind
Smashing: Glenn Thomas. We met at the first Flash Forward
2000 conference in San Francisco. Since then, we have spent a
good deal of time hanging out at conferences, and we are currently working to gather another New Riders book project.

I believe that Smashing Ideas invented the humorous Flash animation genre, and we owe a lot to Glenn and his band of pioneers.

Teaser from the Interview

TP: We're here with Glenn Thomas from Smashing Ideas. So Glenn, who is Glenn Thomas?

GT: You're actually going to go through these questions you sent me, aren't you?

TP: I'm going to go through them, starting with the cheesiest one, too.

GT: Let's see. Want to be more specific on that question? A little broad, a little too big.

TP: That's too big? Glenn Thomas is big, I guess is the answer (laughs) multifaceted, (laughs) multidimensional.

GT: I used to weigh 800 pounds (laughs).

TP: You used to weigh 800 pounds?

GT: And then I went on the Flash diet, and now I weigh 140 (laughs).

Yeah, you know. There's a good quote for you:

"Glenn Thomas lost 660 pounds on the Flash diet."

TP: Hey, don't say it too loud. Macromedia will start using it. So, let's put it this way. Who is Smashing Ideas? That'll probably make it more specific.

GT: Right. I think I'll just give a brief history of us. I think that will somewhat explain it. Let's see. Me personally, when I moved back to Seattle, I started doing independent film and video before the web had really started, and I fell into a job with an online services company before Netscape was a company, and stuff like that.

So in '94, I was building stores on Prodigy when it was 8-bit color and AOL when they were going through their whole get-big-fast thing, when everybody was saying, "But this company is a financial failure, completely false, and they're lying, and they're going to go out of business," and they bought Time Warner.

So when that was going on, I was doing some independent film, animation, and things like that, and I met the other two

founders of the company, Even Clarrissimeaux and Ben Yenter, in an animation class. At that time, the most you could do with animation on the web was animated GIF, which didn't leave a whole lot of room for creativity. So we got to do a project for a local nonprofit here in Seattle and some TV animation, and after we were done with that, we just enjoyed working with each other. So we wanted to try and continue working with each other, and that was when Future Flash came out. And so we saw that and thought that there was a possibility, a future for this sort of stuff on the web, and got involved really early. And then, because we were sort of the first animators to use the tool, we got a lot of the first work in entertainment with animation and the other games and media Flash. And then sort of as the product has evolved, we've evolved.

TP: Yeah.

GT: More application stuff as well as the entertainment side. So that's sort of the history of the company in a nutshell. I guess, you know, our

philosophy is to always try to do interesting work. It turned out to be fun if you could have both in what you create and how you did it.

TP: It's funny, you guys pretty much invented the genre; I mean, you didn't invent animation, but you brought it to the web.

GT: When we first got started, nobody was doing it. You can do this. The Shockwave launch proved it.

Everybody in Hollywood jumped on the bandwagon and threw tons of money at it.

I think it was very exciting for us to be involved with experience on the web. You can do more than you can in traditional places like television or video. Just from a straight narrative standpoint. But we tried to do some interesting stuff with interactive.

To hear this rest of Glenn's response to this question, as well as his answers to the following questions, please go to the Inspirations section of the book's site at www.JUXTinteractive.com/deCONSTRUCTION.

QUESTIONS

02. If you were a fish/sea creature, what would you be?

03. What CD or mp3 is in your player right now?

04. What is your definition of design?

05. What was your very first impression of Flash?

06. If you were walking down the street and came across John Gay and Jakob Nielsen engaged in a fistfight, what would you do?

07. You were a very early developer on the Flash scene. How did Smashing Ideas start out?

08. Are you the man behind all the character animation?

09. You guys do some really fun humor projects, but alongside that, you do some pretty heady application development. How do you balance the staff between the two?

10. In your history, what has been your favorite project and why?

11. Can you tell us a little about your development process?

12. You did a Shockwave single for Madonna. Do you see Shockwave singles as being a viable new content type on the Internet?

13. What is your vision for Smashing Ideas? Do you see a day when you might do some broadcast content?

14. What is it that happens in a typical day that gives you a feeling of satisfaction when you go home at night?

15. Which of your viral marketing projects has been the most successful? Why is that, do you think?

16. If you could do one last project before you had to hang up your designer's cap, what would you want that project to be?

deCONSTRUCTION

The Process, Design, and ActionScript of
Juxt Interactive

Section 03
Deconstructing the Billabong Site

(a)

Pickled.TV was a web site created to promote a feature film being produced by Billabong USA. In the genre of surf flicks, Pickle was a step above. It was filmed on 35mm film, featuring surfers acting. You can call it acting I guess. It was a larger budget project than their typical surf video, and it's also touring the country in a series of movies called *The Adrenaline Series*, in AMC theaters. So it was more than your typical surf flick. This one actually had a bit of a storyline. You wouldn't necessarily call it a plot. To add some humor, there's a character in the industry by the name of Robert Earl, or Aka Toones. Robert is one of those freaks of a culture that has his finger on the pulse of the people and the trends that define it. Robert is very hilarious in his own right. He also understands and relates to the surfing community, and the surfing community relates to him. Billabong retained Robert to work with them on the Pickled movie and he's very much a part of it.

(b)

The movie is basically about Robert and his surf buddies, who are out on a surf adventure touring the world on a yacht. Robert is kind of a "wannabe" to this group. He goes out partying with the surfers, gets a little too intoxicated, and on their trip back to the yacht on the dinghy, he accidentally passes out and gets left on the dinghy. Unknowingly, the surfers take off for their next destination and the dinghy is left adrift in the ocean, leaving Robert stranded. On the dinghy, the only thing with Robert is a jar of pickles. Benji, one of the professional surfers, loves pickles and takes them with him everywhere he goes. Robert on the other hand, hates pickles. So in the end, Robert has to consume pickles to survive. After he eats them, he realizes the pickles are embalmed in alcohol and begins hallucinating the surf adventures of his friends. So that's the storyline of the movie, which as you can see, is pretty deep and emotional stuff.

(c)

The web site needed to capture that loose, comical, tongue-in-cheek feel of the film, but in a way that would be attractive to the target audience. The surf community is very finicky and cynical. They don't tolerate outsiders and can smell a rat a mile away.

We also had the challenge of obtaining the content. The only content we had up front was the storyline and a handful of images. We were actually very inspired by the whole pickled concept. Well, we were actually inspired by the green of Pickles. The essence of the movie also provided it's own inspiration. The movie is, as the director expressed, "a drunken hallucination."

(d)

So, we created this site that was very clumsy: falling over itself, bumping into things. The texture of the site is meant to feel like a torn up circus poster stained with pickle juice. We tried to create the sense of hallucination in the way we treated some of the imagery, animation, and typography. In essence, we attempted to bring the typography to life by the way we animated it. Motion graphics can be very dramatic. They can create a sense of animated life in ordinary things, like a word, just by the way they move across the screen.

(e)

So as you enter each section of the site, a typography animation plays out while other things are crashing into each other; it's kind of surreal in a way. It's all about that drunken hallucination state and being in that state of mind, where, you know, you're shaking and nodding yourself back to consciousness, almost falling asleep. It's very loose, very raw, and very fun.

(f)

That's the bottom line of this site. The movie is about having fun. The surfing culture is a lifestyle of good times, good friends, and surfing good waves. We didn't want this to be taken too seriously, so we tried to have a lot of fun with it.

Behind all that fun, we did some interesting things on the back end with ActionScript. We created a game where Tunes is defending himself and his pickles from rabid seagulls in the Pacific, and the humor that comes out of that makes me chuckle even now.

(g)

We also used ActionScript to help us create this kind of drunken feeling in the navigation of certain elements of the site. Things that go well beyond a simple tween.

c6 CHAPTER

Flash deCONSTRUCTION

BILLABONG-USA.COM—INNOVATIVE ACTIONSCRIPT NAVIGATION

Billabong is a company that makes apparel for people who are into extreme sports and live very active lifestyles. The company's branding is not so much about certain colors and fonts; instead, it's about energy, attitude, and freshness. This branding was a driving force behind the interaction we built into the site.

Many sites I see on the web force interactivity onto a brand or content that has no real need for it. In fact, it works against that brand. Billabong-USA.com is a site that is as perfect a place as ever there was for dynamic and interesting interactivity.

In this chapter, we will be breaking down some of the interesting interactive pieces that work to make the site a total experience.

NOTE

Without the proper server and Generator environment, these files will not work when run from your desktop. However, we have provided files for you to explore and follow along with the examples.

NOTE

This chapter deals with Macromedia Generator application development. It requires that you have the Generator Extensions installed in Flash. If you do not have the extensions installed, you can download them for free from Macromedia's web site at www.macromedia.com/software/generator/download/extensions.html.

6.1 SKATE TEAM RIDERS

In the youth sports apparel market, one of the major marketing tactics used is building teams of riders in specific sports by offering sponsorships to these riders. Billabong has hundreds of pro and amateur sponsored riders spread across several sports. It is a symbiotic relationship because Billabong gives the riders gear and money, and the riders wear the gear to promote the brand. We learned firsthand in creating this site that these guys are always on the move and are hard to pin down at times. Nevertheless, they're always supporting the brand out in the water and on the streets.

6.1.1 NAME CLUSTERER

On the skate team rider page, we abstractly captured this dynamic of the riders through something we call the "name clusterer" or "the swarm." We wanted to display the riders' names in a dynamic and organic manner, as per the dynamics of the relationship we talked about previously. The concept we came up with was similar to a raging virus—a growing mass of graphical elements that spread across the screen in a random, frantic manner, as shown in Figure 6.1.

Figure 6.1 The name clusterer on the riders screen on Billabong-USA.com.

Open the file namecluster.fla (see Figure 6.2). We've isolated the clusterer to demonstrate how it was done.

Start by looking at the actions on the main timeline:

```
nameList = new Array();
nameList[0] = "Scott Van Vliet";
nameList[1] = "Anthony Thompson";
nameList[2] = "Brian Drake";
nameList[3] = "Deborah Schulz";
nameList[4] = "Phil Scott";
nameList[5] = "Lisa Brabender";
nameList[6] = "Sue McDonald";
nameList[7] = "Steve Wages";
nameList[8] = "Todd Purgason";
nameList[9] = "Paul Nguyen";
nameList[10] = "Matt Kipp";
nameList[11] = "Luis Escorial";
```

Figure 6.2 Script on a frame in the main timeline in namecluster.fla.

In the Billabong-USA site, we obtained the skate riders' names from the database. In this similar example, we've created an array called nameList populated by the names of a few Juxt Interactive employees.

Now that we've set up the names we'll use, we'll look at the symbol nameclutter_name in the library (see Figure 6.3). We've set up this movie clip with two frames labeled "black" and "white." Each frame has a stop action to keep the clip from looping. There's a dynamic text field called displayName that, if you look at the character palette, is set to black text on the black frame and white text on the white frame.

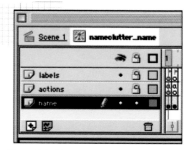

Figure 6.3 The nameclutter_name movie clip-editing mode.

In the Billabong-USA site, we used a lot of 2-bit, black and white bitmaps to create a gritty design aesthetic. For this name clusterer, we chose black and white because it was consistent with the site's feel.

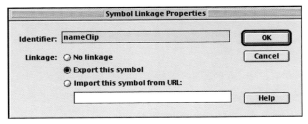

Figure 6.4 The Symbol Linkage Properties dialog box for the
nameclutter_name movie clip.

Notice that this clip isn't actually placed in the stage anywhere. Examine the linkage properties for this clip to see that we're exporting it with an identifier of nameClip (see Figure 6.4).

Now look at the action clip on the name clusterer layer. You'll see later that we've written the cluster script to cluster around wherever this clip is placed. So we've placed it in the center of the stage. Look at the clipEvent on this movie clip (see Figure 6.5):

```
onClipEvent (load) {
    // Set Cluster Area
    clusterWidth = 300;
    clusterHeight = 300;
    clusterLeft = -clusterWidth/2;
    clusterRight = clusterWidth/2;
    clusterTop = -clusterHeight/2;
    clusterBottom = clusterHeight/2;
    // Set Cluster Core
    clusterCoreX = clusterLeft+(Math.round(Math.random()*49)*(clusterWidth/50));
    clusterCoreY = clusterTop+(Math.round(Math.random()*49)*(clusterHeight/50));
    // Initialize Cluster Count
    clusterCount = 1;
}
onClipEvent (enterFrame) {
    if (clusterCount<75) {
        // Attach nameClip
        this.attachMovie("nameClip", "cluster"+clusterCount, clusterCount);
        // Set Name
        randomName = Math.round(Math.random()*(_root.nameList.length));
```

continues

continued

```
    set ("cluster"+clusterCount+".displayName", _root.nameList[randomName]);
    // Set Color
    eval("cluster"+clusterCount).gotoAndStop(Math.round(Math.random()*1)+1);
    // Set Cluster Position
    clusterX = clusterCoreX+(Math.round(Math.random()*(1.5*clusterCount))*(1-Math.round(Math.random()*2)));
    clusterY = clusterCoreY+(Math.round(Math.random()*(1.5*clusterCount))*(1-Math.round(Math.random()*2)));
    if (clusterX>clusterRight) {
        clusterX = clusterRight-Math.round(Math.random()*4);
    } else if (clusterX<clusterLeft) {
        clusterX = clusterLeft+Math.round(Math.random()*4);
    }
    if (clusterY>clusterBottom) {
        clusterY = clusterBottom-Math.round(Math.random()*4);
    } else if (clusterY<clusterTop) {
        clusterY = clusterTop+Math.round(Math.random()*4);
    }
    // Move Cluster to Position
    eval("cluster"+clusterCount)._x = clusterX;
    eval("cluster"+clusterCount)._y = clusterY;
    // Increase clusterCount
    clusterCount = clusterCount+1;
} else {
    // Set Cluster Core
    clusterCoreX = clusterLeft+ (Math.round(Math.random()*49)*(clusterWidth/50));
    clusterCoreY = clusterTop+(Math.round(Math.random()*49)*(clusterHeight/50));
    // Initialize Cluster Count
    clusterCount = 1;
}
}
```

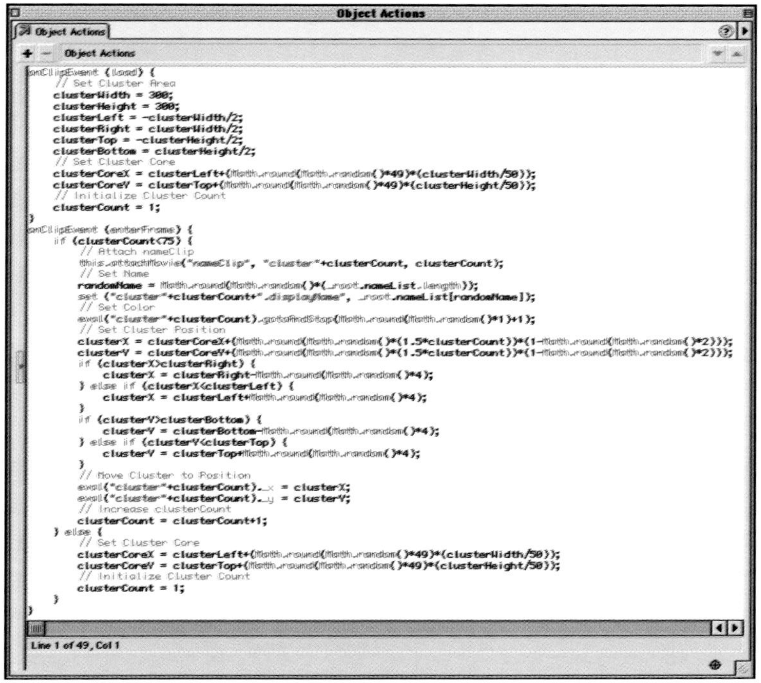

```
onClipEvent (load) {
    // Set Cluster Area
    clusterWidth = 300;
    clusterHeight = 300;
    clusterLeft = -clusterWidth/2;
    clusterRight = clusterWidth/2;
    clusterTop = -clusterHeight/2;
    clusterBottom = clusterHeight/2;
    // Set Cluster Core
    clusterCoreX = clusterLeft+(Math.round(Math.random()*49)*(clusterWidth/50));
    clusterCoreY = clusterTop+(Math.round(Math.random()*49)*(clusterHeight/50));
    // Initialize Cluster Count
    clusterCount = 1;
}
onClipEvent (enterFrame) {
    if (clusterCount<75) {
        // Attach nameClip
        this.attachMovie("nameClip", "cluster"+clusterCount, clusterCount);
        // Set Name
        randomName = Math.round(Math.random()*(_root.nameList.length));
        set ("cluster"+clusterCount+".displayName", _root.nameList[randomName]);
        // Set Color
        eval("cluster"+clusterCount).gotoAndStop(Math.round(Math.random()*1)+1);
        // Set Cluster Position
        clusterX = clusterCoreX+(Math.round(Math.random()*(1.5*clusterCount))*(1-Math.round(Math.random()*2)));
        clusterY = clusterCoreY+(Math.round(Math.random()*(1.5*clusterCount))*(1-Math.round(Math.random()*2)));
        if (clusterX>clusterRight) {
            clusterX = clusterRight-(Math.round(Math.random()*4);
        } else if (clusterX<clusterLeft) {
            clusterX = clusterLeft+(Math.round(Math.random()*4);
        }
        if (clusterY>clusterBottom) {
            clusterY = clusterBottom-(Math.round(Math.random()*4);
        } else if (clusterY<clusterTop) {
            clusterY = clusterTop+(Math.round(Math.random()*4);
        }
        // Move Cluster to Position
        eval("cluster"+clusterCount)._x = clusterX;
        eval("cluster"+clusterCount)._y = clusterY;
        // Increase clusterCount
        clusterCount = clusterCount+1;
    } else {
        // Set Cluster Core
        clusterCoreX = clusterLeft+(Math.round(Math.random()*49)*(clusterWidth/50));
        clusterCoreY = clusterTop+(Math.round(Math.random()*49)*(clusterHeight/50));
        // Initialize Cluster Count
        clusterCount = 1;
    }
}
```

Line 1 of 49, Col 1

Figure 6.5   The script on the name clusterer layer on the main timeline.

First, with the onClipEvent(load), we initialize the script. We'll start by determining the cluster area. We've picked 300 width and 300 height.

We then set variables for the left, right, top, and bottom of the cluster area.

Next we'll set the "cluster core." This is the point from which the cluster will form. For the X and Y position of this core, we divide the cluster area by 50 and then randomize which 50th of the area we'll place the cluster at. You can change out 50 with a higher or lower number, depending on the density of the possible spots you want the cluster to grow out of.

Lastly, we set the clusterCount to 1.

The rest of the actions are contained in an onClipEvent(enterFrame), so they'll be continually looped. First we'll determine if the clusterCount is less than 75. This means that after there are 75 names, the cluster will move to another position and start building again. If the count is less than 75, we'll add names. We start by attaching the nameClip that we previously set to export. Next we'll choose which name from the nameList array we'll display. The variable randomName is a number chosen from the length of the array and then used to transfer the value of a name from the array to the displayName variable in the current cluster clip.

Now we'll set the color of the cluster. As we discussed before, this can either be black or white. By putting gotoandStop(random(2)+1), we'll send the cluster to either frame 1 or frame 2.

Now we'll determine where the current cluster will be positioned. We'll set two position variables, clusterX and clusterY. Let's examine the logic behind clusterX and clusterY, which is the same. We start at the clusterCoreX, which is the center of the cluster. The (1-random(3)) will return either –1, 0, or 1. This will take the result of random(1.5*clusterCount) and either make it negative, leave it positive, or counteract it by setting the X position to the core X position. We chose 1.5 because it fit within our usage. If you use a higher number, the clusters will be spaced out farther. The inverse is also true.

Before we move the cluster to the new X and Y positions, we need to check whether the new position is within the cluster area we initially set through a series of if statements. If the cluster will be out of the cluster area, we manually reposition the X and Y coordinates to the boundary of the cluster area and then break up the numbers with a little randomization.

Finally, we move the cluster to the X and Y positions we just set.

Now we come back to the initial if statement. The preceding actions were to be run if the clusterCount was less than 75. Once the clusterCount exceeds 75, we rerun the initialization script, which randomizes the position of a new "core" and sets the count back to 1.

Now we start again. Notice that we don't remove the clips we attached before starting again. In Flash, only one movie clip can occupy a specific "depth." By restarting to attach the movie clips, we "eat away" at the first cluster by attaching clips to depths that contain the nameClips from the first time the script ran. We intentionally set up the script this way because we were pleased with the way the clusters grew across the screen while slowly "dissolving" after a while.

For this feature, we were conceptually playing with the dynamics of the fluid motion of surf (see Figure 6.6). The content comes into the screen much like swells come to a beach. They roll in as they get closer to shore. They peak, break, and slide back into the sea. So, in this feature, the content rolls to a peak and then falls back down and out of the scene.

Figure 6.6   A Featured Rider screen on the Billabong-USA site.

6.2   BILLABONG-USA.COM SURF FEATURED RIDER

One of the sections of the Billabong-USA.com site that afforded us the most creative experimentation was the featured rider section. Designed to be a frequently updated section of the site, each new featured rider for the three sports received a new design treatment and content navigation experimentation. We used several interesting techniques for each featured rider section. Now we'll look at the Featured Surf Rider for Shane Dorian.

6.2.1   FEATURED RIDER NAVIGATION

Open the file featuredrider.fla. We'll first look at the content navigation system we devised for this particular rider spotlight.

Because this is a surf rider, we tried to develop a navigation system that loosely simulated the feel of a wave. Once the concept was finalized, there were several approaches we could have taken to accomplish the interaction we were looking for. We finally went with a hybrid approach of keyframed/tweened animation and ActionScript because we felt some of the animation control could be done easier without complex mathematical scripts.

First we'll look at the symbol called content on the main timeline (see Figure 6.7). The movie clip is also given an instance name of content. Edit this symbol and observe the timeline. There's a lot of manual animation here. Scrub the timeline to see how we animated the content nodes in and out of the view area.

There's an important issue to remember when you keyframe animation like this. Because the content movie's timeline needs to act in a fluid motion, its play movement could be ActionScripted to stop or start at intervals designated by the tween keyframes. At these tween points, the feature, or node, needs the ability to be ActionScripted to life. It is important to make sure that each keyframe of the tween retains its instance name, thus enabling it to receive actions at any of these points. For example, look at node1 on the layer node1 on all three keyframes. We've made sure the clip has an instance name of node1 on frames 1, 5, and 10.

We'll return to this clip later, but let's move on to the navigation. On the main timeline, there's a clip, featured_nav, with the instance name nav. Edit this symbol. You'll see we have eight copies of the movie clip featured_nav_node. Each has a unique instance name: node1, node2, and so on. Edit this symbol (see Figure 6.8).

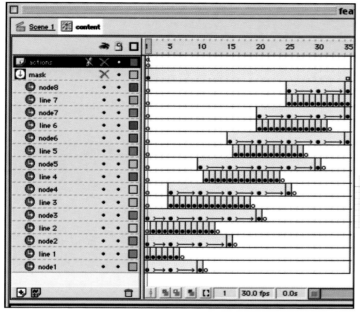

Figure 6.7   The movie clip named content on the main timeline.

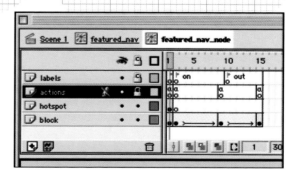

Figure 6.8   The featured_nav_node movie clip is duplicated eight times in the parent clip.

We've set up this clip with a growth animation starting on frame on and a shrink animation starting on frame off. The hotspot on the off frame tells the clip to gotoAndPlay("on"), as shown in Figure 6.9.

On the frame labeled on, we have the following actions:

```
if (_parent.selected != null) {
    _parent[_parent.selected].gotoAndPlay("out");
}
_parent.selected = _name;
```

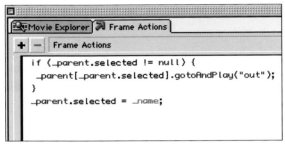

Figure 6.9 The script on the on frame in the featured_nav_node clip
and the action on the button within the hotspot layer.

Because we only want one node to be designated as on at a
time, we've set a variable called selected on the parent timeline
(_root.nav) to the _name of the current on node. If this isn't the first
time we've run this script (_parent.selected != null), we first tell the
current selected node to go to the out sequence. We then set
selected to the current node's _name.

Now that we've seen the structure of the navigation nodes, go back
to the main timeline and view the clip events on the nav clip (see
Figure 6.10).

```
onClipEvent (load) {
    // Set Content Frame  Positions
    node1frame = 1;
    node2frame = 5;
    node3frame = 10;
    node4frame = 15;
    node5frame = 20;
    node6frame = 25;
    node7frame = 30;
    node8frame = 35;
    // Turn Node1 On
    node1.gotoAndPlay("on");
    _root.movingStopped = true;
}
onClipEvent (enterFrame) {
    // Move Content
    if (_root.content._currentframe != this(selected+"frame")) {
        for (a=1; a<=8; ++a) {
            _root.content["node"+a].gotoAndStop("off");
        }
        if (_root.content._currentframe> this[selected+"frame"]) {
            _root.moveDirection = -1;
        } else if (_root.content._currentframe< this[selected+"frame"]) {
            _root.moveDirection = 1;
        }
        _root.content.gotoAndStop(_root.content._currentframe+
            _root.moveDirection);
    } else {
        _root.movingStopped = "true";
        _root.content[onNode].gotoAndStop("on");
    }
}
```

```
onClipEvent (load) {
  // Set Content Frame  Positions
  node1frame = 1;
  node2frame = 5;
  node3frame = 10;
  node4frame = 15;
  node5frame = 20;
  node6frame = 25;
  node7frame = 30;
  node8frame = 35;
  // Turn Node1 On
  node1.gotoAndPlay("on");
  _root.movingStopped = true;
}
onClipEvent (enterFrame) {
  // Move Content
  if (_root.content._currentframe != this[selected+"frame"]) {
    for (a=1; a<=8; ++a) {
      _root.content["node"+a].gotoAndStop("off");
    }
    if (_root.content._currentframe> this[selected+"frame"]) {
      _root.moveDirection = -1;
    } else if (_root.content._currentframe <this[selected+"frame"]) {
      _root.moveDirection = 1;
    }
    _root.content.gotoAndStop(_root.content._currentframe + _root.moveDirection);
  } else {
    _root.movingStopped = true;
    _root.content[selected].gotoAndStop("on");
  }
}
```

Figure 6.10   The clip events on the nav clip.

We start by initializing some settings with onClipEvent(load). The variables node(1-8) frame are the actual frame numbers in which the content is correctly positioned on the stage. Because the content starts out with content node1 focused on, we'll turn the navigation node1 on by telling it to gotoAndPlay("on").

And now for the actions that move the content. Because we want these actions to loop, we put them in an onClipEvent(enterFrame) located on the nav movie clip. We'll start by determining whether the content is at the correct position by comparing the current frame of the content clip against the result of the concatenation of the variable called selected (node1, node2, etc.) and the string called frame. The result of the [selected+"frame"] statement will look something like node1frame. If selected = node3, the concatenation of the variable called selected with the string frame gives us node3frame. If you recall, node3frame is a variable that has already been set to be equal to 10 within the onClipEvent(load) statement we used on the nav clip. To highlight the content for node3, the content movie clip's desired frame location would be at the value of node3frame, or in this case, 10. Using the brackets to concatenate and evaluate the variable selected with the string frame works well, but must be used with the content of a timeline identifier presented before the brackets. In addition, the dot notation usually found between two objects in a timeline reference is dropped directly before the bracket. For example, _root.content["node"+a] .gotoAndStop("off").

Next, we'll determine which "side" of the desired frame the content clip is on. If the current content frame is greater than the desired frame, we'll set the variable moveDirection to –1. Otherwise, we'll set the moveDirection to 1. Once we've determined which direction to move the content clip, we'll move the content to the currentframe plus the direction we've determined. This action will keep looping until the currentframe is the same as the desired frame. Once we've moved the content clip to the desired frame, we'll tell the correct content node to gotoAndStop("on").

Now we've set up the navigation. Go back to the content clip. Edit one of the content nodes (for example, content_node1). Look at the actions on the hotspot on the off frame:

```
on (rollOver) {
    if (_root.movingStopped == true) {
        _root.nav[this._name].gotoAndPlay("on");
        _root.movingStopped = false;
    }
}
```

Because each content node has an instance name of node1, node2, and so on, when we concatenate _root.nav with _name, Flash will return _root.nav.node1,2,3,etc. We tell this clip to gotoAndPlay("on"). By controlling the nav in this manner, the user can roll over either a content node or a navigation node to move the content. The if (_root.movingStopped == "TRUE") checks to make sure the content isn't currently animating. The if statement used here checks to make sure the content isn't currently animating. This prevents the clip action from happening more than once.

6.3 MOVIE CONTROL

In the Shane Dorian featured rider section, we kept the higher res color images and the two movies as external movie clips to help cushion the download time for the user. To demonstrate the controller, we developed for the movies. We've included one of the movies in the featuredrider.fla file.

Before we look at that file, we'll quickly discuss how to use video inside of Flash. As of Flash 5, you cannot directly play a QuickTime, AVI, or MPEG (and so on) movie inside your Flash file. There are times, however, when you need to utilize bitmap movies inside of Flash. To do this, you'll need to import your video as an image sequence. Motion pictures are basically many still images displayed rapidly in a sequence. With just about any 2D effects/compositing/

NLE software available today (that is, After Effects, Premier, Final Cut Pro), you can export digital video to a folder of sequentially named, still images. See your software's manual for specific instructions on how to do this.

If you don't own any of this software, and your budget's not ample, a cheap tool that can do this function is QuickTime Pro, which sells for about $30 at www.apple.com/quicktime. QuickTime Pro can do a variety of tasks, including exporting your movies as image sequences. Regardless of what software you use, we recommend using no compression on the still images. It's advantageous to bring images into Flash as high-quality images and let Flash do the compression. This avoids even further loss of quality from redundant compression. Also, make sure your output files are named with a sequential numeric order. Most software will do this automatically or will offer it as an option.

One great feature of Flash is that it recognizes sequentially named image sequences. All you need to do is import the first image of a sequence, and Flash will recognize the other images. Flash will then prompt you to decide whether or not to import the whole sequence. If you select yes, Flash will create a new keyframe on the currently selected layer of your timeline for every image. Export this and—viola!—your video is playing in Flash. Keep in mind that Flash isn't meant for just displaying video, and you'll start fighting performance issues depending on the size of the video and how many frames it is. Remember, the user has to download every single still image, which can quickly add up.

One technique you can use to deal with this is to delete every other frame of video and leave one frame in between each of the remaining keyframes. The motion will start to be less smooth, but now your user only has to download half as many images. If this isn't enough, delete every other two frames. Experiment until you reach an acceptable equilibrium between quality of the motion and file size.

We used this technique for the two videos controlled in Flash. Let's go back to featuredrider.fla (see Figure 6.11).

Figure 6.11   A screen from the feature rider page.

On the movie layer, we've put the movie clip node3_movie with an instance name of surfmovie on the on frame. Edit this symbol. You'll see that we've imported an image sequence into a movie clip. Go back one level to the node3 clip.

We'll be concentrating on the movie clip content_video_controller, which is on the controls layer (see Figure 6.13). Edit this clip.

Figure 6.13   The timeline on the content_video_controller clip.

Open this file, edit the content clip, and then edit the symbol content_node3 (see Figure 6.12). You'll see that we structured the clip like the other content clips, with an off frame and an on frame.

Figure 6.12   The timeline on the content_node3 clip.

We've structured this clip with a "playing" frame and a "paused" frame. On the first frame, playing, there are the following actions:

```
stop ();
controller.gotoAndPlay("playing");
_parent.surfmovie.play();
```

We start by telling the controller clip (which we'll look at next) to gotoAndPlay("playing"). We also tell the surfmovie to start playing. On the paused frame:

```
stop ();
controller.gotoAndPlay("paused");
_parent.surfmovie.stop();
```

Look at the hotspot layer. The playing frame has a hotspot over the timeline graphic that tells the clip to go to the paused frame. On the paused frame, we have several hotspots with actions to tell the clip to go back to the playing frame.

Now edit the content_video_controller_button movie clip with an instance name of controller (see Figure 6.14).

Figure 6.14 The timeline on content_video_controller_button.

You'll see that we've set up two, two-frame loops. The first loop starts at the playing frame. The first frame has the actions, and the second frame loops back to the first frame. The second loop starts at the paused frame. During the playing loop, the movie is playing, and we want the scrub bar to move in sync with the movie.

Look at the actions on the playing frame:

```
dragLeft = -32;
dragRight = 80;
frame = _parent._parent.surfmovie._currentframe;
step = (dragRight-dragLeft)/(_parent._parent.
    surfmovie._totalframes);
_x = (frame*step)+dragLeft;
```

First, we set the left and right limits of the scrub bar with the variables dragLeft and dragRight. These values were determined by manually moving the scrub bar to the left and right of the timeline and noting the X position.

We next set the frame variable to the currentframe of the surfmovie. Step is a variable determined by taking the drag area (dragRight-dragLeft) and dividing it by the number of frames in the surfmovie (_parent._parent.surfmovie._totalframes).

Lastly, we set the X position of the scrub bar to the frame variable multiplied by the step variable. We offset this variable by the left of the drag area. Now, on every loop, the scrub bar will move along with the surfmovie.

Now that we've set up the scrub bar to move along with the surfmovie, we need to set it up so that when the user rolls over the scrub area, he or she can drag the scrub bar and consequently the surfmovie.

Look at the actions on the paused frame.

```
_root.moviePosition = Math.round((_x-dragLeft)/step);
_parent._parent.surfmovie.gotoAndStop(_root.moviePosition);
```

First, we set the variable moviePosition. This is an inverse equation to the step variable we set in the previous loop. We limit this value to an integer. We tell the surfmove to gotoAndStop(_root.moviePosition).

Finally, look at the actions on the hotspot on the paused frame.

```
on (press) {
    startDrag ("", true, dragLeft, _y, dragRight, _y);
}
on (release) {
    stopDrag ();
}
```

Now the scrub bar is draggable and is constrained to the scrub area. When the user drags the scrub bar, it will evaluate its position and move the surf movie to the appropriate frame. This technique is scalable and can be used to control a movie clip of any length.

6.3.1 JAVASCRIPT POP-UP WINDOW

In our minds, the key to creating a good site is to use technology for its strengths and work around its weaknesses, if possible, with other technologies. We love Flash because it has so many strengths that work around the many weaknesses of HTML. However, Flash has its own weaknesses, and at times we use things like HTML, JavaScript, and QuickTime to provide solutions for those weaknesses. The key is to weave all these elements together to make a consistent presentation that feels seamless. You can opt to make every page a hybrid. In other words, a balance of HTML and Flash together on each page. Or you can isolate the unique elements of content that will need HTML and pop them up in JavaScript windows. This is the method we choose on the Billabong site because it allows the main focus of the content to reach a high level of concentration through Flash without the distracting breaks in experience that come with HTML page loads.

To open a new browser window with JavaScript, the window.open() method is used. The syntax of that JavaScript method is as follows:

```
window.open(theURL,winName,features);
```

The benefit of using JavaScript to open a new window rather than targeting a blank new window is that you are given control over the size and properties of the new window. To control the features, you would use a method similar to this example:

```
window.open('window_url.html','window_name','toolbar=no,
    location=no,status=no,menubar=no,scrollbars=no,
    resizable=no,width=400,height=400');
```

All of the features set to no can be set to yes. At Juxt, if a new window will be filled with Flash (such as Pickled.tv), we'll set status=yes and the other features to no. We do this so that the user can see the browser's status bar, which will display the download status of the files being loaded (see Figure 6.15).

Figure 6.15 We set the status to yes for new windows opening with Flash so that the user can monitor the browser's status.

There are several ways to invoke this JavaScript method from Flash. The most compatible way is to define a JavaScript function in the HTML page where you've embedded your Flash file. Put this in the head of your document:

```
<SCRIPT LANGUAGE="JavaScript">
<!-

function openWindow(theURL,winname,features) {
window.open(theURL,winname,features);
}

//->
</SCRIPT>
```

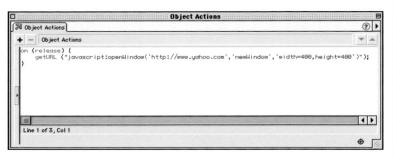

NOTE

This is the only method that works for Internet Explorer 4.5 on the Macintosh.

In Flash, create a button with a getUrl action that calls the JavaScript function (see Figure 6.16). For example:

```
on (release) {
    getURL ("javascript:openWindow('http://www.yahoo.com',
        'newWindow','width=400,height=400')");
}
```

Figure 6.16 A button in Flash with a getUrl action that calls a JavaScript function.

There's another technique we use that involves a hidden frame. When a Flash site is contained in a pop-up window, usually the HTML file that the window contains is actually an HTML frameset with one or more hidden frames. A hidden frame is a frame that isn't allowed any viewable space. Here's a sample frameset for you to see this principle:

```
<html>
<head>
<title></title>
</head>

<frameset rows="100%,*" frameborder="NO" border="0"
   framespacing="0">
<frame src="maincontent.html" name="mainframe"
   marginwidth="0" marginheight="0" scrolling="NO"
   noresize frameborder="NO">
<frame src="blank.html" name="hidden" marginwidth="0"
   marginheight="0" scrolling="NO" noresize frameborder="NO">
</frameset>
<noframes><body bgcolor="#FFFFFF">

</body></noframes>
</html>
```

You'll see that we've given the mainframe frame100% of the viewable size, while the hidden frame is limited to whatever's left (*), which in this case isn't anything.

Through the browser, the only frame you will see is the mainframe. But the hidden frame is still there, and its existence allows us to load data into that frame without the user seeing it. We can use this hidden frame to launch JavaScript functions as well as opening JavaScript windows. Create an HTML file called launch_yahoo.html with the following contents:

```
<HTML>
<HEAD>

<TITLE></TITLE>
<SCRIPT LANGUAGE="JavaScript">
<!--

function openWindow(theURL,winname,features) {
window.open(theURL,winname,features);
}

function openYahoo() {

openWindow('http://www.yahoo.com','yahooWindow','
   toolbar=yes,location=yes,status=yes,menubar=yes,
   scrollbars=yes,resizable=yes,width=400,height=400');
}

//-->
</SCRIPT>
</HEAD>
<BODY onLoad="openYahoo()">

</BODY>
</HTML>
```

In your Flash file, the getURL action will look like this:

```
on (release) {
    getURL ("launch_yahoo.html", "hidden");
}
```

When you invoke this action, the launch_yahoo.html file will be loaded into the hidden frame, and the JavaScript function will run, opening a new window.

6.4 EMBEDDING VIDEOS

Another technology that has strengths in its own right is video. Billabong has lots of great video footage that is great content for the site. As we showed you earlier in this chapter, you can export video as stills and import the stills into Flash as frames to simulate video. But this takes a fair amount of development time to do and would mean we would have to be involved every time Billabong wanted to add a video to the site. For the Footage sections of the site, it was a much better choice to rely on the widely distributed QuickTime and Windows Media players to augment the Flash experience. This enabled us to build a system for Billabong to upload videos at any time on their own without having to call on us. We will cover the content management aspect of this in the next chapter. For now, let's focus on the embedding video formats.

On the Billabong-USA site, we gave the user the option of viewing the surf/skate/snow videos in either QuickTime or Windows Media formats. Embedding these video formats in an HTML page is very easy. For the Windows Media format, the following HTML is used:

```
<OBJECT ID="MediaPlayer" classid="CLSID:22d6f312-b0f6-
    11d0-94ab-0080c74c7e95" width=200 height=160
    CODEBASE="http://activex.microsoft.com/activex/
    controls/mplayer/en/nsmp2inf.cab#Version=5,1,52,701"
    standby="Loading Media Player components..."
    TYPE="application/x-oleobject">
  <PARAM NAME="FileName" VALUE="MEDIA FILE URL">
  <PARAM NAME="AutoStart" VALUE="true">
  <PARAM NAME="ShowControls" VALUE="0">
</OBJECT>
<EMBED TYPE="application/x-mplayer2"
    PLUGINSPAGE="http://www.microsoft.com/Windows/
    MediaPlayer/" SRC="MEDIA FILE URL" NAME="MediaPlayer1"
    SHOWCONTROLS="0" WIDTH="200" HEIGHT="160"
    AUTOSTART="FALSE"></EMBED>
```

Just replace MEDIA FILE URL with the actual URL of the Windows Media file in both the OBJECT and EMBED tags.

For a QuickTime movie, use the following:

```
<EMBED SRC="QUICKTIME FILE URL" WIDTH="200"
    HEIGHT="160" TYPE="video/quicktime">
```

Again, replace QUICKTIME FILE URL with your URL and you're ready to go.

6.4.1 VIDEO LIST

The Footage section of Billabong-USA utilizes Generator to create a dynamic list of the videos available for each sport. We've included the source file for this, but please note that Generator is a web server application for creating dynamic Flash content. Because we have a unique server environment, these files won't "work" upon export. We're examining them to give you insight into how we utilize Generator. We'll be delving more into Dynamic Flash content management in the next chapter.

That being said, look at the file video_list.fla. There aren't many actions on the main timeline. Other than two stops on the last two frames, there is a simple preloader on frame 3 (see Figure 6.17).

```
if (getBytesLoaded ( ) == getBytesTotal ( ) ) {
  _root.loaded = "TRUE";
}
if (_root.loaded == "TRUE") {
  gotoAndStop ("featured");
} else {
  gotoAndPlay ("loop");
}
```

Figure 6.17   The script on frame 3 of the file named video_list.fla.

```
if (getBytesLoaded ( ) == getBytesTotal ( ) ) {
    _root.loaded = "TRUE";
}
if (_root.loaded == "TRUE") {
    gotoAndStop ("featured");
} else {
    gotoAndPlay ("loop");
}
```

The getBytesTotal() function returns the value in bytes of the current timeline. The getBytesLoaded() function returns the value of the bytes loaded. We compare these values and, if they're equal, set the loaded variable to true. Then there is an if statement that continues playing if loaded is true or continues looping if it isn't. The reason for the additional if statement is that it gives the flexibility to add additional requirements before continuing.

An alternative method for this would be to use the movie clip object methods getBytesLoaded() and getBytesTotal() to perform the same function. The getBytesLoaded method returns the number of bytes loaded on a movie clip. The getBytesTotal method returns the size of a movie clip. These methods are used for both internally and externally loaded movie clips.

Go to the frame featured. This is the list of the three featured videos in this sport section. Because we've constrained the featured video section to three videos, there's no need for a scrolling list. We went with a static, hard-coded list (see Figure 6.18).

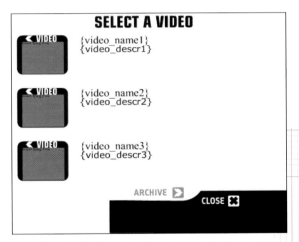

Figure 6.18   The featured videos list on the featured frame.

The data from this list comes from the environment data. The environment data is the first icon of the three icons at the top right of the Flash application window. You'll see that we're using the data source {team}_video_list.txt, as shown in Figure 6.19.

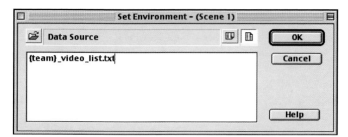

Figure 6.19 The Set Environment dialog box in Flash.

The Generator variable {team} is provided through the URL of the .swt. We'll discuss URL variables and offline Generator in the next chapter. All we need at this point is to know that {team}_video_list.txt will evaluate to surf_video_list.txt (or skate or snow). Here's the contents of snow_video_list.txt:

```
name,value
video_src1,"crawford.jpg"
video_name1,"Crawford"
video_descr1,"Crawford ripping on anything with snow on it"
video_id1,"8"
video_src2,"kevin.jpg"
video_name2,"Kevin"
video_descr2,"Kevin Jones knows how to snowboard"
video_id2,"10"
video_src3,"kevin_2.jpg"
video_name3,"Kevin"
video_descr3,"Kevin at Mammoth 12/01"
video_id3,"16"
```

Look at the stage. If you look at the Generator variables {}, you'll see where the data flows. Select one of the video buttons (see Figure 6.20). Look at the actions:

Figure 6.20 The actions on one of the video buttons.

```
on (release) {
    getURL ("video_media.cfm?video_id={video_id1}", "left");
}
```

You'll see that we use Generator variables here to construct a URL string to pass to Cold Fusion.

In the library, look at the symbols video_thumb1,2,3. We've got an Insert JPG with a source of ../../images/video/{video_src1}.

Now that we've seen the featured section using an environment data source, go to the archive frame, as shown in Figure 6.21. This is the archived list of footage.

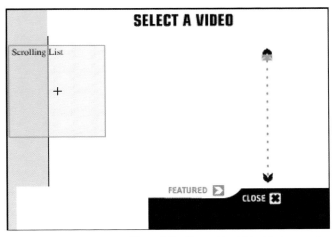

Figure 6.21   The archived list of footage on the archive frame in the main timeline.

The central part of this section is a Generator scrolling list (see Figure 6.22).

Figure 6.22   The Generator template named Scrolling List displays the Generator scrolling list window.

The Data Source is {team}_video_archive.txt, which, like the previous environment data source, will evaluate to snow_video_archive.txt (or skate, surf). Here's the content of snow_video_archive.txt:

clip,video_name,video_descr,video_id

archive_item,"Crawford","Crawford ripping on anything with snow on it",8

archive_item,"Kevin","Kevin Jones knows how to snowboard",10

archive_item,"Kevin","Kevin at Mammoth 12/01",16

A Generator scrolling list uses the clip parameter to decide which movie clip in the library to use for this list. Look at the clip archive_item in the library (see Figure 6.23).

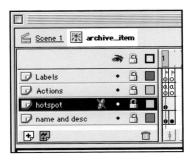

Figure 6.23   The timeline of the clip named archive_item.

The clip is set up like a rollover with off and on frames. The content of the clip is inserted through Generator variables.

6.5 SUMMARY

We are really excited about all of the dynamic, interesting interaction and content we included in the Billabong site. You can see from this example how interactivity can be used not only to create an interesting experience, but also to reinforce creative concepts in your designs. This is the stuff that really excites us. We feel that it makes a site successful and makes us successful as designers and developers.

To clients, however, what really makes a site successful is that they can flawlessly and easily update the content of the site, keeping it current with their business. Even in this hard-core market segment of extreme sports apparel, that is a main concern for these companies. So, in the next chapter, we are going to show you how we married the immersive Flash experience on Billabong-USA.com with a custom-built web application that gives clients the control they want and need for their content so the site can be successful.

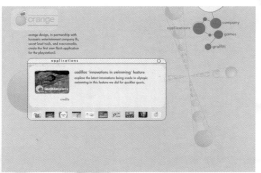

FRED SHARPLES

Fred Sharples Interview
by Todd Purgason

Introduction
www.orangedesign.com

I was introduced to Fred Sharples by Hillman Curtis at a one-day Flash seminar that Hillman had put together back in the very early days of Flash 4.

The three of us were doing a seminar for a couple hundred people at Macromedia. Hillman and I were covering motion and sound stuff, thinking we're all bad. Then Fred gets up there and blows us away with this game he created over the weekend while watching the infamous Yellow Submarine on TV. He called it Blimpo, and it was insanely freaky. But more importantly, it was a sophisticated, interactive experience, which that at that time was just not seen. Games were in the Shockwave space, not in Flash.

Since then, I have worked with Fred on other projects and have followed the progress of Orange Design closely. The company has had the opportunity to do some innovative Flash work for some of the biggest brands around like Coke, Old Navy, and Kodak. In addition, Orange Design will go down in history as the first company to produce a gaming interface in Flash, due to their work for Lucas Arts on the Star Wars Star Fighter game.

Fred is a great guy, and he has more experience with Flash and Director than just about anyone out there.

Teaser from the Interview

TP: So, we're here with Fred Sharples from Orange Design. So, who is Fred Sharples?

FS: Fred Sharples, the enigma.

That's a hard one, Todd.

TP: He's the guy with the bird on his shoulder.

FS: Yeah, I'm the guy with the bird on his shoulder in Hillman's book.

TP: Ok, who is Orange Design? We'll put it that way.

FS: Yeah, that's probably better. Orange Design is a small Flash studio, actually a multimedia studio, I'd say. But we do all Flash stuff, and we just started it so we could have a small company that would be fun to work at, that would make a little money, and you know, stay focused on doing interesting projects. Kind of an escape from working in really big agencies and big companies. That's sort of an antidote to that. And it was an experiment by Pam and myself that turned out really well. We were able to believe that we could have our own sort of creative group that could be independent, that would be able to say no when we needed to, and that would be able to reap the benefits when it was good to say yes. And we were able to, you know, really control what projects we'd take, how we would do them, how we would treat people that worked with us, and how we would be treated by our clients, it worked out really well. So that was the main focus. And then, additionally, it was just to make sure that we had really, really good people that worked for, with us and to ensure that we can deliver in a stress-free environment, I'd say.

TP: Wait, wait, stress free? What's that?

FS: Yeah, well…

TP: Relatively.

FS: Yeah, compared to most places, yeah definitely. So yeah, we all work really hard, obviously, but it's more of a social experiment.

TP: Cool.

FS: That's all. It's turned out really well.

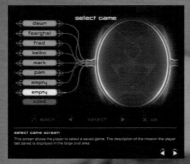

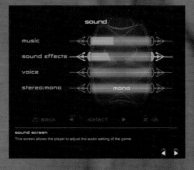

memory card screen

Like most console games, a memory card is essential to prolonged game play. All things memory card related occur here.

select game screen

This screen allows the player to select a saved game. The description of the mission the player last saved is displayed in the large oval area.

options screen

Here the player can choose view the various controller setups, configure sound levels, save the current game, or restore game defaults. The Player does so by using the select right and left arrows keys to toggle between the menu items.

sound screen

This screen allows the player to adjust the audio setting of the game.

To hear the rest of Fred's answer, as well as his answers to the following questions, please go to the Inspirations section of the book's site at www.JUXTinteractive.com/deCONSTRUCTION.

QUESTIONS

02. If you were a fish/sea creature, what would you be?

03. What CD or mp3 is in your player right now?

04. What is your definition of design?

05. What was your very first impression of Flash?

06. If you were walking down the street and came across John Gay and Jakob Nielsen engaged in a fistfight, what would you do?

07. You will go down in history as the first Flash developer to do a game interface. Was Flash a good fit for this, or was it just a crazy idea?

08. You do a ton of games in Flash. Do you think that with Flash 5, Flash ActionScript can finally compete with Lingo in this space?

09. You have a very long history with interactive media. Your experience at Macromedia put you on some very interesting Director projects. The big debate flies was is up with Director now that Flash is getting so smart.

Can you explain, in your perspective, the difference and value of the two?

10. What the hell is up with that bird on your shoulder in your photo in Hillman's book, anyway?

11. Can you tell us a little about your process?

12. You do a lot of games for Old Navy. Do you pitch game concepts to them, or do they come to you with the concepts?

13. You take your staff to Burning Man every year. Is there any risk for them? You must have a fun

office culture. Is that a correct assumption?

14. What is it that happens in a typical day that gives you a feeling of satisfaction when you go home at night?

15. You guys partner with a lot of other companies to do Flash programming work. Does this create coordination and expectation problems?

16. If you could do one last project before you had to hang up your designer's cap, what would you want that project to be?

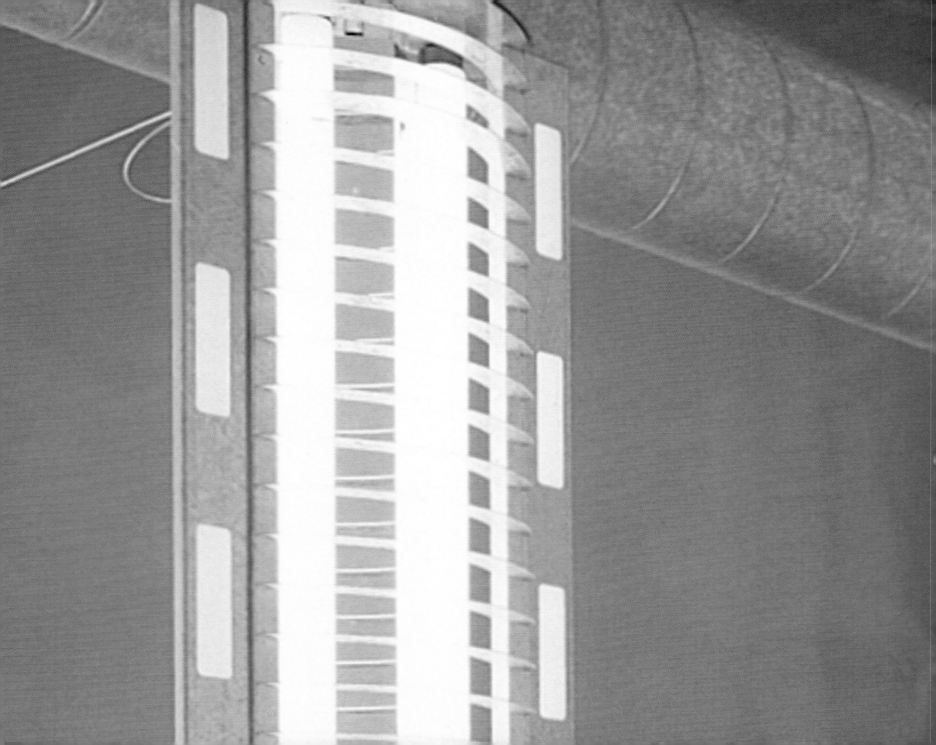

c7 CHAPTER

Flash deCONSTRUCTION

**BILLABONG-USA.COM—
FLASH CONTENT MANAGEMENT**

At Juxt, we strive to reach a level of balance through partnership with our clients. We do this by discovering and defining what it is they ultimately need from us on a long-term basis. We construct systems and tools that empower our clients because what we create for them will ultimately have an impact on their success.

As a medium, the web site is most effective when it's updated continuously. We feel that the time lost when a developer must manually add certain types of content to a site ultimately destroys a site's effectiveness. Billabong could not agree more. In fact, that was the most important issue for the company.

In this chapter, we will deconstruct some of the pieces that make up the content management system for the Billabong-USA.com site.

7.1 USING GENERATOR

For the Billabong-USA.com site, the client wanted the capability to add, update, and delete content at their convenience. Because the site is a fully interactive Flash site, we had to build a dynamic solution that included Macromedia Generator.

When building a dynamic web site with Macromedia Generator, you have to decide whether to provide live dynamic content or offline generated dynamic content. With live content, the user requests a page that contains content served live. Every time the user makes a request, the dynamic application (such as ColdFusion, ASP,

Generator, and so on) on the web server has to retrieve and compile the data. This is a good technique when the content requested is updated frequently, such as sports scores, auctions, and weather reports. Offline generated content is compiled only when the content is updated. These sites behave like a static site.

With the Billabong-USA.com site, we decided to structure the site for offline generation. We planned on building a back-end administration site for the client to add, delete, and update content. We'll discuss this administration application later. Choosing offline generation techniques helped speed up the serving of the site because the web server was only required to make HTTP calls and didn't have to retrieve and compile dynamic data every time a user requested content.

There are many different techniques for creating dynamic Flash-based sites. Most demands for dynamic data in Flash can be met with pure Flash ActionScripting and some type of back-end database scripting language. However, dynamically inserting JPEG and GIF images into a Flash movie is not something ActionScript can do. Also, to get certain dynamic text to display in the correct font, we could not use a pure Flash technique. Luckily, Macromedia Generator provides these two features (among many others).

Generator was specifically used to insert JPEG images and to embed text data into the dynamic portions of the Billabong USA site. Yet Generator only provides part of the content generation solution.

To efficiently and controllably extract information from the Billabong USA content management database, we used ColdFusion. Conveniently, a custom tag is available for ColdFusion that allowed us to control offline Generator from within our ColdFusion scripts. This meant we could easily script ColdFusion to request that Generator create new SWF file for each section of the site that needed updating at the moment the content management database is edited.

To add the data-driven dimension to the page, it was programmed using ColdFusion 4.01 and SQL. SQL is the standard language for controlling databases. Although it is a language, by itself it cannot be used to program an application. For that, we needed an application programming language.

ColdFusion is a fourth-generation programming language. This means it is much more specialized and therefore faster to develop in than other web scripting languages. Other popular web scripting languages like ASP, JSP, Perl, or PHP require significantly more lines of code to accomplish the same tasks as ColdFusion. So ColdFusion typically reduces development and maintenance costs dramatically. Plus, it's easy to learn and use, making it ideal for our customers to take over technical maintenance should they desire to do so. Again, other languages have strengths that tower over ColdFusion for certain types of projects. However, in our experience, ColdFusion has been an excellent and reliable choice for many projects.

In this chapter, we'll cover how these technologies were brought together to create a highly efficient, extremely scalable, and radically dynamic Flash web site.

The section of the site that best demonstrates this technique is the Team Riders section (see Figure 7.1). We'll be looking at the Snow Team Riders, but the same techniques were used for the Skate and Surf sections.

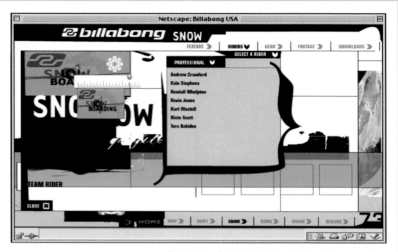

Figure 7.1   The team riders section of the web site.

The user first enters the Team Riders section by selecting Riders from the top navigation. This takes the user to the riders list. Once he clicks on a team rider name, that rider's page is presented with biographical content, interview questions, and thumbnails that link to one to four desktop images of that rider in action.

The content of each rider's page is compiled dynamically from a database that the client maintains through our administration application. To save server bandwidth and processing load, we decided to dynamically generate static SWFs rather than serve Generator templates live to the user. When the client adds or updates a rider in the database, Generator templates are used to generate static SWF files with the rider's content. With the addition or deletion of a rider, the rider list is also updated, and a static SWF of the rider list is created. These new SWFs are kept in a temporary folder on the server. At midnight every night, the server runs a script that copies the new SWFs into the live server.

7.2 RIDER LIST GENERATOR TEMPLATE

The first file we'll look at is the rider list (see Figure 7.2). This list is the navigation tool for the user to select a rider to view. Open the file snow_riders_list.fla.

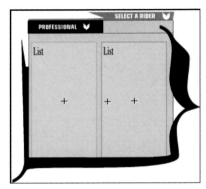

Figure 7.2 The snow riders list template.

Edit the symbol snow_teamriders_selection. We've got two Generator scrolling lists (see Figure 7.3). The snow section was planned to never exceed 22 riders, so creating an "inflexible" solution like this wasn't a problem.

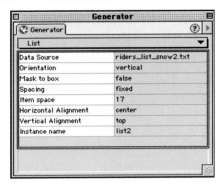

Figure 7.3 The snow riders list Generator list parameters.

The data source for each of these lists is riders_list_snow1.txt and riders_list_snow2.txt. These text files are dynamically generated by ColdFusion with data from the database. Here is some sample content from these text files:

```
clip,rider_id,rider_name
list_item,86,"Andrew Crawford"
list_item,25,"Kale Stephens"
list_item,87,"Kendall Whelpton"
list_item,88,"Kevin Jones"
list_item,24,"Kurt Wastell"
list_item,27,"Risto Scott"
list_item,82,"Tara Dakides"
```

Code 7.1 Data source for the Snow Riders list.

The first column of data is "clip." Clip is a required column for Generator scrolling lists. This value is the name of the movie clip in the library that will be used to populate the list. This is similar in concept to attachMovie and the capability to export symbols with identifier names. The other two columns are the rider's ID, which is a unique identifier number assigned by the database, and the rider's name. The benefit of using a scrolling list with Generator is that for each row of data, the list will "attach" another item to the list. Then each item is assigned data from the corresponding row of data.

Look at the list_item symbol in the library (see Figure 7.4).

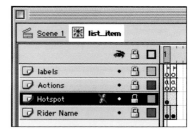

Figure 7.4   The list_item symbol in the library.

You'll see that we set up the movie clip like a button with off and on frames. There's a hotspot with the following actions:

```
on (release) {
    loadMovieNum ("snow/snow_rider{rider_id}.swf", 10);
}
on (rollOver) {
    gotoAndStop ("on");
}
on (rollOut) {
    gotoAndStop ("off");
}
```

Code 7.2   The movie clip is set up like a button.

The on(rollOver) and on(rollOut) actions make the movie clip behave like a button. The on(release) action loads the rider's page onto level 10. The URL is constructed with the Generator variable {rider_id}.

If you look at the text on the rider name layer, you'll see we have a static text block with the contents {rider_name}. This will be replaced by Generator with the data from the data source. This text block has different colors on the off and on frames to facilitate our rollover effect.

7.3 TEAM RIDER GENERATOR TEMPLATE

Once the user has clicked on a rider, the rider's page is loaded. Figure 7.5 shows a snow team rider in the player.

Figure 7.5   The Snow Rider section (snow_rider.fla) in the context of the Billabong site.

Now open the FLA file named snow_rider.fla, as shown in Figure 7.6.

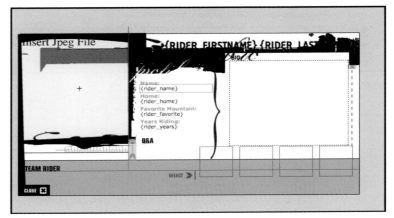

Figure 7.6   The snow _rider.fla file.

Just by comparing the two screen shots (Figures 7.5 and 7.6), you can quickly see the dynamic structure of this file. Let's first look at the data source. We're using an environment data source. If you have the Generator Extensions installed, you will see an iconic button has been added to the bar at the top of the Flash timeline palette immediately preceding the Scene button. This button is identified by a Generator icon and, when clicked, opens the Set Environment dialog box. Click this button to open the dialog box now. We're using another dynamically generated text file called rider_snow{riderid}.txt. The data that this file contains is formatted like this:

```
name,value
rider_id,88
rider_thumb_count,4
rider_favorite,Mammoth
rider_firstname,KEVIN
rider_lastname,JONES
rider_name,Kevin Jones
rider_years,"1"
rider_age,"16"
rider_home,"Mammoth"
rider_bio,"BORN \nSacramento a long time ago\n\nHEIGHT\n5'10\n\nWEIGHT\n170 lbs\n\nSTANCE\nregular\n\n\nBOARD DIMENSIONS
    \n157 Kevin Jones  black snowboard of death\n\nFAVORITE MANEUVER\nOff the lip\n\nWORST SLAM\nMaverics circa '69\n\n\
    nSURFING INFLUENCES\nOccy, Machado \n\nSPONSORS\nNorthwave, Drake, Capita Snowboards, Freestyle, Reef, TSG Helmets,
    Consolidated Skateboards"
    rider_headshot_src,"ACF3CD.jpg"
    rider_thumb1_src,"ACF3B9.jpg"
    rider_thumb2_src,"ACF3BE.jpg"
    rider_thumb3_src,"ACF3C3.jpg"
    rider_thumb4_src,"ACF3C7.jpg"
    rider_image1_src,"ACF3BA.jpg"
    rider_image2_src,"ACF3BF.jpg"
    rider_image3_src,"ACF3C4.jpg"
    rider_image4_src,"ACF3C8.jpg"
    rider_answer1,"Snowboarding."
    rider_answer2,"Frank Zappa."
    rider_answer3,"Heli board for a whole decade."
    rider_answer4,"Ronnie James Dio, Holy Diver."
    rider_answer5,"Skateboarding, and I was in a band called Yukon Cornelius."
    rider_answer6,"Same place I am now, but with gray hair."
    rider_answer7,"Vert ramp skateboard and pads."
    rider_answer8,"J.D. Heís my weiner dog."
    rider_answer9,"Skateboarding."
    rider_answer10,"J.D."
```

Code 7.3   The data of rider_snow{riderid}.txt.

You can see the Generator variables on the main timeline. They're the text that is surrounded by curly braces {}. All of these will be replaced with the correct data. Look at the actions on the first frame of the main timeline.

```
// Convert Variables from  Generator
rider_id = "{rider_id}";
rider_bio = "{rider_bio}";
bio_backup = rider_bio;
rider_thumb_count = "{rider_thumb_count}";
rider_question_count = 10;
```

Code 7.4   ActionScript on the Snow Rider list main timeline.

We convert these variables by putting Generator variables as the values of the Flash variables. When this template compiles, the script will behave like the following:

```
rider_id = "88"
```

We have five "insert jpg" Generator objects. The first is the rider headshot. The source for this image is the Generator variable rider_headshot_src. The other four images are thumbnails of the rider's action images. We required that the client provide at least one action image and limited them to four. The source for these JPEGs is defined in our data source as the variables rider_thumb(1-4)_src.

The action image thumbnails begin offstage. There are four of them, and they each have a unique instance name of "thumb(1-4)." The reason we had to "prepopulate" these movie clips is that Generator compiles a template *before* the SWF actually runs. You have to plan on Generator running before ActionScript.

Edit the movie clip snow_rider_thumb1. Thumbs 2 through 4 are structured the same. Each thumbnail clip has a hotspot that opens the large image viewer. The URL for this viewer is compiled with dynamic data. Look at the frame actions on the actions layer:

```
url_1 = "snow/snow_rider_large.swf?";
url_2 = "rider_id=" + _root.rider_id;
url_3 = "&rider_thumb_count=" + _root.rider_thumb_count;
url_4 = "&rider_thumb=1";
url = url_1 + url_2 + url_3 + url_4;
```

Code 7.5   Frame actions for opening the large image viewer.

The actual hotspot has the following simple action:

```
on (release) {
    loadMovieNum (url, 15);
}
```

Code 7.6   The hotspot's simple action.

Before we look at the large image browser, let's look at the code that places the thumbnails in position. We started the four thumbnails offstage because, as we noted earlier, a rider can have between one and four images. We didn't want thumbnails that didn't link to images to show up on the stage. Look at the actions on the last frame of the main timeline:

```
// Load Thumbnails

for (a=1; a <= rider_thumb_count; ++a) {

    _root["thumb"+a]._x = 353+(75*(a-1));

    _root["thumb"+a]._y = 273;

}

stop ();
```

Code 7.7   The last frame actions.

The rider_thumb_count variable was brought in from Generator. It will be a number between 1 and 4. This for loop positions the correct number of thumbnails. All of the thumbnails are placed at the Y position of 273. For their X position, we start the first thumbnail at 353 and then place each subsequent thumbnail 75 pixels apart.

Now that the thumbnails are placed, we'll look at the large image browser that pops up when a thumbnail is clicked. If you look back at the URL we constructed in the thumbnail hotspot, you'll see we're passing rider_id, rider_thumb_count, and rider_thumb variables. Open the file snow_rider_large.fla (as shown in Figure 7.7).

The file seen in Figure 7.7 is actually a static SWF. The data it uses is passed through the URL we compiled in the thumbnail. This file acts as an image browser for the large versions of the action images. Edit the movie clip snow_rider_large_image. This clip has five frames. The last four frames are reserved for displaying the action images. Look at the actions on one of the frames:

```
_root.image_number = 1;
loadMovie ("snow/snow_rider" + _root.rider_id + "_image1.swf",
    "container");
stop ();
```

Code 7.8   A single frame from the snow_rider_large_image clip.

Figure 7.7   The Snow Large image (snow_rider_large_fla) in the context of the Billabong site.

The important part is the loadMovie command. This command loads a dynamically generated static SWF that contains the large image. The Generator template for this image is snow_rider_image.fla. Look at this file. It's simply an insert jpg Generator object. When the administrative application generates the rider content, it loops through the action images and creates static SWFs for each image.

7.4   CONTENT MANAGEMENT (FEEDING THE MONSTER)

We've looked at the structure of the Generator templates for a team rider list and a team rider page. These templates rely on images and data values for the (insert jpg) and (scrolling list) Generator objects and for the curly-brace Generator variables. How, you might ask, is this data collected, formatted, and eventually turned into a content-rich Flash web site? Content management, that's how! We built a custom web-based content management application for Billabong USA to use. Let's continue our look at the Team Riders section of the site and see how it all ties together.

The Billabong USA content management system is constructed as a separate, password-protected web site that Billabong USA employees can log in to and post web site content. Once the admin user is logged in, he or she can maintain news, opt-in email lists, riders, and videos. We'll continue to focus on maintaining content for the Team Riders section of the web site.

When planning and developing dynamic content for Flash, we follow these key steps:

1. Plan the overall site (site objectives, navigation, and experience).
2. Sketch the page (or scene) elements and suggested layout.
3. Identify static vs. dynamic elements on the page (or scene).
4. Design a database structure to contain the dynamic elements.
5. Design the content management screens and the web site screens.
6. Define the field names and formats for Flash and Generator data sources and create sample text files for early development testing.
7. Produce the designs in the intended medium (Flash, HTML).
8. Write the program logic for the content management screens (SQL, ColdFusion, ASP, JSP, Perl, and so on).
9. Write the program logic that feeds Flash and Generator with source data.

Once the list of dynamic items was decided for the riders section (see step 3), we designed the appropriate database structure to contain those database elements (see Figure 7.8). (If you're familiar with database design, you'll notice that this table is denormalized. We chose to denormalize this table for strategic reasons related to simplifying administrative program code in consideration of project objectives.) Because the web site was planned for a Windows NT environment, we chose Microsoft SQL Server 7 for a database server.

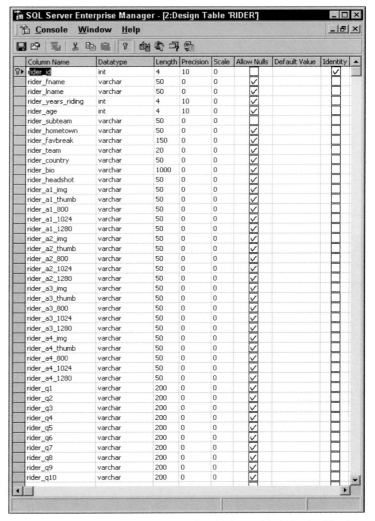

Figure 7.8 The database table design for rider data.

Next we built the content management screens and programming logic.

7.4.1 C.M. RIDERS LIST

Within the content management web site, the admin user can click on Riders in the main navigation to see a list of riders sorted by team. This list page displays only a summary of the rider information. From here, the user can add a new rider, edit or delete an existing rider, or preview what the rider Flash movie will look like for an existing rider.

The Rider List page was developed as HTML because of the flexibility and ease of construction and the lack of need for rich media experience in a purely administrative web site. HTML and Flash each have their strengths and weaknesses. It is our goal to use the right tool for the right job, according to the needs and objectives of the task at hand. In our experience, HTML makes more sense as a medium than Flash for back-end administrative systems, with a few exceptions.

To add the data-driven dimension to the page, it was programmed using ColdFusion and SQL. SQL is the standard language for controlling databases. Although it is a language, by itself it cannot be used to program an application. For that, we need an application programming language. ColdFusion serves nicely as a specialized application programming language for web applications. It is a tag-based language (like HTML), and although it is very easy to use, it is also quite scalable and powerful (when used properly).

Take a look at Code 7.9 for a sample of the ColdFusion code in the Rider List C.M. page. The resulting list page can be seen in Figure 7.9.

```
<cfquery datasource="#Application.dsn#" name="get_riders_surf">
  SELECT rider_id, rider_fname, rider_lname, rider_subteam, rider_age
  FROM RIDER
  WHERE rider_team LIKE '%surf%'
  ORDER BY rider_subteam DESC, rider_fname, rider_age
</cfquery>

<cfset shade = "on">
<cfoutput query="get_riders_surf">

  <tr>
    <td colspan="4"><img src="../../images/ spacer_clear.gif"
    width=420 height=5 alt="" border="0"></td>
  </tr>
```

continues

continued

```
  <tr <cfif shade IS "on">bgcolor="DADADA"<cfset shade = "off"><cfelse><cfset shade = "on"></cfif>>


    <td><img src="../../images/spacer_clear.gif" width=10 height=1 alt="" border="0"><font class="list">#rider_fname# #rider_lname#
      </font></td>


    <td><font class="list">#rider_subteam#  </font></td>


    <td><font class="list">#rider_age#  </font></td>


    <td><a href="add_edit.cfm?rider_id=#rider_id#"> <font
    class="list">Edit</font></a><img
    src="../../images/spacer_clear.gif"
    width=5 height=1 alt="" border="0"><a href="##"
    onClick="window.open(
    '../../tempSite/surf/surf_rider.cfm?rider_id=#rider_id#',
    'test_rider', 'width=700,height=400, scrollbars=no,menus=no');
    return false;"><font class="list">Preview< /font></a><img
    src="../../images/spacer_clear.gif" width=5 height=1 alt=""
    border="0"><a href="index.cfm?del_id=#rider_id#"><font
    class="list">Delete</font></a></td>


  </tr>

</cfoutput>
```

Code 7.9 The content management site rider list ColdFusion code snippet.

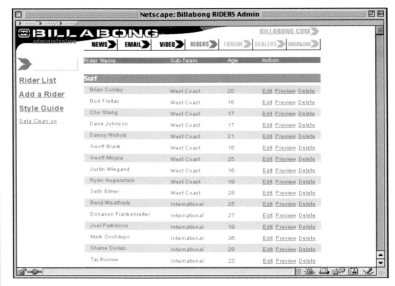

Rider Name	Sub-Team	Age	Action
Surf			
Brian Conley	West Coast	20	Edit Preview Delete
Bud Freitas	West Coast	16	Edit Preview Delete
Che Stang	West Coast	17	Edit Preview Delete
Dane Johnson	West Coast	17	Edit Preview Delete
Danny Nichols	West Coast	21	Edit Preview Delete
Geoff Brack	West Coast	16	Edit Preview Delete
Geoff Moysa	West Coast	25	Edit Preview Delete
Justin Wiegand	West Coast	16	Edit Preview Delete
Ryan Augenstein	West Coast	19	Edit Preview Delete
Seth Elmer	West Coast	28	Edit Preview Delete
Benji Weatherly	International	25	Edit Preview Delete
Donavon Frankenreiter	International	27	Edit Preview Delete
Joel Parkinson	International	19	Edit Preview Delete
Mark Occhilupo	International	36	Edit Preview Delete
Shane Dorian	International	28	Edit Preview Delete
Taj Burrow	International	22	Edit Preview Delete

Rider List
Add a Rider
Style Guide
Data Clean up

Figure 7.9   The Rider List page in the content management web site.

The <cfquery> tag directs ColdFusion to execute the enclosed SQL statement against the database defined in the datasource attribute. In this case, the SQL SELECT statement retrieves the fields rider_id, rider_fname, rider_lname, rider_subteam, and rider_age from the RIDER table. It will only return records where the team name contains the word surf. Finally, the ORDER BY directive tells the database to sort the results by rider_subteam in descending order and then subsort by rider_fname and rider_age.

Next, the script uses <cfset> to set a variable named shade to contain the value on. We use this to alternate the background shading of each row in the HTML list.

We then use the <cfoutput> tag with a query= attribute to direct ColdFusion to loop through the contents of the named database query and output the enclosed HTML tags for each record found in the query results. Within the <cfoutput> tags, anytime ColdFusion encounters something enclosed in pound signs (such as #rider_fname#), it will evaluate the enclosed text as an expression and insert the results into the output HTML. So, where you see #rider_fname#, ColdFusion will read the rider_fname data field from the current database record and output it. In the place of #rider_fname#, it will output something like Donovan. With the exception of the <cfif>, <cfelse>, and <cfset> tags used to toggle the list row shading, the rest of the contents of the <cfoutput> tags is ordinary HTML (and a little JavaScript).

7.4.2   C.M. RIDER DETAILS

When the user clicks on the Edit or Add a Rider link in the Rider List page (refer to Figure 7.9), the Rider Details page is displayed. The Edit link has the rider_id for the selected rider embedded in the URL. If no rider_id is passed to the details page, it assumes that it is in Add Mode and displays a blank form. Otherwise, it does a database query to look up the rider record containing the specified rider_id. An example of the Rider Details page in Edit Mode can be seen in Figure 7.10.

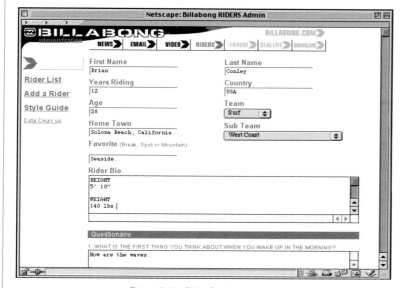

Figure 7.10   Rider Details page editing content for a surf rider.

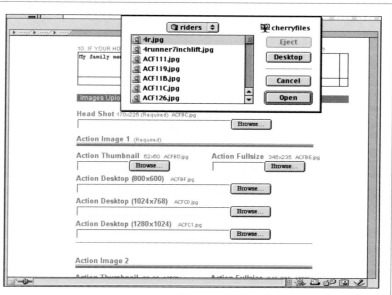

Figure 7.11   The Rider Details page file upload.

Once the Rider Details page is displayed, the user can fill in the form for the selected rider. In addition to simple text content, we used HTML's file upload feature: the <input type="file"> tag. This enables us to program the form to accept files like JPEG images and videos (see Figure 7.11). To upload a file, the user simply presses the Browse button next to the field and browses through the local computer's file system for the file to upload. This puts the full path and filename into the input field to the left of the Browse button.

When the user presses the Save button at the bottom of the page, the contents of all the form fields as well as the contents of any files marked for upload are sent to a ColdFusion script to deal with. Then the user is returned to the Rider List page (refer to Figure 7.9). We built all of the form data processing logic into the rider details script. When the rider details script runs, it first checks to see if it has

received any form data. If so, it determines whether it has been instructed to add, edit, or delete a rider in the database. It then uses the appropriate SQL statement (INSERT, UPDATE, or DELETE) to carry out the database update.

If the user uploads any files, the script uses the <cffile action= "upload"> tag to save the file contents into individual files on the web server. It then records the file names in the database. So the images and videos themselves are not stored in the database, only their filenames. The actual files are stored in certain subdirectories on the web server.

Once the form data and files have been saved, we use offline Generator to construct new SWF files containing the newly posted content.

7.4.3 FORMATTING DATA FOR GENERATOR

Whenever the user edits, adds, or deletes a rider, the system regenerates the Rider List SWF and the SWF files for the particular rider that was changed.

NOTE

Online Generator is a term for the way Generator can be used live to generate a dynamic SWF every time a user requests the file. The Flash/Generator template file (*.swt) is either embedded into an HTML page or loaded by another Flash movie using the loadMovie() or loadMovieNum() actions. This method of employing Generator is meant only for Generator Enterprise Edition, and even then, it is not always the best use of your server's CPU.

Offline Generator refers to the technique of generating static SWF files from a Flash/Generator template file (*.swt) without an online (web) request from a user. Generator 2 provides a command-line program named generate.exe to invoke a conversion from a template file to a supported export format (JPEG, GIF, PNG, SWF, MOV, TXT, SMAP, CMAP, and Flash projectors).

When working with online Generator, data sources can be URLs, JDBC, or simple text files. However, when working with offline Generator, the data source options are limited. We never use the JDBC method of getting data for Generator because the data source formatting requirements of Generator would often require us to design our databases specially just for Generator. We prefer to use either URLs or text files. Because offline Generator does not support URLs, we programmed the system to dynamically create text files and fill them with database information in the special format that Generator craves.

As seen in Code 7.1, earlier in this chapter, we defined a data source for the Flash-based list of riders. For a snippet of ColdFusion code that creates this text file, see Code 7.10. We also generate a text file for the specific rider that has just been added or edited. There is a lot more data included in the Rider Details page, so the ColdFusion code snippet in Code 7.11 is a bit longer than the one that generates the list page details.

```
<cfquery datasource="#Application.dsn#" name="get_riders_p_snow">
    SELECT rider_id, rider_fname, rider_lname
    FROM RIDER
    WHERE rider_team = 'snow' AND rider_subteam = 'Professional'
    ORDER BY rider_fname, rider_lname
</cfquery>

<!--- Format the 1st text output file for a Generator List Object --->
<cfset pageData="clip,rider_id,rider_name" & crlf>
<cfloop query="get_riders_p_snow" startrow="1" endrow="20">
    <cfset pageData = pageData &
      "list_item," & rider_id & "," & quot & rider_fname & " " &
      rider_lname & quot & crlf>
</cfloop>

<cffile action="Write"
 addnewline="No"
 file="#site_gen_root#riders_list_snow1.txt"
 output="#pageData#">
```

Code 7.10 ColdFusion code snippet that creates the riders_list_snow1.txt.file.

```
output="#pageData#">

<!-- Count how many thumbnail images there are -->
<cfset rider_thumb_count = 0>
<cfif this_rider.rider_a1_thumb NEQ "">
  <cfset rider_thumb_count = rider_thumb_count + 1>
</cfif>
<cfif this_rider.rider_a2_thumb NEQ "">
  <cfset rider_thumb_count = rider_thumb_count + 1>
</cfif>
<cfif this_rider.rider_a3_thumb NEQ "">
  <cfset rider_thumb_count = rider_thumb_count + 1>
</cfif>
<cfif this_rider.rider_a4_thumb NEQ "">
  <cfset rider_thumb_count = rider_thumb_count + 1>
</cfif>


<!-- massage the content of the bio, making sure there are no "strange" characters -->
<cfset crlf = CHR(13) & CHR(10)>
<cfset quot = CHR(34)>
<cfset fixed_bio = Replace(this_rider.rider_bio, crlf, "\n", "ALL")>
<cfset fixed_bio = Replace(fixed_bio, quot, "\" & quot, "ALL")>
<cfset fixed_bio = Replace(fixed_bio, CHR(133), "...", "ALL")>
<cfset fixed_bio = Replace(fixed_bio, CHR(145), "'", "ALL")>
<cfset fixed_bio = Replace(fixed_bio, CHR(146), "'", "ALL")>
<cfset fixed_bio = Replace(fixed_bio, CHR(147), "\" & quot, "ALL")>
<cfset fixed_bio = Replace(fixed_bio, CHR(148), "\" & quot, "ALL")>
<cfset fixed_bio = Replace(fixed_bio, CHR(150), "-", "ALL")>


<!-- Create a Rider Text File for Generator -->
```

continues

continued

```
<cfset pageData=
  "name,value" & crlf &
  "rider_id," & this_rider.rider_id & crlf &
  "rider_thumb_count," & rider_thumb_count & crlf &
  "rider_favorite," & this_rider.rider_favbreak & crlf &
  "rider_firstname," & UCase(this_rider.rider_fname) & crlf &
  "rider_lastname," & UCase(this_rider.rider_lname) & crlf &
  "rider_name," & this_rider.rider_fname & " "
        & this_rider.rider_lname & crlf &
  "rider_years," & quot & this_rider.rider_years_riding &quot &crlf &
  "rider_age," & quot & this_rider.rider_age &quot &crlf &
  "rider_home," & quot & Replace(Replace(this_rider.rider_hometown,
        crlf, "\n", "ALL"), quot, "\"&quot, "ALL") & quot & crlf &
  "rider_bio," & quot & fixed_bio & quot & crlf &
  "rider_headshot_src," &quot &this_rider.rider_headshot &quot &crlf &
  "rider_thumb1_src," & quot & this_rider.rider_a1_thumb &quot &crlf &
  "rider_thumb2_src," & quot & this_rider.rider_a2_thumb &quot &crlf &
  "rider_thumb3_src," & quot & this_rider.rider_a3_thumb &quot &crlf &
  "rider_thumb4_src," & quot & this_rider.rider_a4_thumb &quot &crlf &
  "rider_image1_src," & quot & this_rider.rider_a1_img &quot &crlf &
  "rider_image2_src," & quot & this_rider.rider_a2_img &quot &crlf &
  "rider_image3_src," & quot & this_rider.rider_a3_img &quot &crlf &
  "rider_image4_src," & quot & this_rider.rider_a4_img &quot &crlf &
  "rider_answer1," & quot & Replace(Replace(this_rider.rider_q1, crlf,
        "\n", "ALL"), quot, "\"&quot, "ALL") & quot & crlf &
  "rider_answer2," & quot & Replace(Replace(this_rider.rider_q2, crlf,
        "\n", "ALL"), quot, "\"&quot, "ALL") & quot & crlf &
  "rider_answer3," & quot & Replace(Replace(this_rider.rider_q3, crlf,
```

continues

continued

```
      "\n", "ALL"), quot, "\"&quot, "ALL") & quot & crlf &
  "rider_answer4," & quot & Replace(Replace(this_rider.rider_q4, crlf,
      "\n", "ALL"), quot, "\"&quot, "ALL") & quot & crlf &
  "rider_answer5," & quot & Replace(Replace(this_rider.rider_q5, crlf,
      "\n", "ALL"), quot, "\"&quot, "ALL") & quot & crlf &
  "rider_answer6," & quot & Replace(Replace(this_rider.rider_q6, crlf,
      "\n", "ALL"), quot, "\"&quot, "ALL") & quot & crlf &
  "rider_answer7," & quot & Replace(Replace(this_rider.rider_q7, crlf,
      "\n", "ALL"), quot, "\"&quot, "ALL") & quot & crlf &
  "rider_answer8," & quot & Replace(Replace(this_rider.rider_q8, crlf,
      "\n", "ALL"), quot, "\"&quot, "ALL") & quot & crlf &
  "rider_answer9," & quot & Replace(Replace(this_rider.rider_q9, crlf,
      "\n", "ALL"), quot, "\"&quot, "ALL") & quot & crlf &
  "rider_answer10," & quot & Replace(Replace(this_rider.rider_q10,
      crlf, "\n", "ALL"), quot, "\"&quot, "ALL") & quot & crlf   >


<CFSET textFile = site_gen_root & this_team & "\rider" & this_team & this_rider.rider_id & ".txt">


<CFFILE ACTION="Write"
    ADDNEWLINE="No"
    FILE="#textFile#"
    OUTPUT="#pageData#">
```

Code 7.11 ColdFusion code snippet that creates the ridersnow{rider_id}.txt file.

7.5 AUTOMATING OFFLINE GENERATOR

Once the text files have been created, the ColdFusion script kicks in with a few calls to offline Generator. Macromedia provides an extension to ColdFusion, making it easy for ColdFusion scripts to call offline Generator. This extension is named CFX_Generate, and you can find more information about it at the following URLs:

Integrating Generator with Allaire ColdFusion Tutorial:
www.macromedia.com/support/generator/how/subjects/
gen_cf_tut/gen_cf_tut.html

ColdFusion Generator SDK:
http://download.macromedia.com/pub/flash/generator/
sdk/gencf.zip

Here's, basically, how CFX_Generate works. Call the CFX_Generate tag, passing the swt filename in the *template=* attribute, the output SWF filename in the *file=* attribute, and the type of output file (SWF) in the *type=* attribute. See Code 7.12 for a basic ColdFusion sample. There are four other attributes of the CFX_Generate tag as well. Go online to the just-mentioned tutorials for full information on the tag's capabilities.

```
<cfset templateFile = site_gen_root & this_team & "\" & \this_team & "_rider.swt">

<cfset outputFile = site_gen_root & this_team & "\" & this_team & "_rider" & this_rider.rider_id & ".swf">

<cfx_generate
    template="#templateFile#"
    type="swf"
    file="#outputFile#">
```

Code 7.12 A basic ColdFusion example using CFX_Generate.

For the Billabong USA site, when generating a team rider SWF, we had to pass the rider_id value to the Generator template so that it would know which text file to use for its dynamic content. Passing command-line parameters to an swt file through CFX_Generate is a little odd. It required that we create a virtual query result set and populate it with the name/value pairs we wanted to place on the command line. Code 7.13 shows how this was done for the Rider Details movie.

When ColdFusion calls the CFX_Generate extension, the server runs an instance of the generate.exe command from the Generator installation. A nifty little DOS window pops up briefly on the web server. Unfortunately, generator.exe does not complain if it runs into any problems. Under harsh server conditions, it will simply fail to create the desired output file, or it will only partially create the output file. So if you want to reliably automate it, you have to spend a little time with your automation code to ensure that it doesn't run into "harsh" conditions.

```
<cfset templateFile = site_gen_root & this_team & "\" & this_team & "_rider.swt">

<cfset outputFile = site_gen_root & this_team & "\" & this_team & "_rider" & this_rider.rider_id & ".swf">


<!-- Create a virtual query containing the Generator name/values -->
<cfset GenParams = QueryNew("NAME,VALUE")>
<cfset x = QueryAddRow(GenParams)>
<cfset x = QuerySetCell(GenParams,"NAME","riderid")>
<cfset x = QuerySetCell(GenParams,"VALUE",this_rider.rider_id)>

<!-- Call off-line Generator to create a swf -->
<cfx_generate
    template="#templateFile#"
    type="swf"
    query="GenParams"
    file="#outputFile#">
```

Code 7.13 ColdFusion cfx_generate example passing parameters to SWT.

We found that if we tried to sequentially call CFX_Generate (and thus generate.exe) numerous times in a row without pause, something would fail to output properly. CFX_Generate simply calls generate.exe and then frees ColdFusion up to continue running the program, regardless of generate.exe's progress.

When we built an automation script that looped through all of the riders in the database to provide Billabong with a global refresh function, generate.exe was called about 120 times in the space of about 10 seconds. Each instance of generate.exe was vying for memory and CPU attention on the server, creating harsh conditions for themselves. There was no indication of anything wrong until we went to validate the 120 SWF files that were output. Some of them were fine, but most of them were either missing or corrupt.

Two solutions came to mind. One was to do away with a global update script and only provide an automation script that would generate two to five SWF files at a time. This smaller script would be run every time the admin user edited a rider in the content management site and would only output the rider list SWF and rider SWF files.

The other solution was to try and slow down the global update script to give the presently executing instances of generate.exe time to finish their task. This worked reasonably well but still had problems occasionally. The way we caused delay was to insert a loop into the ColdFusion script to continuously check for the existence of the expected output SWF file. Once the file came into existence, the ColdFusion script would continue on its merry way. Unfortunately, this technique only gave generate.exe enough time to *start* outputting the SWF file. Without a straightforward way to detect when generate.exe is finished with its task, we decided to give up on large-scale Generator automation. We're convinced that with enough time and effort, a solution can be concocted, but as pragmatists, we moved on to the next challenge.

There was one final issue we considered when building the offline Generator automation scripts. Should we allow Generator to output SWF files directly into the live web site folders? We chose not to. The first reason was that Generator might take more than a second to generate a particularly beefy file, and during that time, someone visiting the live site would receive an error. The second reason was our concern for what would happen to the live site if an error occurred during generation of a file.

Rather than put the live web site at risk, we chose to create a temporary directory structure where Generator could output SWF files. This also enabled us to create a preview feature in the content management system. The admin user could then view the generated SWF files in the temporary directory and fix content problems before going live.

7.6 SCHEDULING A LIVE SITE UPDATE

Because we automated Generator to output Flash content to a temporary folder, we needed to create a way for the administrative user to post new Flash content to the live site. We built two web scripts, one that copies the files to the live folder immediately (see Code 7.14) and one that schedules the first script to run at midnight (see Code 7.15). Both of these scripts were meant to run in a pop-up HTML window. We provided links on the main menu of the content management web site to Post Now or Post at Midnight.

```
<html>
<head>
  <title>Post Content Live</title>
</head>
<body>

<cfset aDirs = ArrayNew(1)>
<cfset aDirs[1] = "">
<cfset aDirs[2] = "skate\">
<cfset aDirs[3] = "snow\">
<cfset aDirs[4] = "surf\">
<cfset aDirs[5] = "video\">

<cfoutput>
Copying from: #site_gen_root#<BR>
To:  #site_root#<BR>
</cfoutput>

<cfloop index="idx" from="1" to="#ArrayLen(aDirs)#">

  <cfset subDir = aDirs[idx]>
  <cfset theDir="#site_gen_root##subDir#">

  <cfoutput><BR><b>Directory:
  #site_gen_root##subDir#</b><BR></cfoutput>
```

```
<!--
  Copy all generated SWF files from the main directory
-->

<cfdirectory action="LIST" name="qryFiles" directory="#theDir#">
<cfloop query="qryFiles">
  <cfif LCase(Right(qryFiles.Name,4)) EQ ".swf">
    <cfoutput>Found:
      #site_gen_root##subDir##qryFiles.Name#</cfoutput><BR>

    <cffile action="COPY"
      source="#site_gen_root##subDir##qryFiles.Name#"
      destination="#site_root##subDir##qryFiles.Name#"
      attributes="Normal">
  </cfif>
</cfloop>

</cfloop>

</body>
</html>
```

Code 7.14 The ColdFusion script to post flash content live.

```
<CFSETTING enablecfoutputonly="YES">
<CFSET TodaysDate = DateFormat(Now(), "mm-dd-yyyy")>

<CFSET urlPath = GetDirectoryFromPath(CGI.SCRIPT_NAME)>
<CFSET urlPath = Left(urlPath, Len(urlPath)-1)>
<CFSET url = "http://#CGI.SERVER_NAME#:#CGI.SERVER_PORT##urlPath#copy_generated_files.cfm">
<CFSCHEDULE ACTION="UPDATE"
    TASK="PostSiteLive"
    OPERATION="HTTPRequest"
    URL="#url#"
    STARTDATE="#TodaysDate#"
    STARTTIME="11:59 PM"
    INTERVAL="Once"
    RESOLVEURL="No"
    PUBLISH="No"
    REQUESTTIMEOUT="1200">
<CFSETTING enablecfoutputonly="No">
<HTML>
<HEAD>
  <TITLE>Billabong USA - Site Update Scheduler</TITLE>
  <link rel="STYLESHEET" type="text/css" href="admin.css">
</HEAD>

<BODY>

<P class="leftnav">Updating Schedule...</p>
<SCRIPT>
  alert('The schedule has been updated.');
```

continues

```
continued
  top.close()    ;
</script>
</BODY>


</HTML>
```

7.7 SUMMARY

In this chapter, we've looked at how to develop Flash movies using Generator to embed dynamic content. We discussed the strategies used on the Billabong USA web site for content management, automation of offline Generator, and scheduling live content postings. Some of the caveats and solutions for offline Generator were covered as well.

With an understanding of database design, SQL, a web scripting language like ColdFusion, HTML, and creating Flash movies with Generator authoring extensions, you can create amazing web sites that appear to be completely handcrafted but with the lower cost and higher flexibility of a content-driven web site.

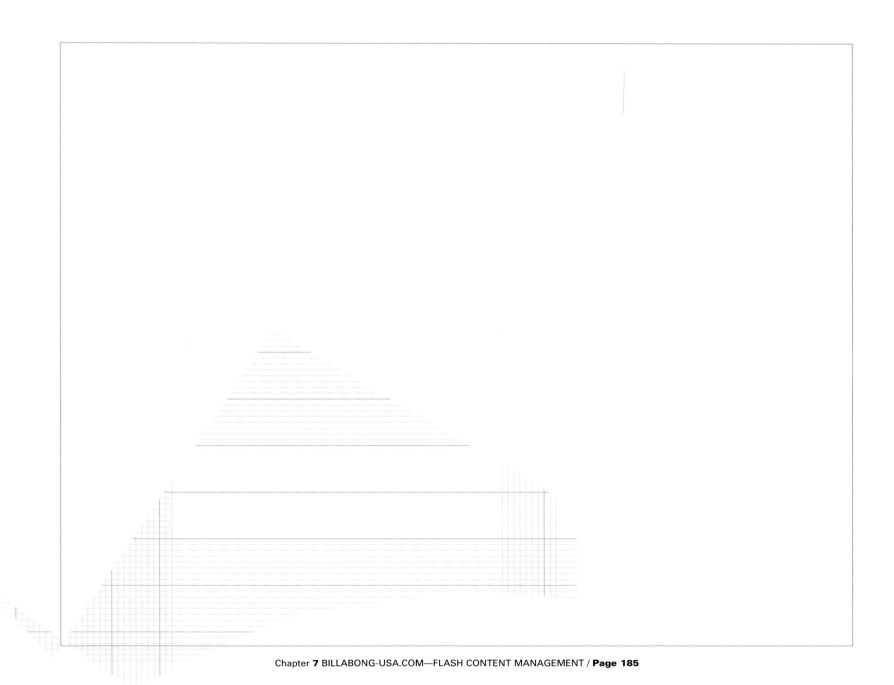

IO RESEARCH

Josh Ulm Interview
by Todd Purgason

Introduction
www.ioresearch.com

IO Research is a team of highly skilled and creative designers and programmers in San Francisco. The founder, Josh Ulm, is well known for his installation site, www.theremediproject.com. This site brings together some of the best minds in web design space to do quarterly installments for the rest of us to enjoy.

I first met Josh at UCON 99, where at a moment's notice, I was thrown into a keynote panel with him. The panel discussion, which was lead by Lynda Weinman (of www.lynda.com), got into some pretty interesting concepts, and after listening to Josh, I was sold on his genius. After talking with him personally, I have

found that not only is he brilliant, he is a genuinely nice guy as well. I think he would be the first to agree with me that he has a great team of people behind him, and we can expect this group to maintain its impact on the web.

Teaser from the Interview

TP: Okay, so Josh Ulm, what is IO Research?

JU: IO Research is a multi–disciplinary design studio in San Francisco. There are four of us right now. On occasion, we kind of drift in and out; we have some people that work on other projects, so they're sometimes here and some-times not. The two principals are myself and Chris Griffith, my partner, who is our studio director. I'm the creative direc-tor. Basically, we specialize in interactive storytelling and documentary work.

To hear the rest of Josh's answer to this question, as well as his answers to the following questions, please go to the Inspirations section of the book's site at www.JUXTinteractive.com/deCONSTRUCTION.

QUESTIONS

02. If IO Research were a fish/sea creature, what would it be?

03. What CD or mp3 is in your player right now?

04. What is your definition of design?

05. What was your very first impression of Flash?

06. If you were walking down the street and came across John Gay and Jakob Nielsen engaged in a fistfight, what would you do?

07. You guys are creating some very interesting technology with Flash. What has been the biggest technological challenge you have faced thus far?

08. What is your vision for IO Research?

09. Is it hard to sell Flash as a technology tool to your clients? Is the stereotypical IT director anti-Flash for one reason or another?

10. How did you select the members of your team? What were you looking for in potential candidates?

11. Can you tell us a little about your development process?

12. How do you balance the R&D work with client work?

13. Being the leader, Josh, how does your background in film influence IO Research?

14. What is it that happens in a typical day that gives you a feeling of satisfaction when you go home at night?

15. Many designers criticize some Flash work as being driven by the tool. Do you feel that is the case with IO Research, being that it is so tied to the technology? Do you care?

16. If you could do one last project before you had to hang up your designer's cap, what would you want that project to be?

c8 CHAPTER
Flash deCONSTRUCTION
OTHER BILLABONG SITES

C8 CHAPTER
Flash deCONSTRUCTION
OTHER BILLABONG SITES

In working with a client as a partner, you put yourself in a position not only to garner more work but to also pitch ideas for projects that the client might or might not have considered.

Today, marketing on the Internet is much more like marketing in the real world. You need to be hitting the market with frequent and consistent efforts that will keep your brand in the faces and minds of existing and potential customers. Many people mistakenly believe that just creating a web site is all they need to do to take full advantage of the marketing potential of the web. To use an analogy, how many companies that you know would use a marketing strategy like the following? Imagine a company that produces one catalog every two years. They actively distribute this catalog in its first month of publication. After that, catalogs are just left in piles at various locations for people to pick up at their leisure. You would have to have one heck of an amazing product to be successful with such a limited strategy. Unfortunately, this is often what companies are doing on the web. There is no blame to be placed on anyone. After all, the web is still very new to most people, and they don't understand the dynamics of it. This is where Juxt, and groups like us, can and should step in and advise our clients on actions that should be taken. This way, they can fully harness the web to support their brand and marketing efforts.

8.1 PICKLED.TV

In working with Billabong, we have released two phases of their site this year and are currently working on the third. All of these phases extend their brand and marketing efforts on the web. In addition, we identified a couple of unique opportunities that enabled Billabong to extend their branding efforts even further on the web and to explore some new revenue streams.

First was the Pickled.tv site (www.pickled.tv), which was created to promote a new surf film produced by Billabong (see Figure 8.1). Every year, Billabong, like many other surf brands, makes a film that features their team riders. This is a key part of their marketing strategy. It keeps the kids (their customers) stoked on the Billabong-sponsored riders.

This year Billabong went a step further with *Pickled the Movie* (see Figure 8.1). Traditionally, these films are shot and put on video. For Pickled, they hooked up with an extreme film series, called the Adrenaline Series, that is touring theaters across the nation. To do this, they have to shoot in 35mm and make a much higher investment in the film. They also brought in Robert Earl, a well-known personality in the extreme sports industry, and built a plot (technically you can call it a plot) for the film.

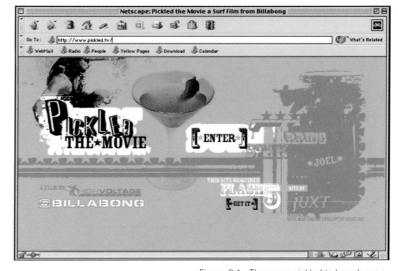

Figure 8.1   The www.pickled.tv launch page.

We saw this as a great opportunity to build a micro site that would promote the film. More importantly, it was another way to assert the Billabong brand to its market through the web. The kids that see and buy these films are typically isolated in geographic areas that have a surf culture that supports surf shops. The films are mostly seen or purchased in these surf shops. With the web, we took the amazing content and tongue-in-cheek nature of the film and built a great experience that breaks free of geographic barriers (see Figure 8.2).

Figure 8.2   The Pickled call-to-action link on the Billabong-USA.com home page.

The real goal of the film is not to be a profit vehicle but a branding vehicle. We have now taken the film, which is one vehicle, and made and leveraged it to create a second vehicle. These two vehicles travel in opposite directions, yet they achieve the same objective—to promote the Billabong brand in the surf culture.

Pickled.tv was a very fun project both in design and technology. To be absolutely honest, when we started this book, we had intended to deconstruct a great deal of Pickled content. However, disaster struck during the writing of this book, and a large portion of the source files became corrupt. After much effort and heartache, we had to move on and use other source content. We feel that although this experience was a letdown for us, in the end it worked in our favor. The alternative content is even better than the Pickled content would have been. Fortunately, a few portions of the site did not get corrupted, and we will share them with you.

8.1.1   PICKLED.TV MAIN NAVIGATION

For the Pickled.tv site to be a successful representation of the movie, we needed to give the site a real personality. It needed to reflect the personality of the movie and that of Robert Earl, the movie's star. Robert is a funny big goofball who's animated and off the wall. He makes you laugh until your sides hurt. We felt the site's personality had to capture some of the spontaneous, off-the-wall silliness of the movie. Many site elements work together to achieve this personality. A major element of this is the main navigation.

The navigation on Pickled is as much design as it is technology. At first glance, it's kind of odd looking and subdued, so you don't think too much of it. However, as soon as you touch it, it jumps to life with spontaneous, in-your-face motion and audio. As you roll across the bar, it feels like you're tickling it and eliciting a spasm of interaction. Navigation for a web site, in general, forces people to make assumptions about what content lies behind each button. We designers have developed tricks, like showing more detailed information on a rollover, that we've been using for years. On this project, we used voiceover by Robert to subtly explain what users can expect. We give more information to help users make a decision as to where to go. At the same time, we've added a huge amount of personality to the site experience.

Lets take a look at how Figure 8.3 is constructed. Open the file nav.fla. The first three frames of the file contain a preloading system that consists of four elements. The first element is a label on frame 3 named loaded. Next, on frame 1, we have our standard loading movie clip that plays while the user waits.

Figure 8.3   The Pickled.tv main navigation rollover effect.

NOTE

In the Pickled site, this loading movie clip is loaded at the beginning of the site from a shared library. This enables us to reuse the movie clip every time we need to communicate to the user that we are loading new content without having to download it over and over. For our example file, we broke the linkage to the shared library. Now it's self-contained in nav.fla.

Also, frame 1 has the following frame ActionScript:

```
if (_framesloaded>=_totalframes) {
    gotoAndPlay("loaded");
}
```

This script gets the property _framesloaded, which is how many frames have currently been loaded. Then it checks to see if this number is greater than or equal to (>=) the total number of frames in the movie clip, which is determined by getting the property _totalframes. If the results of this are true, the playback head jumps to our label on frame 3 named loaded. If this is not true, the playback head simply moves on to the next frame. In the next frame, frame 2, we have our last element, which is the simple script:

```
gotoAndPlay(1);
```

This line of code simply sends the playhead back to frame 1, which will again check to see if the number of total frames loaded is greater than or equal to the total frames in the movie clip. This cycle will repeat itself until the statement returns true, which will allow the movie clip to play itself out.

Following our preloader mechanism is a motion graphic sequence that animates the movie clip to the screen. This culminates on frame 24, which is labeled static, and has a stop frame action on the labels layer. The rest of the timeline is divided into seven segments of six frames each. Each of these segments corresponds to one of the buttons on the main navigation. Each segment is identical in structure, but they are individualized for each particular button. For this example, we'll just deconstruct one of these sections. You can check out the other segments, too.

In the main timeline, move the playhead down to the sixth segment, which starts on frame 55 and is labeled game (see Figure 8.4).

Let's take a look at what's going on, starting at the top layer (named labels) and moving down to the last layer (named text white). The first layer, labels, is simple enough. It has keyframes with label markers that help distinguish segments. We can also target them with our button actions, which we discuss later in this chapter. Next, we have the actions layer. On this layer, at the beginning of each segment, we have an ActionScript that tells the player to start playing the correct sound for the button and to stop all other sounds that might be playing.

Let's take a deeper look at how this works. For this to work properly, we used Flash 5's new sound object, which was covered in detail in Chapter 5, "JuxtInteractive.com Environment Scripting." To review, let's talk about how to create a sound object in Flash 5 and control it using ActionScript.

The first step is to import a sound you want into Flash. Next, open the library and select that sound. Once it's selected, click on Linkage in the Library Palette pop-up menu to open the Symbol Linkage Properties dialog box, as shown in Figure 8.5.

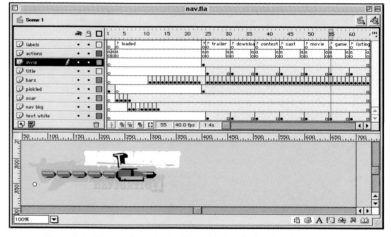

Figure 8.4   The nav.fla main timeline with the playhead at the game button label.

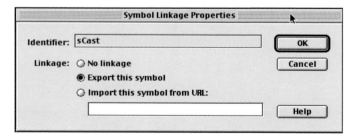

Figure 8.5   The Symbol Linkage Properties dialog box.

Next, give the sound object a unique name in the Identifier field. Then click on the Export this symbol radio button and click OK. For the main navigation, we had to create eight unique sound objects, one for each button.

Back to the frame action: In the game segment, if you look at that action, you will see the following eight lines of code, as shown in Figure 8.6.

```
sTrailer.stop("sTrailer");
sDownload.stop("sDownload");
sContest.stop("sContest");
sCast.stop("sCast");
sMovie.stop("sMovie");
sGame.stop("sGame");
sGame.start(0,1);
sListing.stop("sListing");
```

Figure 8.6 Frame script that controls the sound for the game button.

Seven of the lines are there to stop other button sounds that might be playing when you roll over the game button. They're identical in structure, but they're each talking to a unique sound object. For example, sTrailer.stop("sTrailer"); identifies the sound object to control (sTrailer) and then tells it what you want it to do (.stop). Because a sound object can have more than one sound, we finish off by identifying which specific sound in the object controls sTrailer within the parentheses.

The only unique line of code is the one that controls the sound for the game button, sGame.start(0,1);. This script again starts by identifying the sound object to control (sGame) and then follows with the command (.start). This, of course, starts the sound object. This is followed by two parameters within the parentheses, (0,1). The first one specifies the number of seconds to offset within the sound. In this case, it's set to 0, which means that the sound will start playing from its beginning. The next number specifies the loop, which in this case is set to 1. The result is that the sound will only play once.

> **NOTE**
> We also have a stop action for the sGame sound object immediately above the start action. This will prevent sound overlap if the user quickly rolls over the button, out of the button, and then back in.

On the next layer, invis, we have all our buttons for the main navigation. Each one is a duplicate of the same invisible button (all states are empty except the hit state) symbol that has a different action attached to it. Select the second invisible button from the right over the Game button bar (refer to the preceding game label) to inspect the script. Figure 8.7 shows the ActionScript for the game button.

```
on (release) {
    _level0.gotoAndStop("game");
    logo.gotoAndStop(2);
    unloadMovieNum (100);
}
on (rollOver) {
    gotoAndPlay ("game");
}
on (rollOut) {
    gotoAndStop ("static");
}
```

The rollover action is very simple, gotoAndPlay ("game"); it just tells the main playhead to go to the label "game" on the main timeline of this movie and play. This jumps the playhead to the game segment of frames, executes the frame action we deconstructed above, and plays out the segment until it hits the stop action at the end of the segment. Then, on rollout, it sends the playhead back to our "static" label and stops. All the buttons are basically the same as this one. The only difference is they point to other labels.

The dynamics of the buttons are brought to the stage as the playhead plays through the frame segment of each button. These are made up of four key components that exist on the remainder of the frames. The first one is on the next layer down, called title. On this layer, in the first frame of the segment, we have the game title movie clip, which contains the text build motion graphics (see Figure 8.8).

Figure 8.7   ActionScript for the game button.

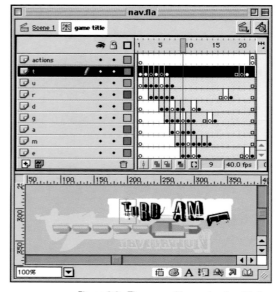

Figure 8.8   The game title movie clip with the button title build-out motion graphics.

The first section of the script controls the actions that will take place when this button is clicked. These only work in the context of the main site; you will not be able to see these results in the files you have downloaded, but you can see them on the live site. So, for our purposes, we'll skip over the on (release) action and focus on the rollover and out.

If you edit this symbol, you can see the keyframe animations for each letter that ultimately build out the title for the button.

The next component is the button bar jitter motion that plays out as a keyframe animation on the bars layer. We chose to do this on the main timeline as opposed to in a separate movie clip so that we could keep track of the button graphic in relationship to the actual buttons on the invis layer.

The next three layers contain elements that make up the static graphics on the nav bar.

Finally, our last piece is on the layer named text white. It contains a movie clip named text white bkg, which is the background for our button label that will build out. It simply slides in position from left to right based on which button you're over.

As you can see, this section achieves a balanced mix of scripting, movie clips, and motion graphics.

8.1.2 PICKLED.TV CAST SECTION

Another fun feature of the Pickled site is the image scroller in the cast section. Image scrollers are kind of popular in Flash development these days because they typically do two things for a site. First, they add an easy-to-use yet interesting interactive experience to the site. Second, they help solve screen real-estate issues. These scrollers are very popular in fashion sites and typically function in a similar manner. For Pickled, we wanted to give this effect a twist that would make the transitions between images more dynamic and in tune with the personality of the site, in addition to capturing the energy of the sport of surfing.

8.1.3 IMAGE SCROLLER

Open the file imageflipper.fla and we'll show you how this is done (see Figure 8.9).

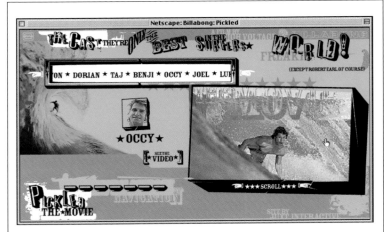

Figure 8.9 The Pickled cast image scroller in the context of the site.

On the scroller layer, we've put a movie clip named image_scroller_masked with an instance name of image. Edit that symbol to see that it contains another movie clip that is masked. The movie clip is image scroller, with an instance name of scroller (see Figure 8.10). Edit this symbol and you'll see the keyframed animation. This animation transitions three images between each other and is structured to loop seamlessly.

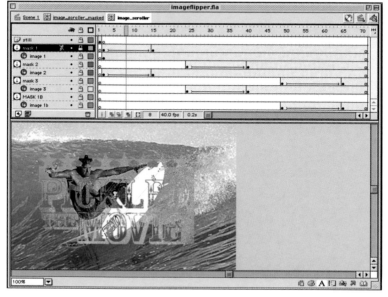

Figure 8.10 The image_scroller movie clip.

Notice how we're animating both the images and the masks. The movie clip basically has three motion sequences, each of which is a transition from one image to the next. The transition is achieved by tweening the first image from 150% down to 100% and then tweening a mask that slides up into the scene to reveal the next image. All of these transitions will be masked one movie clip up in the structure so that they will fit nicely into our view box. The animation is set to play all the way through and loop. We'll be controlling the playback and looping with scripting, so we don't need to add any stop() or play() actions here. Because we need this clip to seamlessly loop backward and forward, notice how we've replicated the animation of image one at the end of the movie clip as well. If we didn't do this, the animated transitions would "jump" between image three and image one as the clip looped.

Go back to the main timeline. There's only one action on the actions layer:

```
image.scroller.stop();
```

This is just to initially stop the scroller animation. All of the important actions are on a clipEvent(enterFrame) on the movie clip named scroller clip (see Figure 8.11).

```
onClipEvent (enterFrame) {
    maxspeed = 3;
    // Set Stage Variables
    stageWidth = 365;
    stageCenter = stageWidth/2;
    // Set Dead Area
    deadArea = 80;
    deadAreaLeft = stageCenter-(deadarea/2);
    deadAreaRight = stageCenter+(deadarea/2);
    // Set Speed                              continues
```

continued

```
    if (_root._xmouse>=deadAreaLeft &&_root._xmouse<=
    deadAreaRight) {

        _root.speed = 0;

    } else if (_root._xmouse<deadAreaLeft) {

        if (_root._xmouse>0) {

            _root.speed = -(Math.round((deadAreaLeft
            _root._xmouse)/(deadAreaLeft/maxspeed)))-1;

        } else {

            _root.speed = -maxspeed;

        }

    } else if (_root._xmouse>deadAreaRight) {

        if (_root._xmouse<stageWidth) {

            _root.speed = -(int((deadAreaRight
            _root._xmouse)/(deadAreaLeft/maxspeed)))+1;

        } else {

            _root.speed = maxspeed;

        }

    }

    // Move Scroller

    _root.nextframe = _root.image.scroller._currentframe+_root.speed;

    if (_root.nextframe<=0) {

        _root.nextframe = _root.image.scroller.
        totalframes+_root.nextframe;

    } else if (_root.nextframe>=_root.image.scroller._totalframes) {

        _root.nextframe -=_root.image.scroller._totalframes+1;

    }

    _root.image.scroller.gotoAndStop(_root.nextframe);

}
```

Figure 8.11 The image scroller script.

The purpose of this script is to set a speed variable and move the scroller animation using this speed. The speed variable is determined by the mouse position with a "dead area" in the middle of the stage. We want to limit the speed to three frames, and we don't want to track the mouse outside the stage area.

As with most scripts, we begin by setting variables that set the environment of our script. First, we'll start off by setting the maxspeed variable to 3 because we don't want the scroller to ever move faster than three frames at a time. The next step is to set variables for the stage dimensions, stageWidth and stageCenter. We'll set the stageWidth to 365. The reason we don't use the property _root._width is because that property is not determined by the stage width but by the content width. The stageCenter will be half of the stageWidth. Next we'll set up the dead area. The dead area is an area in the center where the user can position his or her mouse to stop the scroller. We've used a dead area of 80 pixels. The left and right borders of the dead area are determined by dividing the deadArea variable in half and adding and subtracting that result from the stageCenter.

```
deadAreaLeft = stageCenter-(deadarea/2);
deadAreaRight = stageCenter+(deadarea/2);
```

Now we'll dynamically set the speed based on the current mouse position. First we'll deal with the dead area. If the mouse is within the dead area, we'll set the speed to 0 because we want the scroller to stop when the mouse is positioned here, in the center of the stage. This is done with an if statement evaluating whether the _root._xmouse value is to the right of (greater than) the left border of the dead area or to the left of (less than) the right border.

```
if (_root._xmouse>=deadAreaLeft &&
    _root._xmouse<=deadAreaRight) {
    _root.speed = 0;
```

If the mouse is to the left of the dead area,

```
} else if (_root._xmouse<deadAreaLeft) {
```

we'll check to see if it's within the stage. Because the left border of the stage is the pixel position 0, if the mouse position is greater than 0 (in the stage), we perform a mathematic conversion of the mouse position value into a speed value.

```
if (_root._xmouse>0) {
    _root.speed = -(Math.round((deadAreaLeft-
    _root._xmouse)/(deadAreaLeft/maxspeed)))-1;
```

If it is outside the stage (less than 0), we'll set the speed to maxspeed.

```
} else {
    _root.speed = -maxspeed;
```

We use the same routine if the mouse is to the right of the dead area.

Finally, we'll move the scroller. We'll be moving the scroller to the variable *nextframe*, which is on the main timeline. We determine this variable based on the current frame of the scroller and then add the speed we just set.

```
_root.nextframe = _root.image.scroller._currentframe+_root.speed;
```

Before we use this *nextframe* variable, we need to calculate whether moving the scroller will necessitate that it loop. We first test whether the *nextframe* will be less than the first frame.

```
if (_root.nextframe<=0) {
```

If it is, we'll loop the clip to the end. Because, in this case, *nextframe* is a negative number, by adding it to the scroller's *_totalframes* property, it will evaluate to a frame value less than the *_totalframes* at the end of the clip.

```
_root.nextframe = _root.image.scroller.
    _totalframes+_root.nextframe;
```

If the *nextframe* is greater than the last frame, we loop the clip around to the beginning.

```
} else if (_root.nextframe>=_root.image.scroller._totalframes) {
        _root.nextframe -= _root.image.scroller._totalframes + 1;
    }
```

Finally, we'll move the scroller by the *nextframe*.

```
        _root.image.scroller.gotoAndStop(_root.nextframe);
}
```

8.2 BILLABONG STORE

The Billabong store (www.billabong-usa.com/store) provided another opportunity to expand Billabong's brand on the Internet. It arose somewhat in conjunction with Pickled.tv (see Figure 8.12).

Figure 8.12   The Billabong store (www.billabong-usa.com/store).

Billabong was founded in Australia in 1973. Since then, Billabong has developed very important and trusted relationships with the vendors that sell Billabong products. Because of this, the last thing Billabong wants to do is take money out of vendors' pockets by selling all their products directly online. However, certain products are more "brand centric" than others and are really not of great consequence to retail partners. In fact, the products on the Internet help promote the Billabong brand more than they generate direct revenues. These products include videos and DVDs like *Pickled* that Billabong produces. So we suggested to Billabong that we test the waters of e-commerce and further promote the brand through the web by building a Billabong store. It was important to them that this site not have the feeling of a cheesy e-comm site that would degrade the Billabong brand. If they were going to do it, they wanted the store to be very cool but also very functional. To us, this presented the perfect opportunity to employ Flash to make an e-commerce experience that is functional and cool.

We happen to believe that many aspects of the traditional HTML based e-commerce experience devastate the success of online shopping. In this scenario, there are many timely page jumps that are annoying and painful for modem users. This makes the alternative of the 800 order line a much easier choice in most cases. Businesses sometimes forget that no matter how advanced the technology, if it goes against human nature, it will fail.

We have always felt that, with Flash, you can create a much more intuitive and human experience on the web, and for commerce, this is a huge advantage! Most companies write off Flash for e-commerce from the beginning, which is a big mistake. This decision is typically a result of software engineers not understanding the capabilities of Flash. They see it as an intro maker and not a UI builder. With the Billabong store, we were given the opportunity to prove that Flash not only can do e-commerce, but can improve on it. I challenge everyone of you reading this book; if you find a better shopping experience on the web, let us know. We will have a special place on the book's site (www.JUXTinteractive.com/deCONSTRUCTION) forum for posting links to better online shopping experiences.

We wanted to deconstruct some of the code behind the Billabong store to show you how simple it is to build.

8.2.1 BILLABONG STORE SHOPPING CART

Everyone has become familiar with shopping carts on e-commerce sites. They serve as effective tools in supporting communication with the user during the online shopping experience.

On HTML-based e-commerce sites, shopping carts are simultaneously a blessing and a curse. It's important for a user to get feedback when he or she puts something in a cart. But typically, the transaction is several page loads later, meaning a customer using a modem has to endure a long waiting time. In contrast to HTML, with Flash we can send and get data from the server without forcing a page load. As such, we can make a shopping cart that simply updates itself with new information, communicating to the user immediately with no page reload. The end result is a very painless shopping experience. Let's take a look at how we constructed the shopping cart in the Billabong store (see Figure 8.13).

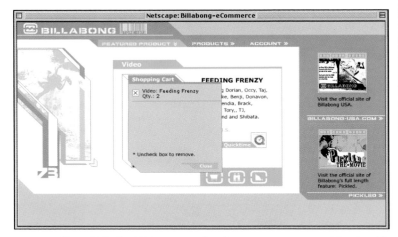

Figure 8.13   The Billabong store shopping cart pops up on top of the store UI.

Open the file billabongstore.fla. In the main timeline, edit the symbol viewcart on the view cart layer. This is our floating shopping cart movie clip (see Figure 8.14).

Figure 8.14   The "viewcart" movie clip.

You'll see that we have four instances of the movie clip named viewcart_item with unique instance names of list_item(1-4). Edit the viewcart_item movie clip to see that this clip has two visible dynamic text fields called video and quantity, respectively. Go back to the main timeline and view the clip events on the viewcart clip (see Figure 8.15).

```
onClipEvent (enterFrame) {
    if (_x < 0) {
        list_count = 0;
        for (a=1; a<=_root.item_count; ++a) {
            if (["_root.product"+a+"_quantity"] > 0) {
                list_count = list_count+1;
                ["list_item"+list_count].quantity =
                    ["_root.product"+a+"_quantity"];
                ["list_item"+list_count].video = ["_root.product"+a+"_name"];
                ["list_item"+list_count].product = a;
                ["list_item"+list_count]._visible = 1;
                ["list_item"+list_count].gotoAndStop("on");
            }
        }
        for (b=list_count+1; b<=_root.item_count; ++b) {
            ["list_item"+b]._visible = 0;
            ["list_item"+b].quantity = 0;
            ["list_item"+b].video = "";
        }
    }
}
```

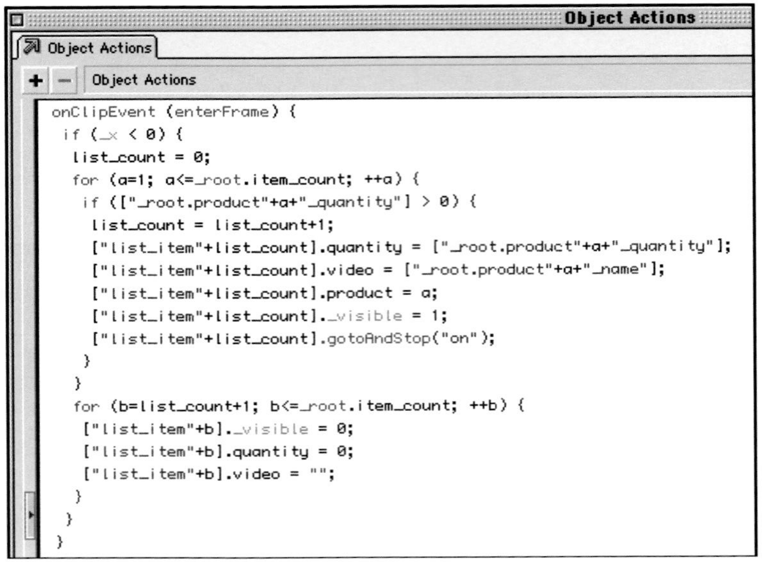

Figure 8.15 The shopping cart script.

```
onClipEvent (enterFrame) {
  if (_x < 0) {
    list_count = 0;
    for (a=1; a<=_root.item_count; ++a) {
      if (["_root.product"+a+"_quantity"] > 0) {
        list_count = list_count+1;
        ["list_item"+list_count].quantity = ["_root.product"+a+"_quantity"];
        ["list_item"+list_count].video = ["_root.product"+a+"_name"];
        ["list_item"+list_count].product = a;
        ["list_item"+list_count]._visible = 1;
        ["list_item"+list_count].gotoAndStop("on");
      }
    }
    for (b=list_count+1; b<=_root.item_count; ++b) {
      ["list_item"+b]._visible = 0;
      ["list_item"+b].quantity = 0;
      ["list_item"+b].video = "";
    }
  }
}
```

This script loops every frame if the shopping cart clip is positioned off the stage.

```
if(_x < 0){
```

We start by setting the variable *list_count* to 0. This variable will be a tally of the list positions that are occupied. Next, with a for loop, we cycle through the products. If a product's quantity is greater than zero,

```
if (["_root.product"+a+"_quantity"] > 0) {
```

the variables *quantity* and *video* are transferred to the appropriate list_item.

```
["list_item"+list_count].quantity = ["_root.product"+a+"_quantity"];
["list_item"+list_count].video = ["_root.product"+a+"_name"];
```

Then the item position's visibility is set to true.

```
["list_item"+list_count]._visible = 1;
```

Finally, for all the items that have zero quantity, we set the list_item's visibility to false.

```
for (b=list_count+1; b<=_root.item_count; ++b) {
    ["list_item"+b]._visible = 0;
```

With a floating palette, you can position it wherever you want. For the Billabong store, we positioned it off stage until the user requested it. In the library, edit the symbol product1_feeding frenzy. On the second frame, look at the action of the second navigation button:

```
on (release) {
    _root.viewcart._x = 300;
}
```

By setting the X position of the cart to 300, we bring the cart back on stage for the user to see.

8.2.2 BILLABONG STORE FLASH FORMS

When you're designing a form in Flash, it's a good habit to question each aspect of the form to aid in the planning process (see Figure 8.16):

- What is the purpose of the form?
- What is the type of data that will be collected or modified?
- How will that data be handled?
- Will the form prepopulate with pre-existing data?

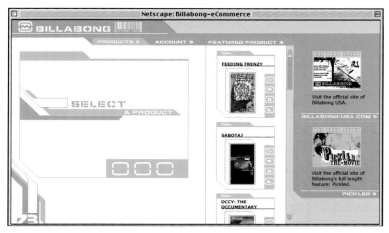

Figure 8.16   The Billabong store product selection.

Questions like these help you define the purpose and parameters of the form and save restructuring time later if you've set up your form correctly the first time.

Forms in Flash are essentially editable variables that are formatted for output. A standard approach is to create visible input text fields for the variables, along the lines of a standard HTML form. For the Billabong store, we used this approach for data relating to the customer (such as shipping address, credit card, and so on) and set data variables with other means such as buttons.

When you're considering the format your data needs to be in, make sure you plan to pass the data efficiently for the method you've chosen. Again, you must ask yourself some questions. Is the data going to be passed with GET or POST methods? XML socket? URL string? When you're sending data with GET or POST, make sure all the variables you are sending are in the same timeline as the action sending the data. For example, if you were setting variables in timeline checkout but were sending the data from the root, you'll need to add script that transfers these variables to the correct timeline.

Here's an example:

```
_root.variableOne = _root.checkout.variableOne
```

The account section is a good example of handling a substantial amount of data with Flash. Go back to the billabongstore.fla file. On the main timeline, go to the frame labeled account. On the account layer, edit the movie clip named checkout (see Figure 8.17).

The first set of actions is on the first frame of this clip:

```
// Set Item 1 Videos
list_item1_video = "Feeding Frenzy";
list_item1_quantity = _root.product1_quantity;
list_item1_price = 27.00;
// Set Item 2 Videos
list_item2_video = "Sabotaj";
list_item2_quantity = _root.product2_quantity;
list_item2_price = 27.00;
// Set Item 3 Videos
list_item3_video = "Occy: The Occumentary";
list_item3_quantity = _root.product3_quantity;
list_item3_price = 27.00;
// Set Item 4 Videos
list_item4_video = "9 Lives";
list_item4_quantity = _root.product4_quantity;
list_item4_price = 27.00;
stop ();
```

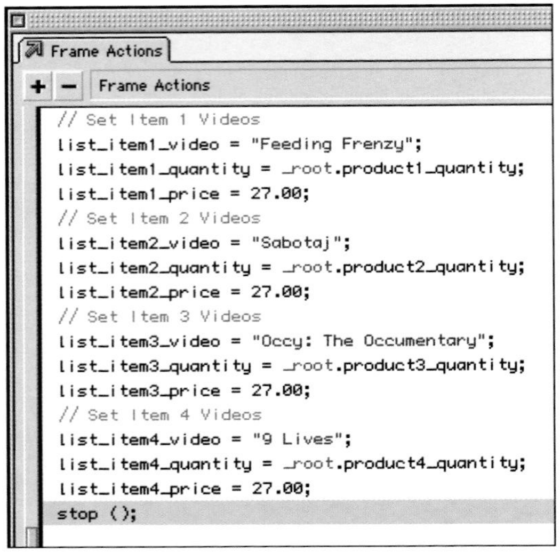

Figure 8.17 The store checkout script.

These actions initialize variables for each of the four videos. The *list_item(1-4)_quantity* variable is exchanged from the root timeline, where it is set as the user adds items to his or her shopping cart.

The "meat" of the checkout application is in clip events attached to the movie clip named checkout_list clip on the list clip layer:

```
onClipEvent (load) {
    list_count = 0;
    for (a=1; a<=_root.item_count; ++a) {
        if (["_root.product"+a+"_quantity"]>0) {
            list_count = list_count+1;
            ["_parent.list_item"+list_count].video = ["_parent.list_item"+a+"_video"];
            if (["_parent.list_item"+list_count+".qset"] != "TRUE") {
                ["_parent.list_item"+list_count].quantity = ["_parent.list_item"+a+"_quantity"];
            }
            ["_parent.list_item"+list_count].product = "product"+a;
            ["_parent.list_item"+list_count].price = ["_parent.list_item"+a+"_price"];
            ["_parent.list_item"+list_count].gotoAndStop("on");
        }
    }
    for (b=list_count+1; b<=_root.item_count; ++b) {
        ["_parent.list_item"+b].gotoAndStop("off");
    }
}
onClipEvent (enterFrame) {
    // Initialize
    list_count = 0;
    _parent.subtotal = 0;
    _parent.total = 0;
    _root.quantity = 0;
    // Figure Subtotal
    for (a=1; a<=_root.item_count; ++a) {
```

continues

```
continued
    if (["_root.product"+a+"_quantity"]>0) {
        list_count = list_count+1;
        _parent.subtotal = _parent.subtotal+(["_parent.list_item"+list_count+".quantity"]*["_parent.list_item"+list_count+".price"]);
    }
}
// Figure Tax
if (_root.billState == "CA" or _root.billState == "California" or _root.billState == "california" or _root.billState == "CALIFORNIA") {
    _parent.tax = _parent.subtotal*.0775;
    taxstring = String(_parent.tax);
    decimalPosition = taxstring.indexOf('.');
    decimalValue = Math.round(100*Number(substring(taxstring+"000", decimalPosition+1, 4)))/100;
    _parent.tax = Number(substring(taxstring, 0, decimalPosition))+decimalValue;
} else {
    _parent.tax = 0;
}
// Figure Shipping
for (b=1; b<=_root.item_count; ++b) {
    _root.quantity = _root.quantity+["_root.product"+b+"_quantity"];
}
_parent.shipping = _root.quantity*5;
// Figure Total
_root.total = _parent.subtotal+_parent.tax+_parent.shipping;
// Output
_parent.subtotal = _parent.subtotal+" U.S.";
_parent.tax = _parent.tax+" U.S.";
_parent.shipping = _parent.shipping+" U.S.";
_parent.total = _root.total+" U.S.";
}
```

The first set of actions in the onClipEvent (load) is for displaying the itemized shopping cart (see Figure 8.18).

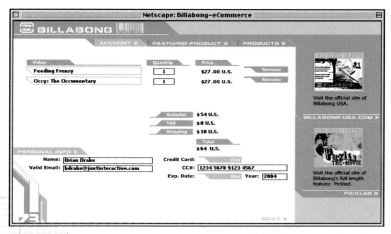

Figure 8.18   The store checkout form.

The shopping cart list is composed of four movie clips on the Checkout List layer. These four movie clips are instances of the movie clip checkout_list item. If you edit this clip, you'll see that it has two frames, an off and an on frame.

If the list position is unoccupied, the clip remains on the off frame. If there's an item for that position, the clip moves to the on frame, where it displays the name, quantity, and price of the item as well as a button to remove the item by setting its quantity to zero (see Figure 8.19).

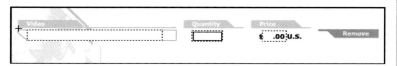

Figure 8.19   The checkout_list item movie clip.

Back to the clip event, we start by resetting the list_count variable to zero. With a for loop, we cycle through the items. With an if statement, we determine whether the current clip's quantity is greater than zero.

```
if (["_root.product"+a+"_quantity"]>0) {
```

If a certain product's quantity is greater than zero, we increase the list_count variable, which is a record of how many items are displayed on the list.

```
list_count++;
```

Next, we set the *video*, *quantity*, *product*, and *price* variables for that clip.

```
["_parent.list_item"+list_count].video =
    ["_parent.list_item"+a+"_video"];
["_parent.list_item"+list_count].product = "product"+a;
["_parent.list_item"+list_count].price =
    ["_parent.list_item"+a+"_price"];
```

The clip is then told to gotoAndStop("on") to display the data we just set. Finally, we loop through the remaining clips and turn them off.

```
for (b=list_count+1; b<=_root.item_count; ++b) {
    ["_parent.list_item"+b].gotoAndStop("off");
}
```

The next set of actions is contained in an onClipEvent (enterFrame). These actions will be continually looped. We start by initializing the list_count, subtotal, total, and quantity variables to zero.

```
list_count = 0;
_parent.subtotal = 0;
_parent.total = 0;
_root.quantity = 0;
```

Next we calculate the subtotal for the shopping cart. For each item that has a quantity greater than zero, we add the total price for that item to the subtotal. The item's total price is the item's unit price multiplied by the quantity.

```
_parent.subtotal = _parent.subtotal+
    (["_parent.list_item"+list_count+".quantity"]
    *["_parent.list_item"+list_count+".price"]);
```

Next, we determine the sales tax. Because the Billabong USA store is located in California, we'll only charge sales tax if the customer is buying from California. We determine this by checking the billstate variable that has been set by the user when filling out his or her billing and shipping information. If the user lives in another state, we set the tax to zero; if the person is a California resident:

```
if (_root.billState == "CA" or _root.billState ==
    "California" or _root.billState == "california" or
    _root.billState == "CALIFORNIA") {
```

We first figure the tax by taking 7.75% (the current California sales tax) of the current subtotal:

```
_parent.tax = _parent.subtotal*.0775;
```

We could just add this to the subtotal; however, we want to limit the tax to a correct cent amount. For example, if the subtotal were $81, the tax would be $6.2775. We want to round this to $6.28. After we've figured out the actual tax, we convert it to a string by setting the variable taxstring to the string of the tax.

```
taxstring = String(_parent.tax);
```

Then, using the indexOf() method, we find the position of the decimal point in the string and set that number to the variable decimalPosition.

```
decimalPosition = taxstring.indexOf('.');
```

We then find the value of the decimal numbers. We start by finding the numbers to the right of the decimal point by extracting a substring from the taxstring using the decimalPosition to start the substring.

```
decimalValue = Math.round
    (100*Number(substring(taxstring+"000",
    decimalPosition+1, 4)))/100;
```

For our previous example of $6.2775, this will result in .277. The reason we add three zeros before getting the substring is to keep the script from erroring out if there aren't three decimal numbers. Now that we have the decimal numbers, we convert the string back to a number and multiply it by 100. For our example, this will yield 27.7. We then use the Math.round() function, which will take 27.7 and round it to 28.0. Then we divide this number by 100, and the result is 28. Finally, we add this number to the whole numbers to the left, which in this case results in the number 6.28.

```
_parent.tax = Number(substring(taxstring, 0,
    decimalPosition))+decimalValue;
```

Now we'll determine the shipping cost. For each item, we tack on $5.

```
parent.shipping = _root.quantity*5;
```

Then we output the total by adding the subtotal, the tax, and the shipping.

```
_root.total = _parent.subtotal+_parent.tax+_parent.shipping;
```

Lastly, we output each variable by taking the numerical value and adding the string U.S.

```
_parent.subtotal = _parent.subtotal+" U.S.";
_parent.tax = _parent.tax+" U.S.";
_parent.shipping = _parent.shipping+" U.S.";
_parent.total = _root.total+" U.S.";
```

8.3 SUMMARY

From navigation to shipping calculation, this chapter covered a full spectrum of ActionScript capabilities. To work effectively with a client as a partner, you need to be able to wear many hats and take advantage of the many opportunities that arise. Client relationships, like the one we have with Billabong, push us to continually explore new things and to grow ourselves. Hopefully, you have pulled some inspiration from the deconstruction we've shared with you in this section. Our work is not only about Flash, it also is about partnering with our clients.

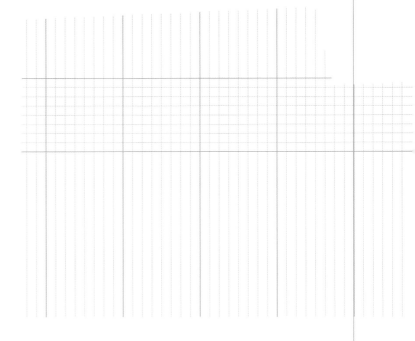

SOUND OFF

...umn by shawn stru...

NEWS

COLD PACIFIC STORM HITS COCHRAN AVENUE, HUNDREDS OF WET DOGS.
POWER CRISIS PREVENTED OPERATION OF HAIR DRYERS.
WET PAVEMENT CAUSED FATAL FALL.

ENTER

GRATUITOUS ANIMATIONS, MEANINGLESS CONTENT.
TYPOGRAPHIC, TESTED BY APES, APPROVED BY MONKEYS.

SOMETIMES WE DO SOME WORK

MAYBE SOME PRESS WILL HELP

PREVIOUS VERSIONS
ONE   TWO   THREE

WORK STUFF

EMAIL

the process is simple, you do th... that... ot this into that, it's done

version info
DISCLOSE   APPROACH   OUTPUT   CONNECT

JIMMY CHEN

Jimmy Chen Interview
by Todd Purgason

Introduction
www.typographic.com

My history with Jimmy goes back to my very beginning in web design. It was very early in 1996, and there was all kinds of trash on the net and not much you could even call design of any sort.

I came across this cool site that was actually well designed (barring the huge limitations of HTML in those days). I sent my first email to a site designer to complement him. I didn't expect to get a response. This was back in the days when the web wasn't the community it's become today. It was still a new experience for everyone. I was surprised to get a response from this guy named Jimmy Chen. Well, years passed and the web attracted more and more creative minds. We began to see a kind of design revolution going on.

In the middle of all that was going on, Josh Ulm launched his first version of www.theremediaproject.com, and there was this

Jimmy Chen guy again with this site called Typographic.com. Being that I was hugely into typography myself, I loved the site.

We finally met in person at the Flash Forward 2001 conference in San Francisco. Since then, we have hooked up to hang a bit. It turns out that this guy, who was a total hero to me, is extremely down to earth and totally humble. Jimmy has done some very powerful and beautiful work on the web and continues to explore and perfect the art of motion graphics on the web. He has developed some very successful and solid techniques for working with After Effects and Flash. These techniques have opened our eyes to the potential of our medium. But more than anything, his work graces the screen like a complete vision of color and design. Jimmy's work doesn't follow the commonly cheap clichés that cover the web. Rather, it radiates its own uniqueness that has become Jimmy's trademark style.

Teaser from the Interview

TP: We're here with Jimmy Chen from Typographic.com. So, who is Jimmy Chen?

JC: Well, I guess first of all, I would just, first and foremost, be a designer, mainly digital, interactive design, but with focus on the web aspect of the design. That's pretty much how I can describe myself since I don't really have an outside life.

TP: You don't have an outside life?

JC: Right.

TP: You're a typical workaholic designer.

JC: Yeah, once in a while I do go out, but you know, sometimes. And when I do go out, I talk about work. This is sort of the universe we live in.

TP: Yeah, you're unbalanced like the rest of us.

JC: Half the people know that they're not balanced.

TP: I think that happens to a lot of people that have a passion.

JC: Yeah, you know, it's the Internet life; it's a good life.

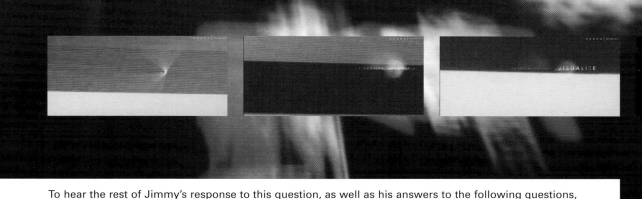

To hear the rest of Jimmy's response to this question, as well as his answers to the following questions, please go to the Inspirations section of the book's site at www.JUXTinteractive.com/deCONSTRUCTION.

QUESTIONS

02. If you were a fish/sea creature, what would you be?

03. What CD or mp3 is in your player right now?

04. What is your definition of design?

05. What was your very first impression of Flash?

06. If you were walking down the street and came across John Gay and Jakob Nielsen engaged in a fistfight, what would you do?

07. What was your inspiration for creating Typographic.com?

08. Of all the studies you have created for Typographic, which is your personal favorite?

09. The imagery you use is beautifully rich. Do you go into Photoshop with a structure in mind, or do you just nurture the images by working in Photoshop until your satisfied?

10. Where do you get your inspiration?

11. Can you tell us a little about your design process?

12. Your work is very raster based. Do you ever use FreeHand or Illustrator?

13. You have done work for Imaginary Forces. What did you do for them, and was it a good working relationship?

14. What is it that happens in a typical day that gives you a feeling of satisfaction when you go home at night?

15. Who is your favorite font designer? Foundry? Face?

16. If you could do one last project before you had to hang up your designer's cap, what would you want that project to be?

deCONSTRUCTION

The Process, Design, and ActionScript of
Juxt Interactive

Section 04
Creative Concept for nDecision

(a)

nDecision was created as an issue for Kaliber 10000 (www.k10k.com). This is a design portal run by a couple of psychos, Mschmidt and Token, out of Sweden. Well, they were in Sweden, but now they're in several different places at once, I think. Anyway, the project was created as an issue for K10K, and for us internally, it was an exploration of Flash and XML.

(b)

The site was inspired by a conversation I had over dinner with Jeffrey Zeldman and Joshua Davis at a Design Conference in Denver, Colorado. We were discussing the different approaches to design, the factors involved, the anxieties some feel in creating, and the confidences that others feel. In summary, we discussed what design is, and the following concept was born as a result. We created a tool that lets users design a motion graphics sequence. It enables them work in a fixed environment, where they can explore different rationales for creating a design. It was also a fun opportunity for us to work with the newer features of Flash and XML. As part of our first project, we were opening an XML socket and talking back and forth from Flash to the server through XML. The whole experience was quite an adventure.

(c)

In design, there are an infinite number of decisions that we will refer to as "n." In essence, the site, nDecision, is based on the following fact: Numerous decisions are made in creating things. The patterns and processes that people use in creating decisions are unique, in and of themselves. There are certain methodologies and processes that are typically followed. These processes are consistent, but every designer relies on their training, world view, confidence level, boss, and whatever else, to make these decisions. This presented us with the opportunity to explore the idea of studying the thinking behind the process of design. Can good design come in with a good designer and a fixed environment, or is it the environment and assets that make a designer good. We don't know ourselves; we were just exploring this concept with nDecision.

(d)

nDecision is an application in which you make a movie on the web: not a new concept, we know. However, we were trying to take it to the next level for our own R&D purposes. For instance, we strung together a group of movie clips in which we can control two tracks, the alpha, the color channels RGB, and the speed and scale of a movie to build your own motion graphic segment. It seems simple enough, but using Flash and XML was quite an adventure.

(e)

In this section, we hope to shed some light on some of the things that we learned in the adventure of working with XML and Flash.

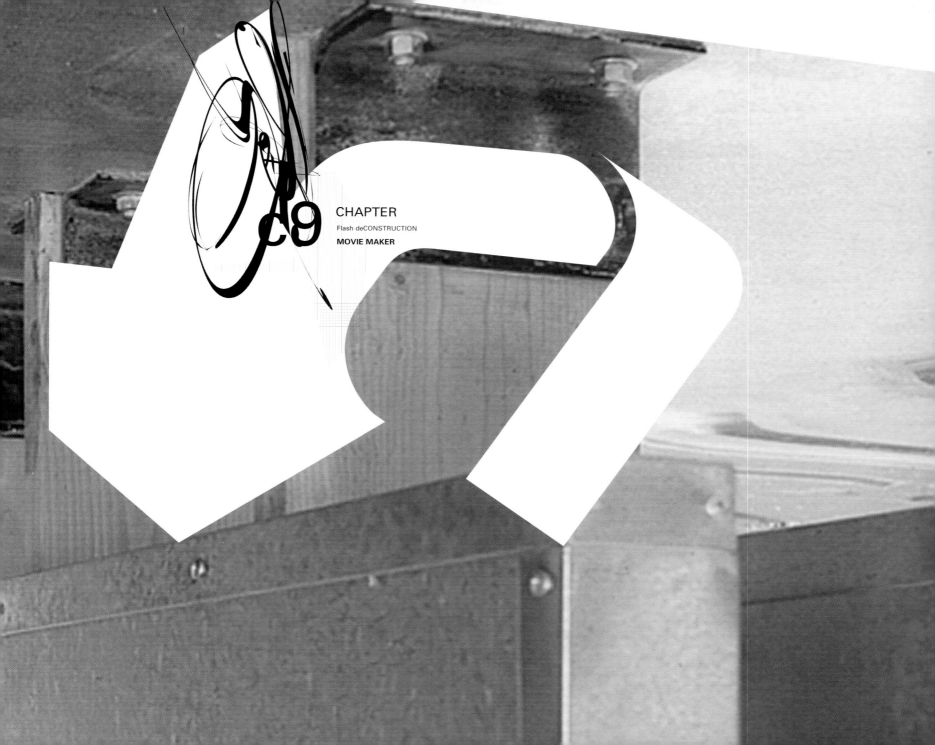

CHAPTER

Flash deCONSTRUCTION

MOVIE MAKER

c9 CHAPTER

Flash deCONSTRUCTION

MOVIE MAKER

As an R&D project, we wanted to develop something that was interesting and that enabled us to explore both the design and the technology behind the design. nDecision was an exploration into what an application could be and how user interaction could impact design. Knowing that its launch would take place on Kaliber 10000 (http://k10k.com, which is a hub for the web design community), we knew that the people playing with this would have curiosities about design and UI that are similar to ours. We wanted to create an experience in which the interaction was part of the design and the design would evolve with that interaction. All the while, we would be carrying out the purpose of the application, which is basically a movie maker. But even in that vein, we wanted to explore areas of this kind of application that we hadn't seen done in Flash. Finally, we wanted to explore Flash's new XML capabilities and see what could be achieved using them.

We hope that this chapter will seed some curiosity of your own as to what a UI can be and how interactivity and application development can be explored.

9.1 DRAG-AND-DROP EVENTS

The nDecision movie maker uses drag-and-drop techniques in several ways. The user can drag video clips from the palette into the 10 drop slots to organize play sequence. One of three sound clips can be dragged onto the headphones to select the sound track. Slider bars that edit the colors, speed, scale, and alpha all use a draggable handle. Finally, the user can drag and drop video clips from the 10 drop slots onto the Trash can to delete them.

9.1.1 NDECISION MOVIE MAKER: MEET THE PLAYERS

Before we get started, it's important to describe the layout of the movie maker. Figure 9.1 calls out the elements that are key to the drag-and-drop functionality, and Table 9.1 describes each element.

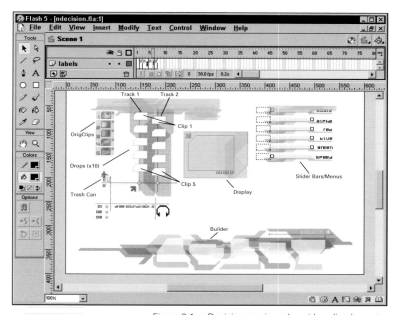

Figure 9.1 nDecision movie maker video clip elements.

Element	Target Path	Description
Orig Clips	K.clip2 thru K.clip6	These five clips represent the palette of original video clips that can be dragged and dropped onto any of the 10 drops.
Drops	K.drop2 thru K.drop11	These 10 movie clips represent the slots where the user can drop Orig Clips. They are organized into two columns of five. Column 1 represents track 1 (the foreground track), while column 2 represents track 2 (the background track). The five rows of drops represent the sequence in which the video clips will be played.
Track 1	K.drop2 thru K.drop6	These five drops contain the video clips played in the foreground.
Track 2	Kdrop7 thru Kdrop11	These five drops contain the video clips played in the background.
Clip 1	Kdrop2 and Kdrop7	These two drops represent the first pair of video clips to be played simultaneously: one in the foreground and one in the background.
Clip 5	Kdrop6 and Kdrop11	These two drops represent the last pair of video clips to be played simultaneously: one in the foreground and one in the background.
Display	Ddisplay	This movie clip plays the currently selected video clip.
Trash can	Kdump	This movie clip is used as a drop target for removing video clips from the Drops.
Menus	1 through 6	These six sliders allow the user to edit the attributes of the selected movie shown in the central display.

Table 9.1   Movie maker elements.

9.1.2 ACTIONS: SET DROP VS. CLEAR DROP

In this application, we enabled two types of drag-and-drop for the video clips. First, the user can drag any of the five Orig Clips and drop the selected clip onto one of the Drop clips. Once a Drop contains a video clip, it can be dragged to the Trash can. Although we do not constrain the draggable area of the movie clip, we do check the _droptarget to restrict what the clip can be dropped onto.

NOTE

Most everything in Flash 5 supports the dot syntax (where movie clips are separated by periods rather than slashes). However, the MovieClip._droptarget property still uses that old slash syntax. So, if you are programming some drag-and-drop functionality that uses the _droptarget property, beware of slashing. For example, a target named K.clip6 would show up in the MovieClip._droptarget property as /K/clip6. This makes a big difference when trying to match target names or extract values from the _droptarget value.

9.1.3 MEET DUMMYDRAG

The palette of Orig Clips needed to remain intact after the user drags them into place within the panel of Drops. We also needed to allow the user to drag any given Orig Clip out into the Drops as many times as desired. It wouldn't do to let the user actually drag the *real* Orig Clip (like K.clip2).

Our solution was to create another movie clip, one that appears out of view of the stage until the user starts a drag operation. Once the user starts trying to drag a clip (whether it's from the Orig Clips to the Drops or from the Drops to the Trash can), this hidden movie clip does a gotoAndStop() to a frame that contains the appropriate image of the video clip being dragged and then locks itself to the mouse. We affectionately call this special little movie clip "K.dummyDrag."

So, when the user is dragging a video clip around, it is not a copy of the actual Orig Clip or Drop; it's dummyDrag. This makes the programming and targeting much simpler. It keeps us from having to use the duplicateMovieClip() and removeMovieClip() actions to make real copies of the clips that get dragged around.

In the ndecision_dragdrop.fla example, notice that the dummyDrag movie clip contains six frames (see Figure 9.2). Frame 1 is an empty clip (outline and arrow but no bitmap). Frames 2 through 6 contain images of the five original video clips. Because the Orig Clip instances are named clip2 through clip6, this makes it easy to figure out which frame dummyDrag should advance to. We simply extract the digit from the end of the Orig Clip instance name and tell dummyDrag to gotoAndStop(digit).

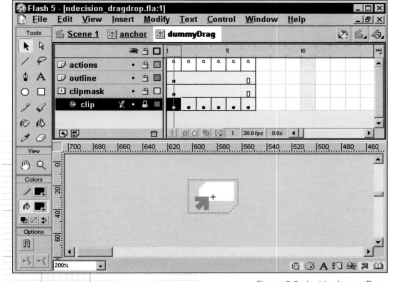

Figure 9.2 Inside dummyDrag.

9.1.4 STARTDRAG()

When the user clicks the mouse on one of the Orig Clips, the on(press) event handler is triggered (see Figure 9.3). First, we use a variable named *fromdrops* to indicate whether the click occurred in one of the Drops. Because the click has occurred in one of the Orig Clips, we set this variable to *false*. This value will be used by the getTarget() and releaseTarget() functions during the drag-and-drop process.

We kept the code in the on(press) event handler to a minimum by calling a function to do all of the dirty work. This was useful because we would have had to put the same logic in each of the five Orig Clips' button hot spots. By defining the getTarget() function in the main timeline, we've also made it easily accessible to any movie clip in the application from the convenient target of _root.

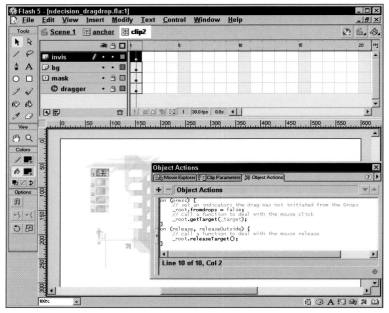

Figure 9.3   Button event handlers for Orig Clip.

```
on (press) {
  // set an indicator: the drag was not initiated from the Drops
  _root.fromdrops = false;
  // call a function to deal with the mouse click
  _root.getTarget(_target);
}
on (release, releaseOutside) {
  // call a function to deal with the mouse release
  _root.releaseTarget();
}
```

The getTarget() function is defined in frame 1 of the main timeline (see Figure 9.4). We've stripped out the comments in the code here to make it easier to read. Let's look at what all it does.

```
function getTarget (targ, origClipNum) {

  clicked = targ;

  K.dummyDrag.saveX = K.dummyDrag._x;
  K.dummyDrag.saveY = K.dummyDrag._y;

  startDrag ("K.dummyDrag", true);

  if (fromdrops) {
    K.dummyDrag.gotoAndStop(origClipNum);
  } else {
    swap = targ.substr(7);
    K.dummyDrag.gotoAndStop(swap);
  }

}
```

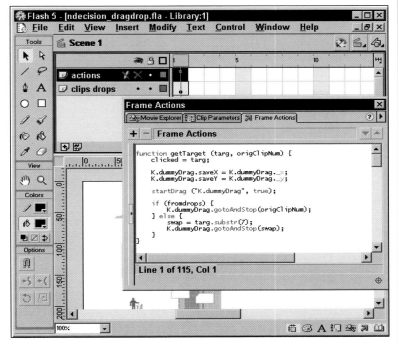

Figure 9.4   The getTarget() function.

First, the two parameters help tell it what to do. The targ parameter contains a string value with the target path of the movie clip that was clicked on. It should contain something like "/K/clip2" or "/K/drop10." The origClipNum parameter is only passed in when the user clicks on a Drop. So, when the user clicks on an Orig Clip, the second parameter is empty (null).

We save some variables related to this drag operation for the benefit of the drop operation later. First, we set the *clicked* global variable to contain the passed-in *targ* value. Then the original X and Y coordinates of the dummyDrag clip are saved into *saveX* and *saveY* variables so that dummyDrag can be restored to its former location when the drag operation is finished.

Next, we check whether the drag operation was initiated from the Drops (using the *fromdrops* Boolean variable). If it was initiated from the Drops, the origClipNum parameter would contain the appropriate frame number for the dummyDrag clip to gotoAndStop(). If it was initiated from the Orig Clips, the frame number is acquired by extracting the numeric value at the end of the targ string (for example, "5" from "/K/clip5"). We save this extracted number into a global variable named *swap* for future use. (Don't ask us about the name.)

Finally, we turn on drag mode by calling the startDrag() action and passing the target name for dummyDrag and a value of *true* for the lock to mouse parameter. This causes the dummyDrag clip to instantly center itself on the mouse pointer. Now, so long as the user holds the mouse button down, the dummyDrag clip is dragged around the stage.

9.1.5 RESPONDING TO A DROP

Let's take a look again at the event handler code for the Orig Clip buttons. Here, we define an on(release, releaseOutside) event handler (see Figure 9.5).

Again, we have set up the event handler to simply call a function that has been defined elsewhere. The releaseTarget() function is defined in frame 1 of the main timeline. As before, we're showing it here, stripped of comments for readability (see Figure 9.6).

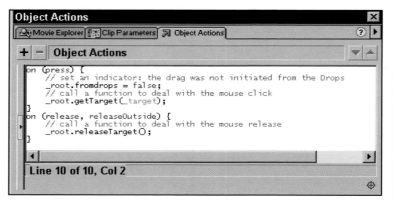

Figure 9.5 Button event handlers for Orig clips.

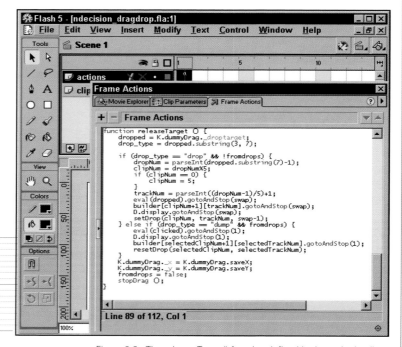

Figure 9.6 The release Target() function defined in the main timeline.

```
function releaseTarget () {
  dropped = K.dummyDrag._droptarget;
  drop_type = dropped.substring(3, 7);
  if (drop_type == "drop" && !fromdrops) {
    dropNum = parseInt(dropped.substring(7)) - 1;
    clipNum = dropNum % 5;
    if (clipNum == 0) {
      clipNum = 5;
    }
    trackNum = ((dropNum-1)/5)+1;
    eval(dropped).gotoAndStop(swap);
    builder[clipNum+1][trackNum].gotoAndStop(swap);
    D.display.gotoAndStop(swap);
    setDrop(clipNum, trackNum, swap-1);
  } else if (drop_type == "dump" && fromdrops) {
    eval(clicked).gotoAndStop(1);
    D.display.gotoAndStop(1);

builder[selectedClipNum+1][selectedTrackNum].gotoAndStop(1);
    resetDrop(selectedClipNum, selectedTrackNum);
  }
  stopDrag ();
  K.dummyDrag._x = K.dummyDrag.saveX;
  K.dummyDrag._y = K.dummyDrag.saveY;
  fromdrops = false;
}
```

The first thing releaseTarget() does is grab the _droptarget property from the K.dummyDrag movie clip. Because dummyDrag is the clip we used when we called the startDrag() action, that is where the _droptarget property is updated by Flash.

Two valid scenarios that could take place here:

1. User drags from one of the Orig Clips and drops onto one of the 10 Drops.
2. User drags from a populated Drop onto the Trash can.

If the user does anything else with drag-and-drop, the application will ignore the user's action and move dummyDrag off the stage again.

If the user drags an Orig Clip onto a Drop, the fromdrops variable will be false, and the drop_type will contain the string drop (extracted from _droptarget like "/K/drop9"). We then extract the dropNum from the drop target string and use it to compute which row (clipNum) and column (trackNum) Drop is in. To make the Drop clip display the appropriate video icon, we tell it to gotoAndStop() the appropriate frame (based on the contents of the swap variable previously saved by the getTarget() function). We do the same thing with the builder clip (at the bottom of the stage) and the D.display clip (in the center of the stage). Finally, we call a function named setDrop() to request that the user's selection be saved to an array for later.

If the user drags from a populated Drop onto the Trash can, then the fromdrops variable will be true and the drop_type will contain the string dump (extracted from the _droptarget of "/K/dump"). In this case, we tell the Drop clip (the one that started the drag operation) to gotoAndStop() frame 1, which contains a blank video clip. We do the same with the D.display and the builder clips. Finally, we call a function named resetDrop() to clear out the values from the array for the selected Drop.

When we've finished updating or trashing a Drop, we set things back to normal by telling Flash to stopDrag(), hiding the dummyDrag clip and clearing the fromdrops variable.

When creating drag-and-drop interactivity, it is important to consider the valid scenarios and how they'll be supported. The _droptarget attribute makes life easy in evaluating scenarios.

9.2 CONTROLLING MOVIE CLIP ATTRIBUTES

Sometimes in Flash it is easiest to use keyframes and tweens to transform imagery on the screen. For motion video pieces, this is usually the best choice because the animation is easy to predetermine and construct in the timeline. However, for interactive projects in which the user is placed in control of animated elements, there is often no way to anticipate all possible combinations of animations that the user may cause. Besides, why would we want to? Using ActionScript to change movie clip properties can provide significant interactive control to the user.

9.2.1 ACTIONSCRIPTING AND MOVIE CLIP PROPERTIES

Every movie clip has a series of attributes that can be easily modified using ActionScript. The main properties that can be directly modified using the dot syntax can be found in Table 9.2.

Property	Value Range	Usage Notes
_alpha	0 to 100	A value of 0 effectively renders the movie clip invisible. A value of 100 makes the movie clip opaque. Everything in between 0 and 100 simply changes the percent of opacity (technically known as the alpha channel).
_height	>= 0	Height (in pixels) of the movie clip. Using this property, you can get or set the height of the movie clip.
_rotation	0 to 360	Degrees of rotation. Default = 0.
_visible	true or false	Sets the visibility of the movie clip. Unlike the alpha property, the visible property really renders the movie clip invisible. When a movie clip's visibility is set to false, any buttons that are inside it will not be active.
_width	>= 0	Width (in pixels) of the movie clip. Using this property, you can get or set the width of the movie clip.
_x	+/- number	Horizontal coordinate of the movie clip center point.
_xscale	>= 0	Controls the horizontal scale of the movie clip as a percentage value. Default = 100.
_y	+/- number	Vertical coordinate of the movie clip center point.
_yscale	>= 0	Controls the vertical scale of the movie clip as a percentage value. Default = 100.

Table 9.2   Editable movie clip parameters.

Here are a few examples of movie clip properties being directly modified using the dot syntax:

- Set the alpha channel to 50% (which makes ball_1 50% opaque):

  ball_1._alpha = 50;

- Divide the current height (in pixels) of ball_1 by 2 (making it half as tall):

  ball_1._height /= 2;

- Multiply the current width (in pixels) of ball_1 by 0.75 (now 75% as wide):

  ball_1._width *= 0.75;

- Add 15 degrees to the current rotation of ball_1:

  ball_1._rotation += 15;

- Make ball_1 visible (not hidden):

  ball_1._visible = true;

- Add 10 pixels to the current x coordinate of ball_1 (shifting to the right):

  ball_1._x += 10;

- Subtract 12 pixels to the current y coordinate of ball_1 (shifting it up):

  ball_1._y -= 12;

- Add 20% to the horizontal (x) scale of ball_1 (making it that much fatter!):

  ball_1._xscale += 20;

- Set the vertical (y) scale of ball_1 to equal that of the horizontal scale:

  ball_1._yscale = ball_1._xscale;

9.2.2 THE COLOR OBJECT

In addition to directly editable movie clip properties, Flash 5 introduced the Color object, which can update movie clip colors.

There are two different ways to change a movie clip's colors using the Color object. One way uses the Color.setRGB() method. The other uses the Color.setTransform() method. These two methods have different effects on movie clip colors.

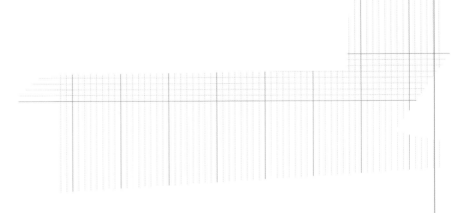

9.2.3 USING COLOR.SETRGB()

The Color.setRGB() method works well if you have an RGB number (like the ones you see in HTML but formatted as follows: 0xRRGGBB). But this only works for movie clips that are solid. An example is if you have a movie clip that only contains a circle and that circle is only one color (no border lines, just fill color). Once Color.setRGB() gets through with the movie clip, all contents become the specified color. This is usually not the intended effect.

If Color.setRGB() is in fact what you're looking for, then the changeColor() function listed here (and in the example colorRGB.fla file) will make it easier to work with (see Figure 9.7).

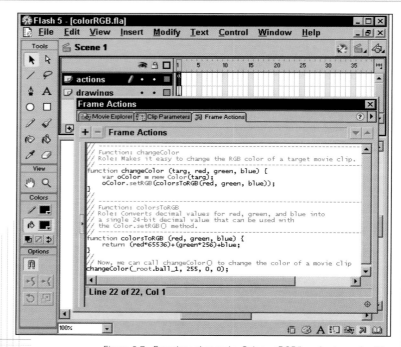

Figure 9.7 Functions that make Color.setRGB() easier to work with.

```
//--------------------------------------------------
// Function: changeColor
// Role: Makes it easy to change the RGB color of a target movie clip.
//--------------------------------------------------
function changeColor (targ, red, green, blue) {
  var oColor = new Color(targ);
  oColor.setRGB( colorsToRGB(red, green, blue) );
}
//
//--------------------------------------------------
// Function: colorsToRGB
// Role: Converts decimal values for red, green, and blue into
//       a single 24-bit decimal value that can be used with
//       the Color.setRGB() method.
//--------------------------------------------------
function colorsToRGB( red, green, blue ) {
  return (red <<16) + (green <<8 + blue;
}
//
// Now, we can call changeColor() to change the color of a movie clip
changeColor( _root.ball_1, 255, 0, 0 );
```

9.2.4 USING COLOR.SETTRANSFORM()

The Color.setTransform() method gives more control over color than the Color.setRGB() method. However, Color.setTransform() takes a bit more study to understand how it works. The best way to learn how it works is to experiment with the transform values. Let's take a look at some sample code. In theColorObject.fla example and Figure 9.8, we demonstrate the use of Color.setTransform() and show the differences between the transformation attributes {ra, ga, ba} and {rb, gb, bb}.

For the purposes of this example, we've written a useful function that makes it easier to deal with the Color object's setTransform() method. Our transformColor() function accepts 7 parameters. The first parameter is the target (movie clip) on which to perform the color transformation. The remaining 6 parameters correspond to the various values used by the Color object's setTransform() method. We'll explain these momentarily.

```
function transformColor (targ, red_percent, green_percent, blue_percent,
                red_offset, green_offset, blue_offset)
{
    var oTrans = new Object();
    // Set percent colors (saturation or alpha) : 0 - 100
    if (red_percent != null) {  oTrans.ra = red_percent;}
    if (green_percent != null) { oTrans.ga = green_percent;}
    if (blue_percent != null) {  oTrans.ba = blue_percent; }
    // Set offset color channels : -255 to 255
    if (red_offset != null) {    oTrans.rb = red_offset; }
    if (green_offset != null) { oTrans.gb = green_offset; }
    if (blue_offset != null) {   oTrans.bb = blue_offset; }
    // Use Color.setTransform() method to change colors
    var oColor = new Color(targ);
    oColor.setTransform(oTrans);
}
```

When using the Color.setTransform() method, the first step is to create a generic object (as in oTrans = new Object();). Next we must add properties to that object to direct the Color object in how to transform the colors of the target, but we must use the six special properties that setTransform() understands. Table 9.3 describes these special color transformation properties. Not all of the six transformation properties must be present. If we only want to alter the red saturation of a target, we would use only the ra property.

In our custom function, we wanted each of the 6 color parameters to be optional. If the caller of the function uses a null value as a placeholder for a parameter, then we want to exclude that parameter from the transformation. This is why we have the if statements that only set the {ra, ga, ba, rb, gb, bb} if their values contain something other than null.

Once we've set up the transformation object, we can create a new Color object, passing the target as a parameter in the constructor (as in *var* oColor = new Color(**targ**);). Finally, to complete the transformation, we use our instance of the Color object to invoke the setTransform() method, passing our transform object (as in oColor.setTransform(oTrans);).

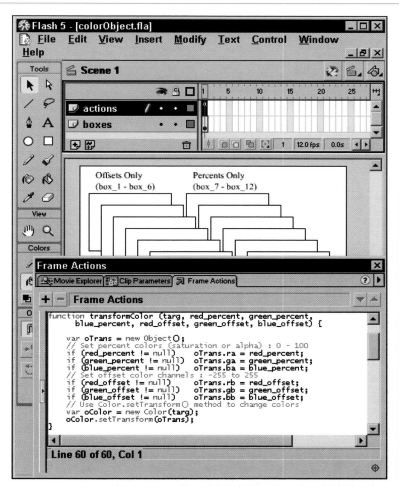

Figure 9.8 Definition of transformColor() function.

Property	Value Range	Usage Notes
ra	0 to 100	Red Alpha (percent saturation of original red)
ga	0 to 100	Green Alpha (percent saturation of original green)
ba	0 to 100	Blue Alpha (percent saturation of original blue)
rb	−255 to 255	Red Offset (offset value to be applied to original red)
gb	−255 to 255	Green Offset (offset value to be applied to original green)
bb	−255 to 255	Blue Offset (offset value to be applied to original blue)

Table 9.3   Color Transform Object properties.

A limitation of the three alpha properties (ra, ga, ba) is that they cannot alter the color black. Because black has an RGB value of 0x000000 (or 0,0,0), increasing the saturation of any of the three base colors will have no effect. The saturation for all three color channels is already at 100%. The closer each color channel is to a value of zero, the less of an effect the alpha transformations will have on the transformed color.

In the following six transformations, the black border will be unaltered, since black is RGB (0,0,0) and applying any percentage value (0 to 100) will remain black (0,0,0). The white fill, however, will be modified by applying the appropriate percent value (0 to 100) to each RGB channel individually.

```
transformColor(box_7, 100, 0, 0); //red fill
transformColor(box_8, 0, 100, 0); //green fill
transformColor(box_9, 0, 0, 100); //blue fill
transformColor(box_10, 50, 0, 0); //dark red fill
transformColor(box_11, 0, 50, 0); //dark green fill
transformColor(box_12, 0, 0, 50); //dark blue fill
```

A strength of the three offset properties (rb, gb, bb) is that they can affect both black and white colors. If we want to transform something that is white (RGB 0xFFFFFF or 255,255,255), we use negative offset properties to directly reduce the saturation of each color channel. For example, a transformation of {rb: -255, gb: -255} on a white target will change that target to blue (RGB 0x0000FF or 0,0,255) by subtracting 255 from the red and green channels, thus reducing red and green to zero and leaving only blue. Conversely, to transform something that is black (RGB 0x000000 or 0,0,0), we use positive offset properties to directly increase the saturation of each color channel. For example, a transformation of {rb: 255} on a black target will change that target to red (RGB 0xFF0000 or 255,0,0) by adding 255 to the blue channel while leaving red and green at zero.

In the following three transformations, we affect the white fill color, since white is RGB (255, 255, 255) and subtracting values from white will cause it to change color. The black border will be unaltered, since black is RGB (0,0,0), and subtracting values from black cannot reduce its value below zero. Notice, that we are using null values for the three percentage values, and only utilizing the offset values.

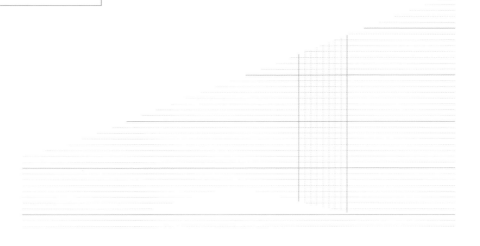

```
transformColor(box_1, null,null,null, 0, -255, -255); //red fill
transformColor(box_2, null,null,null, -255, 0, -255); //green fill
transformColor(box_3, null,null,null, -255, -255, 0); //blue fill
```

The next three transformations once again focus only on the offset values. For these, the black border will be modified, since black is RGB (0,0,0), and adding positive values to black changes its color. The white fill color will be unaltered, since white is RGB (255,255,255), and adding positive values cannot make it go any higher.

```
transformColor(box_4, null,null,null, 255, 0, 0); //red border
transformColor(box_5, null,null,null, 0, 255, 0); //green border
transformColor(box_6, null,null,null, 0, 0, 255); //blue border
```

Figure 9.9 shows the results of our labor with our transformColor() function and the Color.setTransform() method.

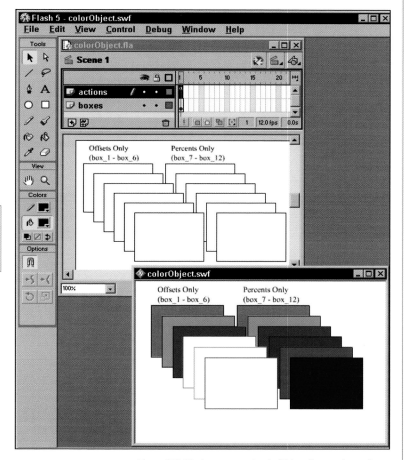

Figure 9.9 Final outcome of colorObject.fla transformations.

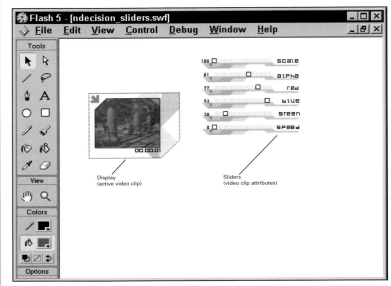

Figure 9.10 Updating video clip attributes with ndecision_sliders.fla.

9.3 COLOR, ALPHA, AND SCALE CONTROL

In the nDecision movie maker, we used _alpha, _xscale, and _yscale movie clip properties as well as the Color.setTransform() method to interactively alter alpha, scale, and color for each video clip.

To the right of the stage, we built a set of slider bars that enable the user to alter the settings of the video clip in the center display (see Figure 9.10). These sliders control six attributes of the video clip: scale, alpha, red, blue, green, and speed. The first two (scale and alpha) were easily manipulated using the movie clip _xscale, _yscale, and _alpha properties. The red, blue, and green attributes were used to control percent of color saturation using the {ra, ba, ga} color transformation properties and the Color.setTransform() method.

The following code shows how we use the values from the sliders to update the D.display and builder.* targets. The attributes() function is called by an onClipEvent(enterFrame) event handler so that the display is constantly updated, giving the sliders a real-time effect.

```
function attributes () {
    speed = _root["6"].speed;
    displayAttributes(D.display);
}
function displayAttributes (targ) {
    // Set Alpha using slider #2 value
    targ._alpha = _root["2"].alpha;
    // Set Scale using slider #1 value
    targ._xscale = targ._yscale = _root["1"].scale;
    // Transform color using slider #3, 4, & 5 values
    var oColor = new Color(targ);
    oColor.setTransform( {ra: _root["3"].red, ba: _root["4"].blue,
        ga: _root["5"].green} );
}
```

The first thing the attributes() function does is set the global speed variable to contain whatever value is presently shown in the speed slider bar (slider #6). Since the speed slider bar has an instance name of 6, we cannot directly refer to it as _root.6—Flash would complain about this syntax. So, we've used the alternate syntax for referring to movie clip instances (the associative array syntax): _root["6"]. Conveniently, our speed slider bar has created a variable named speed within its scope.

Next, the attributes() function calls the displayAttributes() function, passing it a target of D.display (see Figure 9.11). We broke this function out separately from the attributes() function so that we can update the display attributes of several targets easily. In the fully built version of the movie maker, the attributes() function calls the displayAttributes() function twice to update both the D.display and the appropriate builder movie clip (the clips along the bottom of the movie maker).

The displayAttributes() function uses the same syntax to retrieve the current values of the alpha, scale, red, green, and blue slider bars as we used for the speed value. The targ._alpha, targ._xscale, and targ._yscale attributes are all simple enough to update. We just use the values found in the slider bars, and set these attributes of the target referenced by the targ variable.

In the last two lines of code within the displayAttributes() function, we use the technique described earlier in this chapter to transform the red, green, and blue color channels. The effect we were looking for worked best with the {ra, ga, ba} attributes in the Color.setTransform() method. By setting a value of 0 to 100 for each color channel with the slider bars, we can directly apply these numbers as saturation levels for each of the three base colors.

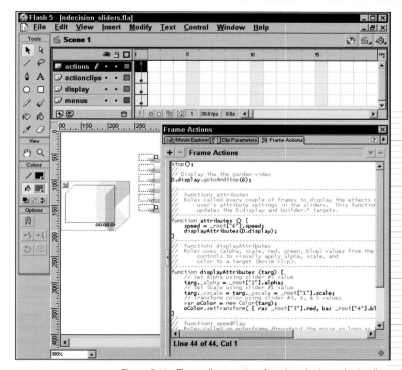

Figure 9.11   The attribute update functions in the main timeline.

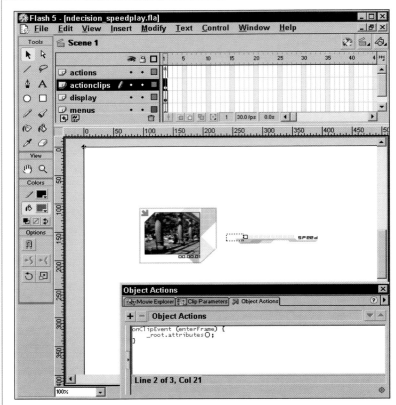

Figure 9.12 ClipEvent handler in the ndecision_speedplay.fla.

9.4 MOVIE MAKER VIDEO CLIP SPEED CONTROL

Wouldn't it be nice if Flash let you control frame rate for each movie clip or level? Well, unfortunately, it doesn't. So, on the movie maker project, we had to come up with a way to vary the rate of play for a movie clip. Here's how we did it.

9.4.1 ADVANCING FRAMES ACCORDING TO DESIRED SPEED

We set up a slider (_root["6"]) to give the user control over a variable named speed. This variable contains a value in the range of 0 to 3. A speed of 0 will cause the video clip to play at the normal frame rate. Conversely, a speed of 3 will cause the video clip to skip over three frames for every one frame it plays, causing the clip to play at four times its normal frame rate. If the clip contains 40 frames and the speed is 3, only 10 frames will play (1, 5, 9…).

If it weren't for the wonderful onClipEvent feature introduced in Flash 5, we would have had to add ActionScript to every frame within each video clip to take care of skipping the proper number of frames. Fortunately, we were able to add an onClipEvent(enterFrame) event handler to a movie clip so that whenever the playhead advances to a new frame, we can call a function to do the dirty work (see Figure 9.12).

On the main timeline, in the upper-left corner of the stage, we have an empty movie clip. This movie clip serves the sole purpose of providing us with a place to put onClipEvent() code. The only thing we need it to do (for the purposes of this example) is to call the speedplay() function that we defined in the _root (main timeline).

```
onClipEvent (enterFrame) {
  _root.speedPlay();
}
```

The speedPlay() function is quite simple. It tells the display video clip to gotoAndPlay() using the video clip's _currentframe attribute plus the speed value from slider 6 (see Figure 9.13).

```
function speedPlay () {
    var curframe = D.display.vid._currentframe;
    var speed = _root["6"].speed;
    D.display.vid.gotoAndPlay( curframe + speed);
}
```

Because speedPlay() was called by onClipEvent(enterFrame), we can assume that the playhead has already advanced by one frame. So, if we add a speed of 0 to this already advanced _currentframe, we are essentially letting the movie play one frame at a time. However, if we add a speed of 3 to the already advanced _currentframe, we are skipping over 3 frames. That's it.

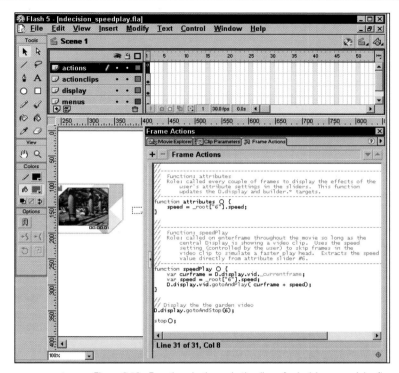

Figure 9.13 Functions in the main timeline of ndecision_speedplay.fla.

9.5   SLIDER CONTROLS

In all likelihood, you've used slider controls in one user interface or another. Perhaps you've used one in a design tool or more commonly in a speaker volume control or graphic equalizer. Sliders let the user drag some sort of handle back and forth across a track with the purpose of easily changing a value within a range.

Sliders can be horizontal or vertical. Actually, they can be curved or odd shaped, too, but only if you're crazy about writing ActionScript and frightening your users. Sliders usually have three visual elements: a track, a handle, and a value display.

9.5.1   CHOOSING SLIDERS

The nDecision movie maker was the perfect application for sliders. We needed to give the user an easy way of editing six attributes for each of 10 video clips. That's a possible 60 attributes to edit.

If we were to give the user the capability to directly edit attribute values in simple text fields, we would then have to build in some sort of data validation to make sure each attribute value stays within the expected range. We would also have to use something to indicate when the attribute should be applied. Using an Apply button adds a step, and requiring that the user press the Enter key when finished with a text field is a bit clumsy. Sliders enforce valid numerical data because they directly represent value ranges. They can also be applied in real-time while the user is still in the middle of dragging the handle.

We chose to set up the user interface so that the user can work with one video clip at a time and edit the active clip's six attributes using one slider for each attribute. See Figure 9.10 for a picture of the user interface.

9.5.2   BUILDING A SLIDER

Let's focus on just one slider: slider 2, the alpha control. First we set up a movie clip for a slider, which will contain all the components of the slider. In the movie maker (and the ndecisionsliders.fla example), we set up the alpha slider with the structure described in Table 9.4 and shown in Figure 9.14.

Path or item	Symbol	Description
_root.2	menu2	A container movie clip for all the components of the slider control that edits alpha.
_root.2: text "alpha"		A dynamic text field that the field displays current numeric value from 0 to 100.
_root.2.alpha	slider	A generic slider movie clip used by all six slider controls.
_root.2.alpha .sliderbutton	sliderbutton_clip	A generic movie clip containing the button or handle.
_root.2.alpha .slidertrack	slidertrack_clip	A generic movie clip containing the visual track along which the slider handle glides.

Table 9.4   Movie clip structure for the alpha slider.

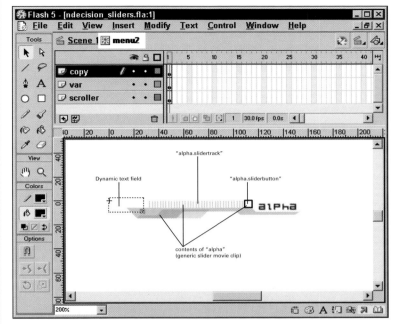

Figure 9.14 Contents of the menu2 movie clip (alpha slider).

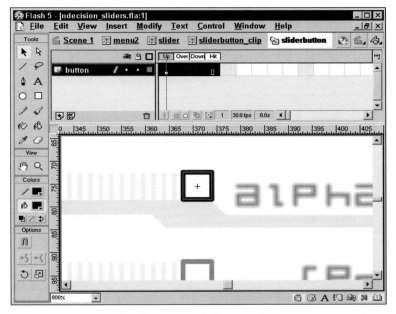

Figure 9.15 Using a button to provide cursor change on rollover.

9.5.3 DRAG-AND-DROP FOR THE SLIDER BUTTON

To enable drag-and-drop functionality for the handle, we added an invisible button inside the movie clip symbol sliderbutton_clip (see Figure 9.15). Although we could have used the movie clip's onClipEvent(mouseDown) event handler to do this, we would miss out on a handy little mouse feature that comes with buttons. When the mouse rolls over a button in Flash, the mouse pointer changes to a hand, giving the user a clue that he can click here. We could simulate this type of behavior ourselves with movie clips, but that would just add unneeded complexity in this case.

When we initiate the startDrag(), we want to lock the draggable area to the slider track. In the on(press) event handler for

_root.2.alpha.sliderbutton listed in the following code, we calculate the left and right coordinates for the draggable area using the width of the _parent.slidertrack clip (see Figure 9.16).

```
on (press) {
    var left = _parent.slidertrack._x -
        Math.floor(_parent.slidertrack._width/2);
    var right = left + _parent.slidertrack._width;
    startDrag (this, true, left, this._y, right, this._y);
}
on (release) {
    stopDrag();
}
```

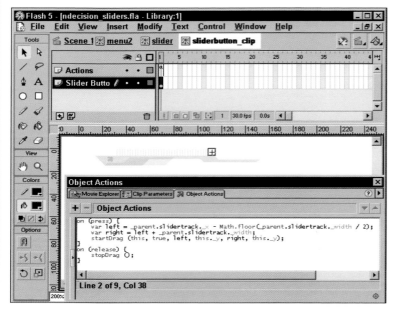

Figure 9.16   Slider button event handlers.

While the user is busy dragging the handle around, the onClipEvent(enterFrame) for _root.2.alpha takes care of the rest (see the following code). It calculates the slider value according to the X coordinate of the slider button relative to the slider track and based on a minimum value and a maximum value. Once we've calculated the slider value, we copy that value to the root (making it easy to access by the rest of the project) and to the dynamic text field that displays the current slider value.

```
onClipEvent(enterFrame) {
  // calculate slider value, and update the display
  var sliderVal = Math.floor((sliderbutton._x+halfwidth)/step)+minval;
  // update root variable
  _root[ _name ] = sliderVal;
  // update slider display text field
  _parent[ _name ] = sliderVal;
}
//
onClipEvent(load) {
```

continues

continued

```
// change minval and maxval to set slider's value range

minval = 0;

maxval = 100;

// set up some constants to be used when calculating slider values

trackrange = this.slidertrack._width;

halfwidth = Math.floor(trackrange / 2);

step = trackrange/(maxval-minval);

}
```

9.6 SUMMARY

In this chapter, we introduced the nDecision movie maker project. We deconstructed the most essential elements of the user interface. In the process, we explored how to set up drag-and-drop, dynamically change movie clip properties, use the Color object, simulate dynamic movie clip frame rates, and even build slider controls.

Once the concepts underlying these techniques are well understood, the possibilities become almost endless. For example, there's no reason a slider couldn't be adapted to move within a square or a circle to select from a color wheel. The movie clip speed technique could be adapted to not only speed up the frame rate but to slow it down as well.

Take these techniques, break them apart, question their inner workings, and apply their concepts to anything you will. The more you can use ActionScript, the more creative and powerful your projects can become.

In the next chapter, we will dig into the back end of this application, showing how the client and server interaction is constructed.

HARD-CODING VS. CALCULATING

We could have hard-coded the constraint coordinates, but hard-coding coordinates is bad form. Not only would it make it harder to change the design of the sliders in the future, it would make the code harder to understand.

Programmers refer to these undocumented hard-coded numbers as "magic cookies." They're magic because innocent bystanders who read the code later on won't know anything about them or how they work. So it is assumed that they contain magical properties, the likes of which the bystander will never come to understand.

Even though calculations sometimes look more complex than hard-coded numbers, at least a calculation gives a clue as to how a numerical value was derived. But the best medicine for convoluted code is the use of comments!

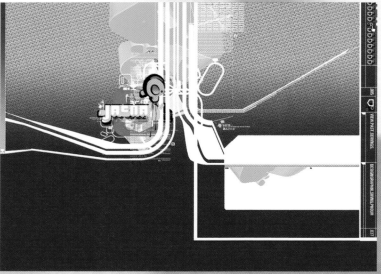

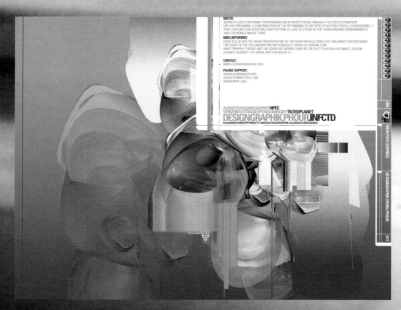

ARCHINE C1. TWOTHSND01

INFCTD
SEVEN STUDIES EXPLORING THE IMAGINATION OF WHAT'S SEEN THROUGH THE EYES OF EVERYDAY
LIFE (MY DREAMING). A CONTINUATION OF THE RETHINKING OF ARTISTIC STUDY FOR CODEX 1 / CODEX SERIES 3
THAT EXPLORES AN ADDITION, SUBTRACTION, 2D, AND 3D STUDY OF THE SURROUNDING ENVIRONMENTS
AND THE BEINGS INSIDE THEM.

MISC ARTWORKS
EIGHT IS A 3D SKETCH BOOK PRESENTATION OF THE EARLY MODELS DONE FOR ARCHINECT BEFORE ENDING
THE START OF THE COLLABORATION WITH BRADLEY GROSH OF GMUNK.COM.
NINE THROUGH TWELVE ARE THE COVER ARTWORKS DONE IN THE PAST YEAR FOR ARCHINECT, DESIGN
IS KINKY AGAINST THE GRAIN, AND HOLDER OF 7S.

CONTACT:
MIKE@DESIGNGRAPHIK.COM

PLEASE SUPPORT:
WWW.ASSEMBLER.ORG
WWW.TSFBASTARD.COM
WWW.NPFC.ORG

AUDIO TRANSMISSION BY NPFC
SERVER HOSTING & SPONSORING BY TILTED PLANET
DESIGNGRAPHIKPHOUR.INFCTD
ALL 2003 & 2004 COPYRIGHT.COM DESIGNGRAPHIK. ALL RIGHTS RESERVED

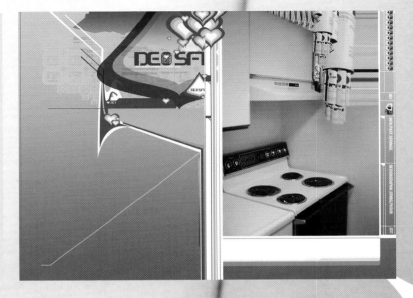

MIKE YOUNG

Mike Young Interview
by Todd Purgason

Introduction
www.designgraphik.com

I distinctly remember the "wow" that silently slipped from my lips during that late-night, after-work, warm-down surf. It was in response to seeing http://designgraphik.com. This site was an object of beauty to behold. This was a rare site on the web at the time. I emailed Mike, giving him props, and we later hooked up at Flash Forward 2000 New York. Mike patiently put up with all my questions about Vir2l, the mysterious company he was working for at that time. We talked about design, about Flash, and we talked about work. It was a good conversation, and I picked up on the fact that Mike is just beginning to realize his potential in design. If there is one amazing guy to watch out for, it is Mike Young.

In addition to Designgraphik and his work for vir2l, Mike has been involved with another great project called www.submethod.com. In fact, at Flash Forward, we sat next to each other during the Film Fest in which www.submethod.com was up against one of our projects, www.shorn.com, for best sound. I was honored to lose to a great designer like Mike. He is currently freelancing and putting out more of his innovative visuals for his own clients.

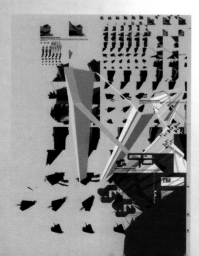

Teaser from the Interview

TP: Here we are with the very talented Mike Young from Designgraphik.com, formerly of Virtual, also Submethod, and lots of other stuff. So Mike, who is Mike Young?

MY: I don't know. I guess, right now, I'm still kind of, trying to find out since I left Vir2l, so I think now it's been about three months, maybe four, since I worked there and I've just been doing my own thing, and I'm just trying to find out where I kind of fit into place right now on my own. And, right now, I'm just lookin' more to kind of do a little bit of everything. The past few months I've been doing a lot of smaller work, a lot of sites that probably consist of about five pages or something and now I'm looking to, like, art direct a lot of bigger projects, maybe something like a really huge site, you know?

TP: Uh-huh.

MY: I think that would be like a midlevel, I guess, kind of like a site design. So I guess I'm kind of anywhere right now. You ask who I am. I'm little bit less on the personal work right now because I'm trying to figure out how to make my client work my personal work also, like trying to combine the two so that my client work becomes fun. I think that was the main reason I went solo, so I could have fun, you know, and do it my way but with the client knowing who I am and them wanting my way, and then me pleasing them.

TP: Are you getting a lot of clients contacting you, asking for that stuff?

MY: Yeah, pretty much. I mean, right now a lot of it is smaller work because it's hard to get in with the bigger names unless you are a design house or a large agency. So I'm just trying to work my way up, I guess, trying to get my foot in the door and that stuff but yeah, it's been a lot of small work but I'm eating and I'm living fine. That's what matters.

TP: Planet of the Drums… That thing was way, way solid.

MY: That was the one for Diesel Boy, I'm getting in with him right now on a new record label they have going and everything. So luckily, I'll be getting in with that label and doing a lot of artwork for them and I guess kind of being the main visual artist for them.

TP: That's cool.

MY: That should be a lot of fun.

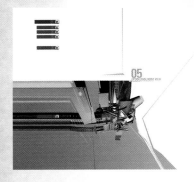

To hear the rest of Mike's response to this question, as well as his answers to the following questions, please go to the Inspirations section of the book's site at www.JUXTinteractive.com/deCONSTRUCTION.

QUESTIONS

02. If you were a fish/sea creature, what would you be?

03. What CD or mp3 is in your player right now?

04. What is your definition of design?

05. What was your very first impression of Flash?

06. Your personal site, Designgraphik, has always been one of my personal favorite spots on the web. It is like a surrealistic visual garden. Is there conceptual thought behind your studies, or are they just visual explorations?

07. The recent design of Designgraphik has a lot of 3D. Is that your 3D? What application was used to create it?

08. Your color work is some of the freshest on the web. Where do you draw the colors out of the photos you're using, or do you create a palette and select or colorize the images?

09. What is Submethod all about?

10. You have been working for Vir2l. We don't see much client work from them. Is the stuff you guys are working on as dynamic as your personal work?

11. Can you tell us a little about your design process?

12. Do you always try to break new ground exploring wholly new directions with each issue of Designgraphik?

13. Do you do any After Effects work as well as Flash?

14. What is it that happens in a typical day that gives you a feeling of satisfaction when you go home at night?

15. Where do you see yourself in two years?

16. If you could do one last project before you had to hang up your designer's cap, what would you want that project to be?

c10 CHAPTER

Flash deCONSTRUCTION
MOVIE MAKER XML

In Chapter 9, "Movie Maker," we deconstructed a number of user-interface elements from the nDecision movie maker project. The movie maker enables the user to drag and drop motion video clips into a sequence; edit the color, speed, scale, and alpha properties of each clip; add sound; and play the sequence. As an added dimension to the project, we developed it to be able to save and load these settings to the web server and email the movie sequence to friends and enemies. We accomplished this using XML within Flash.

In this chapter, we'll look at how the nDecision movie maker used XML to load and save structured information on the web server.

10.1   WHAT IS XML?

The first step to using XML is to understand what it is. To the uninitiated, XML sounds complicated and mysterious. Well, let's demystify it.

10.1.1   XML FACTOIDS

XML stands for eXtensible Markup Language. XML is a derivative of the Standard Generalized Markup Language (SGML). It offers a far less complicated format than SGML and, as such, has been well received by programmers and toolmakers. XML is now widely used, while SGML's complexity puts it out of reach for most. XML is a structured data format that is much more flexible than comma-delimited (CSV) and much cleaner than URL-encoded name=value pairs.

10.1.2   XML BASICS

Sound scary? Well, it's not. It is really quite simple. Here are the basics:

1. XML looks very similar to HTML.
2. XML is a tag-based document format.
3. Tags use the less-than (<) and greater-than (>) symbols.
4. Tags contain the tag name and an optional list of attributes.
5. Unlike HTML, XML tag names and attribute names are case sensitive.
6. When authoring an XML document, you get to make up your own tags.
7. Attribute values must be surrounded by double quotes (for example, firstName="Joe").
8. Any self-closing tag must end with a forward slash (/), as in ("<BR/>").
9. Any closing tag must begin with a forward slash (/), as in ("</BODY>").
10. All tags must be closed (self-closing or with a separate closing tag).
11. Tags must be properly nested:

    Wrong: bold <i>italics</i>

    Right: bold <i>italics</i>

Did we mention that you get to define the tags yourself?! Yep, you just make up your own tags and stuff data into them. That's about all there is to creating XML files (well, mostly anyway). So now that you're an expert, you can add XML to your resume, too.

Most of the rules governing XML are the same as HTML, but XML has just a few extra rules. In fact, the relatively new standard called XHTML is little more than HTML with the additional rules imposed by XML (case sensitivity, self-closing tags, quoted attributes) and a few required tags (like <head>, <title>, and <body>). As an example, because Rule 8 requires that standalone tags must self-close, HTML tags like <hr> and <br> would need to be <hr/> and <br/> to be XHTML compliant. Similarly, the HTML paragraph tag <p> would need to follow Rule 8 or 9 for proper closure (<p>blah blah blah</p> or <p/> for a blank paragraph). Because XHTML follows XML rules, Flash can load XHTML files just as it does any other XML file. Then it can work with the contents of each individual tag as desired. This might be an interesting way to share content between HTML web sites and Flash web sites.

See Code 10.1 for an example of a small XML file.

```
<?xml version="1.0"?>
<Customer firstName="Sally" lastName="Booth" ID="424924">
  <ShoppingCart>
      <CartItem sku="AV-294" price="45.95" ID="9049"/>
      <CartItem sku="AV-313" price="12.95" ID="9134"/>
      <CartItem sku="SC-106" price="19.95" ID="10249"/>
  </ShoppingCart>
</Customer>
```

Code 10.1   A small XML file (customer.xml).

10.2   WHY XML?

Flash designers and programmers have gotten along pretty well so far without XML. This begs the question, "So why would I want to use XML in my Flash projects?" Although XML might not be the right solution for every dynamic Flash project, it definitely has its advantages. Let's look at some of them.

10.2.1   XML IS GOOD AT HIERARCHY

XML lends itself nicely to data that is hierarchical. In contrast, the loadVariables() action in Flash does not. Let's say we want to create an XML document that describes a multilevel cascading navigation menu. There is no limit to the number of levels in submenus. It would be quite complicated and messy to attempt this with a loadVariables() technique.

One common example of hierarchical data is a cascading menu. If a project we were creating in Flash required a cascading menu that could be externally defined by dynamic data, we would need to find a way to load the data into Flash. The sample XML document in Code 10.2 shows a hypothetical structure for a cascading menu system that could be developed in Flash. It has multiple <Menu> tags (called nodes in XML-speak), which can be embedded within other <Menu> tags. The very order in which these tags are nested or embedded within each other determines the structure and hierarchy of the Flash cascading menu.

Although we would love to show a full example of an XML-based cascading menu in Flash with ActionScript here, it is beyond the scope of this chapter. Several source code examples of XML-based Flash menus are posted on several of the Flash resource sites like www.ultrashock.com and www.flashkit.com.

```xml
<?xml version="1.0"?>
<Menu type="submenu">
  <Menu caption="Company" type="submenu">
    <Menu caption="Mission" type="eval" action="showCoMission()"/>
    <Menu caption="History" type="eval" action="showCoHistory()"/>
    <Menu caption="Management" type="eval" action="showCoMgmt()"/>
    <Menu caption="News" type="submenu">
      <Menu caption="Articles" type="submenu">
        <Menu caption="Product of the Year 2001"
            type="url" action="showNews.asp?newsid=294"/>
        <Menu caption="Best in Show, Internet World 2001"
            type="url" action="showNews.asp?newsid=295"/>
        <Menu caption="InfoWeek interview with Hank Jimmyhack"
            type="url" action="showNews.asp?newsid=299"/>
      </Menu>
      <Menu caption="Events" type="submenu">
        <Menu caption="Visit us at Internet World Spring 2001"
            type="url" action="showNews.asp?newsid=293"/>
        <Menu caption="Our CEO speaks on code generation"
            type="url" action="showNews.asp?newsid=297"/>
      </Menu>
      <Menu caption="Press Releases" type="submenu">
        <Menu caption="CodeGen 2.0 release"
            type="url" action="showNews.asp?newsid=290"/>
        <Menu caption="AppGen 1.5 release"
            type="url" action="showNews.asp?newsid=291"/>
      </Menu>
    </Menu>
  </Menu>
```

continues

```
continued
  </Menu>
  <Menu caption="Products" type="submenu">
    <Menu caption="Application Servers" type="submenu">
      <Menu caption="BizServe"
          type="eval" action="showProd('BizServe')"/>
      <Menu caption="EduServe"
          type="eval" action="showProd('EduServe')"/>
    </Menu>
    <Menu caption="Code Generators" type="submenu">
      <Menu caption="AppGen"
          type="eval" action="showProd('AppGen')"/>
      <Menu caption="CodeGen"
          type="eval" action="showProd('CodeGen')"/>
    </Menu>
  </Menu>
</Menu>
```

Code 10.2   A sample XML document to define cascading menus.

10.2.2 COMPATIBILITY

More and more web-based tools and systems are being developed to output data in XML format. Currently, many web content feeds (like news, stocks, and even product catalogs) are being served in XML format. This means that Flash users will be able to access far more in terms of pre-existing documents with XML.

The URL-encoded format used by Flash's loadVariables() action is really only used by Flash, so it must be custom built for Flash applications. In contrast, XML is a standard format that any programming language (and many tools) can read and write. As a result, XML documents are proliferating throughout the world of information systems.

10.2.3 A CLEANER WAY TO GET DATA

The Flash loadVariables() action dumps all of the data it receives from the server into some timeline. This is fine for just a handful of variables, but the Flash XML object allows the Flash developer to retrieve data from a URL into a single structured data object.

This single, self-contained XML variable keeps the timeline free of clutter. Compare the structured XML object results in Figure 10.1 to the variables loaded by loadVariables() in Figure 10.2.

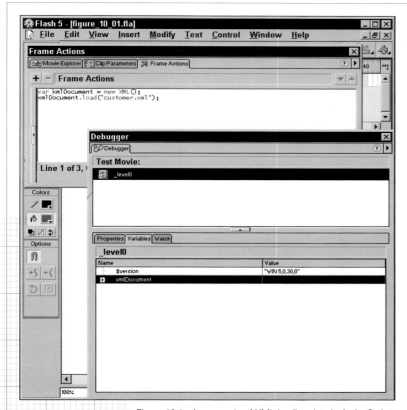

Figure 10.1   An example of XML loading data in ActionScript.

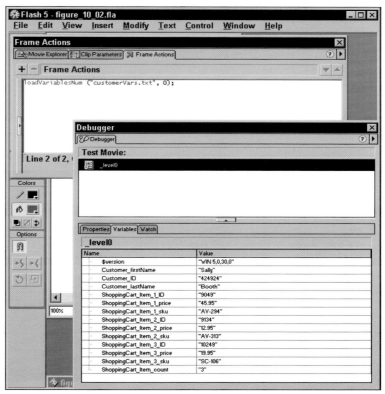

Figure 10.2   The Flash loadVariables() command in this script results in a cluttered timeline.

The raw data from the web server used in Figure 10.2 can be seen in Code 10.3.

Customer_firstName=Sally&Customer_lastName=Booth&Customer_ID=424924&ShoppingCart_Item_count=3&ShoppingCart_Item_
  1_sku=AV%2D294&ShoppingCart_Item_1_price=45%2E95&ShoppingCart_Item_1_ID=9049&ShoppingCart_Item_2_sku=AV%2D313&
  ShoppingCart_Item_2_price=12%2E95&ShoppingCart_Item_2_ID=9134&ShoppingCart_Item_3_sku=SC%2D106&ShoppingCart_
  Item_3_price=19%2E95&ShoppingCart_Item_3_ID=10249

Code 10.3 The raw data from the web server that feeds Figure 10.2.

Which file format would you prefer to work with? The XML found in Code 10.1 or the URL-encoded data found in Code 10.3? The answer is obvious. On both the server side and in Flash, XML is a cleaner and friendlier alternative to URL-encoded data used by the Flash loadVariables() action.

10.2.4 XML AND THE NDECISION MOVIE MAKER

When Juxt designs web applications, one of the key questions is, "How can the project leverage technology for a higher impact on user experience?" The nDecision movie maker was faced with this question, too. It's cool to develop a site that lets people mix movie clips and sounds with the ease of drag-and-drop. It's even cooler to allow users to save their movie creations to a database and send them to their friends.

To save to a database, a project needed some way of sending the user's selections to a script on the web server. Then the user could send email messages to friends, and nDecision would include in the email a link to the "viewer". Because the project would not be using Generator, the Flash movie needed to retrieve the original user's settings to decide what to display. So a database record ID would be passed to the viewer from the email link (see Figure 10.3).

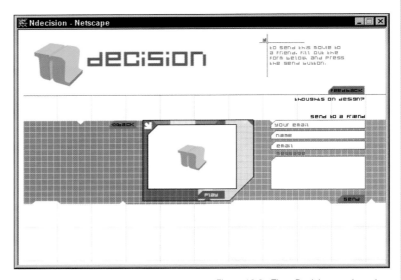

Figure 10.3 The nDecision movie maker.

Once the flow of information was worked out between the movie builder, the email sender, and the viewer components, it was time to decide between using XML and loadVariables. The choice was simple: XML won out and here's why.

Because the movie maker enables the user to assign movie clips to 10 slots, and each slot can be customized with 6 settings (scale, alpha, red, green, blue, speed), there are a lot of variables to keep track of. Inside the Flash movie, the most efficient way to keep the settings in variables would be in a multidimensional array:

```
aClips[ clipNum ][ trackNum ][ attribute ];
```

But how could we send a multidimensional array to a script on the web server for saving to the database? And how could we get the array back from the database? The Flash loadVariables() and getURL() actions have the capability to GET or POST "all" of the variables in the specified timeline (scope) to a server script. But it can't send a multidimensional array very well. Besides, those methods would send all the other variables in the timeline to the script—how messy that would be!

Because XML is so good at structuring data into a hierarchy (which is exactly what a multidimensional array is), XML was a perfect choice for the nDecision movie maker!

10.3 HOW DOES FLASH INTERACT WITH XML?

XML is simply a data format (or more specifically, a markup language). In and of itself, XML doesn't actually *do* anything. It can, however, be used by applications (like Flash) to work with the contents as structured information. In version 5, Flash introduced the capability to work with XML. Let's look at how the Flash XML interface works.

10.3.1 THE FLASH XML OBJECT

Flash uses the built-in XML object to interact with XML data. (Flash also uses an XMLSocket object, which will not be covered here.) As with other objects in Flash, the XML object has a constructor, several methods (built-in functions), and properties.

Some programmers might also refer to this XML object as an "XML parser." A parser is something that reads through a stream of text and uses rules of syntax to create a different version of that text (usually a structure like an array). This is, in fact, only part of what the Flash XML object does. It can also perform the following services:

- Send and receive XML data using URLs
- Call a designated function when a send command or load command finishes
- Convert its contents to and from a string value
- Read or edit individual items in the XML data structure

10.3.2 LOADING DATA INTO THE XML OBJECT

The built-in XML object can get XML data in one of four ways, as shown in Table 10.1.

XML Method	Description
myXML = **new XML**(xmlString);	When assigning a variable to contain a new XML object, an XML string might optionally be passed into the XML() constructor. If an XML string is not passed, then the XML object will be created, but it will contain an empty structure.
myXML.**parseXML**(xmlString);	The XML object's parseXML method will overwrite the XML object's data structure with the XML data found in the xmlString parameter.
myXML.**load**(url);	The XML object's load method will set the XML object's data structure to contain the XML data read from the given URL.

myXML.**sendAndLoad**(url, resultXML);	After sending the XML object's contents to the given URL, the sendAndLoad method receives data back from that URL into the separate resultXML object. Note: You have to first create resultXML as an XML object, as in:
	        var myXML = new XML();
	        var resultXML = new XML();
	        myXML.sendAndLoad(strURL, resultURL);

Table 10.1 Methods that load data Into the XML object.

In the first two cases in Table 10.1, an XML string is passed to the XML object. The XML object simply slices and dices that string (a process called parsing) into a structured format it uses internally to store the XML data. In these cases, there is no need to look to an external file or URL for XML. So, if you have a very small set of XML, or if some XML data is being acquired from somewhere (like the HTML <embed> tag), you can just pass the XML to the **new XML**() constructor or the **parseXML**() method.

In the latter two cases in Table 10.1, we are asking Flash to go and retrieve some XML data from a URL. One of the tricky bits about these methods is that Flash doesn't necessarily finish loading the XML data instantly. These things take time. Flash has to contact the server, request the XML file, get it back, parse the data, and then finally it becomes available to our Flash movie. (Note that the same is true for the loadVariables() action).

So how can we make sure the data is done being loaded before we attempt to use it? The XML object provides two mechanisms to let us know when the XML is done loading:

1. The XML.loaded property
2. The XML.onLoad property

The XML.loaded property is simple. It starts out having a value of *false*. Then, when the data is finished loading, it has a value of *true*. So you can make your Flash movie sit in a loading sequence, looping through frames until (myXML.loaded == true).

The XML.onLoad property is a touch more advanced and in some cases more useful. First, you write a function that you want to be called by the XML object when it finishes loading the data. Then you set the XML.onLoad property to have a pointer to that function. See Code 10.4 for an example of the XML.onLoad property.

```
function xmlLoaded( success ) {
    //
    // In case we want to do something with the XML data,
    // we can use "this" to get a copy of the XML Object
    // that has just been loaded.
    var oXML = this;
    //
    if (success) {
        _root.gotoAndPlay("dataLoaded");
    } else {
        _root.gotoAndStop("dataError");
    }
}
//
var myXML = new XML();
myXML.onLoad = xmlLoaded;
myXML.load("http://www.juxtinteractive.com/deconstruction/samples/customer.xml");
```

Code 10.4   Sample ActionScript that uses the XML.onLoad property.

10.3.3 READING ELEMENTS IN THE XML OBJECT

XML *elements* are also called *nodes*. Think of an element as an individual tag in the XML document. See Table 10.2 for a list of methods provided by the XML object to navigate through elements in the document.

There are several ways to navigate through an XML data structure. One way is using the *childNodes* array. For those most familiar with how arrays work, this might be the easiest (see Code 10.5). Another way to read through an XML object is using the properties *firstChild* and *nextSibling*, or *lastChild* and *previousSibling*. (See Code 10.6 and the corresponding output found in Figure 10.4.)

XML Navigation Methods and Properties	Description
xmlNode.**attributes**[attribName]	If the specified node has any attributes, this property is an associative array of attributes. Use the attribute name as a string value for an array index.
xmlNode.**childNodes**[i]	If the specified node has child nodes, this property is a simple array of child nodes.
xmlNode.**firstChild**	If the specified node has child nodes, this property contains the first child node in the list of child nodes. Otherwise, this property contains a *null* value.
xmlNode.**hasChildNodes**()	Has a value of *true* if the current XML node contains child nodes or *false* if not.
xmlNode.**lastChild**	If the specified node has child nodes, this property contains the last child node in the list of child nodes. Otherwise, this property contains a *null* value.
xmlNode.**nextSibling**	If the specified node has a sibling (same parent node) that comes after it, this property points to it. Otherwise, this property contains a *null* value.
xmlNode.**parentNode**	Unless the specified node is at the top level, this property points to the node's parent.
xmlNode.**previousSibling**	If the specified node has a sibling (same parent node) that comes before it, this property points to it. Otherwise, this property contains a *null* value.

Table 10.2   Methods used by an XML object to navigate a document.

```
//
//— Define a function that gets called when the  —
//— customer XML document is finished loading    —
function customerLoaded(success) {
    //— to access the xml object, use "this" —
    traceNodeNames( this.childNodes );
}
//
//— Define a function that recursively outputs —
//— node names of each node in an XML document —
    function traceNodeNames( xmlNodeArray, tabCount ) {
    //
    //— Set up tabs based on how deep in the XML structure we are —
    if (tabCount == null) {
        tabCount = 0;
    }
    var tabs = "";
    for (var idx=1; idx<=tabCount; idx++) {
        tabs += "   ";
    }
    //
    //— Loop through each sibling nodes —
    for (var idx = 0; idx<xmlNodeArray.length; idx++) {
        //— Output the current node's name —
        trace(tabs + xmlNodeArray[idx].nodeName);
        //
        //— If this node has children, dig down one level —
        if (xmlNodeArray[idx].hasChildNodes()) {
```

continues

continued

```
        //— Call myself recursively (without loosing my place) —
        var childNodeArray = xmlNodeArray[idx].childNodes;
        traceNodeNames(childNodeArray, tabCount+1);
      }
    }
  }
//
//— Now, start loading the XML document from a URL —
var xmlDoc = new XML();
xmlDoc.load("http://www.juxtinteractive.com/deconstruction/samples/customer.xml");
xmlDoc.onLoad = customerLoaded;
stop()
```

Code 10.5   Sample ActionScript using XML.childNodes array.

```
//
//— Define a function that gets called when the  —
//— customer XML document is finished loading     —
function customerLoaded(success) {
   //— to access the xml object, use "this" —
   traceNodeNames( this );
}
//
//— Define a function that recursively outputs —
//— node names of each node in an XML document —
function traceNodeNames( xmlNode, tabCount ) {
   //
   //— Set up tabs based on how deep in the XML structure we are —
   if (tabCount == null) {
      tabCount = 0;
```

continues

```
continued
  }
  var tabs = "";
  for (var idx=1; idx<=tabCount; idx++) {
     tabs += "  ";
  }
  //
  //— Loop through each sibling nodes —
  do {
     //— Output the current node's name —
     trace(tabs + xmlNode.nodeName);
     //
     //— If this node has children, dig down one level —
     if (xmlNode.hasChildNodes()) {
        //— Call myself recursively (without loosing my place) —
        var childNode = xmlNode.firstChild;
        traceNodeNames(childNode, tabCount+1);
           }
     //
     //— Get the next sibling node for the next loop iteration —
     xmlNode = xmlNode.nextSibling;
     //
  } while (xmlNode != null);
}
//
//— Now, start loading the XML document from a URL —
var xmlDoc = new XML();
xmlDoc.load("http://www.juxtinteractive.com/deconstruction/samples/customer.xml");
xmlDoc.onLoad = customerLoaded;
stop();
```

Code 10.6   Sample ActionScript that loads and traces the structure of an XML file.

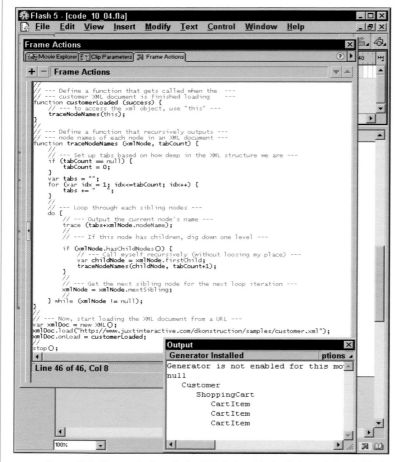

First, we define two functions: customerLoaded() and traceNodeNames(). Then we create an instance of the XML object in a variable called xmlDoc. Next, we tell xmlDoc to start loading the XML file at a certain URL. Finally, we tell the xmlDoc object to call the customerLoaded function when it is done loading the XML data from the URL.

When the customerLoaded function gets called by the xmlDoc object, the XML data has finished loading, and we can use the keyword *this* to gain access to the XML object that has finished loading data. (Notice that you could use the same customerLoaded function for several different XML objects; therefore, it should not assume it is being called by xmlDoc.) Next, customerLoaded() calls traceNodeNames() and passes this as a reference to the XML object.

When the traceNodeNames() function is first called, it is only passed one parameter. We used a variable tabCount to count the levels of indentation for the hierarchy. But the tabCount parameter is initially left as null. For this purpose, we check whether tabCount is null and initialize it to zero the first time around. Then we create a string variable called tabs and use a loop to add three spaces to it for every indentation level indicated by tabCount. This tabs string is used later in the function.

Next we use a do…while loop to iterate through each XML node at the same hierarchical level (otherwise known as sibling nodes). At the end of the do….while loop, we set the xmlNode variable equal to xmlNode.nextSibling and then check to see if xmlNode is still a valid node. If after advancing to the next sibling in this way we find that xmlNode contains a null value, the loop finishes and the function returns to its caller.

Figure 10.4 The results from Code 10.6 displayed in the Debug window in Flash.

In Code 10.6 and Figure 10.4, we see a sample Flash script that loads an XML file and then walks through the hierarchy of the XML data to output the tag names (node names). Let's look at what this code sample is doing.

Within the do…while loop, we first process the current value in xmlNode by outputting (with the trace() command) the tabs string (created earlier in the function) plus the xmlNode.nodeName property. This will display the name of the XML tag for the current node and indent it appropriately.

As soon as the current node name has been output, we check whether it has any child nodes using xmlNode.hasChildNodes(). If so, we get a reference to the first child node with xmlNode.firstChild and pass that child node to another copy of the same traceNodeNames() function while adding a value of one (1) to the tabCount. When a function conditionally calls itself like this, it is referred to as a recursive function. Recursive functions are nice for winding your way through hierarchical data and unwinding again. We'll discuss recursive functions later in this chapter.

10.4   HOW DOES THE SERVER DEAL WITH XML?

We've looked at how Flash interfaces with XML data. Just like Flash, to work with XML, other programming languages and tools must have an XML document interface. Most web scripting languages now have XML parsers. Each language's implementation of an XML parser differs from the next. If you will be developing server-side web scripts to work with XML, you'll need to learn the XML interface for your web scripting language. Let's look at some of the issues surrounding XML on the server side.

10.4.1   STATIC VS. DYNAMIC XML FILES

XML data can be stored in static files on the web server, or it can be dynamically generated using any number of web scripting languages.

In some cases, it makes sense to create a static XML file on the server, to store content or menu structures for a Flash project. If the data only changes occasionally (or not at all) and can be edited by people who know how to edit XML, there's no reason to build a database and a whole system of screens and web scripts to

manipulate the XML data. Web servers don't really do much with static files except serve them. However, if static XML files only change occasionally but are highly complex, it sometimes makes sense to develop server-side solutions using a database and a programming language to generate the static XML files. This technique reduces the day-to-day burden of the server yet allows XML to be produced from a database.

In other cases, the data Flash projects need will be fully dynamic. This data typically comes from a database and is formatted into XML using a web scripting language like ASP, JSP, Perl, PHP, or ColdFusion.

XML can be generated in two ways. One way is to use what is called an XML parser. Much like Flash's XML object, an XML parser can do many things with XML for you. The primary purpose of a parser, however, is to convert a chunk of XML from a string format into a data structure that the program can navigate through using the parser's methods and properties. Although an XML parser does have the capability to assemble data elements into an XML structure and then output it to XML, it is often too complex to program.

The second (and easier) way is to output XML tags in a way that's similar to how HTML tags are output in a dynamic web page. Here are the basic steps to outputting XML from a dynamic script:

1. Set the content-type to text/xml.
   a. In ASP, the command is: Response.ContentType = "text/xml".
   b. In ColdFusion, it's: <cfcontent type="text/xml">.
   c. In Perl, it's: $cgi->print($cgi->header (-type=>'text/xml'));.
   d. In PHP, it's: <?php Header("Content-type: text/xml"); ?>.
   e. In JSP, it's: response.setcontenttype("Content-type: text/xml");.

2. Get the source data that is going to be output as XML (like a database query).

3. Loop through each item in the source data and output the XML tags and attributes necessary to represent the intended data.

   a. In ASP, you can use: Response.Write ("<myXmlTag>" & myData & "</myXmlTag>").

   b. In ColdFusion, you can use: <cfoutput><myXmlTag> #myData#</myXmlTag></cfoutput>.

```
<CFSETTING enablecfoutputonly="YES"><!--- No Whitespace --->

<!--- NOTE:  CustomerID must be passed on the URL --->

<CFQUERY datasource="SalesDB" name="cart">
  SELECT Customer.CS_FName, Customer.CS_LName, Customer.CS_ID,
     CartItem.CI_ID, CartItem.CI_SKU, CartItem.CI_Price
  FROM Customer LEFT JOIN CartItem ON Customer.CS_ID = CartItem.CS_ID
  WHERE Customer.CS_ID = #URL.CustomerID#
</CFQUERY>

<CFCONTENT type="text/xml">


<CFOUTPUT><?xml version="1.0"?></cfoutput>
<CFOUTPUT><Customer firstName="#cart.CS_FName#" lastName="#cart.CS_LName#" ID="#cart.CS_ID#"></cfoutput>
<CFOUTPUT><ShoppingCart></cfoutput>

<!--- Loop through query results, and output it as a cart item --->
<CFOUTPUT QUERY="cart"><CartItem sku="#CI_SKU#" price="#CI_Price#" ID="#CI_ID#"/></cfoutput>

<CFOUTPUT></ShoppingCart></cfoutput>
<CFOUTPUT></Customer></cfoutput>

<CFSETTING enablecfoutputonly="NO">
```

Code 10.7   A sample ColdFusion script that converts a database query to XML.

10.4.2 USING A SERVER-SIDE XML PARSER

To read XML data that has been sent (posted) to a server-side script, the script must parse the XML before inspecting the nodes. It would be too hard to use something like substr() or InStr() string functions to work our way through an XML string.

Given the choice of ColdFusion or ASP for the nDecision movie maker's save script, we chose ASP. Although ColdFusion does have the capability to use COM objects, and there is a freeCOM object that implements an XML parser, ColdFusion does not work well with hierarchical data structures in COM (their "dot syntax" is very limited). So nDecision used the Microsoft XML parser (msxml.dll) as a COM Object in an ASP script. The full source code listings for nDecision movie maker in Flash, ColdFusion, and ASP can all be found on the book's web site.

10.5 SENDING XML IN FLASH

Although the most common use for XML in Flash is to load information dynamically from a URL, Flash can also send XML to a URL. This feature makes it possible to send complex data (that XML handles so well) to the server, which can process the contents in whatever way it wants. Server scripts can save the XML as is into a static XML file and catalog it somewhere, or they can read through the contents and take some sort of action, such as saving records to a database. Let's look at how Flash sends XML data to the server.

10.5.1 XML.SEND() VS. XML.SENDANDLOAD()

As the names say, the *.send()* method sends XML data, while the *XML.sendAndLoad()* method sends XML data and then loads a response as XML. When using the .send() and XML.sendAndLoad() methods, we must deal with custom scripts on the server that will receive the XML data we're sending.

We could use either the XML.send() or XML.sendAndLoad() method. Of course, the XML.send() method is the easiest because we do not have to deal with response data. So the question is, "Do we want to blindly send the XML data and keep it simple, or are we willing to write a few more lines of code to get a response telling us whether the XML was received and, if so, was it received properly?" If we're sending some XML data to a server script that will use it to save the information to a database, it might be useful to have the server script return some XML in response that indicates the status of the transaction as well as the resulting database record ID.

See Code 10.8 and Code 10.9 for simple examples of XML.send() and XML.sendAndLoad(), respectively.

```
//
//— Create a new "instance" of an XML object —
var xmlDoc = new XML();
//
//— Create an XML string, and stuff it into the XML object —
var strXML = '<?xml version="1.0"?><Customer firstName="' + cust_fname + '" lastName="' + cust_lname + '"/>';
xmlDoc.parseXML(strXML);
//
//— Now, send the XML document to a URL —
xmlDoc.send("http://www.juxtinteractive.com/deconstruction/samples/saveCustomer.asp");
```

Code 10.8   Sample ActionScript using the XML.send() method.

10.5.2   USING XML.ONLOAD WITH XML.SENDANDLOAD()

When sending XML data, one might wonder whether or not the XML.onLoad event handler is used. The answer is a tad tricky but makes sense nonetheless. When we use the XML.send() method, the XML.onLoad event handler is never called. This is because we send off the data, and because we're never going to receive a response, there's no point in notifying us when the transaction finishes. However, when we use XML.sendAndLoad(), the XML.onLoad event handler is called when the response data finishes loading into the response object.

The tricky bit is that we don't set the XML.onLoad property on the original XML object we are sending. We set it on the XML object that will receive the response data. Of course, if we think of the XML.onLoad event handler as being called by the "load" portion of the XML.load() or XML.sendAndLoad() method, it all makes sense. For an example of the .onLoad event handler being used with .sendAndLoad(), see Code 10.9.

```
//
//— Define a function that gets called when the  —
//— XML response is finished loading            —
function responseLoaded(success) {
    if (success) {
        //— assuming the XML response data looks something like:
        //—   <?xml version="1.0"?><Customer ID="24"/>
        _root.cust_ID = this.firstChild.attributes["ID"];
        //
        _root.gotoAndStop("customerOK");
    } else {
        _root.gotoAndStop("customerError");
    }
}
//
//— Create a new "instance" of an XML object —
var xmlDoc = new XML();
//
//— Create an XML string, and stuff it into the XML object —
var strXML = '<?xml version="1.0"?><Customer firstName="' + cust_fname + '" lastName="' + cust_lname + '"/>';
xmlDoc.parseXML(strXML);
//
//— Set up the response XML object —
var xmlResponse = new XML();
xmlResponse.onLoad = responseLoaded;
//
//— Now, send the XML document to a URL —
xmlDoc.sendAndLoad("http://www.juxtinteractive.com/deconstruction/samples/saveCustomer.asp", xmlResponse);
stop();
```

Code 10.9   Sample ActionScript using XML.sendAndLoad() array.

10.5.3 RECEIVING A RESPONSE

Once the XML.sendAndLoad() method sends our XML data to the server script for processing, the response data comes back from the server and feeds the response XML object that was passed as the second parameter to XML.sendAndLoad(). If we set up a function in the response XML object's XML.onLoad property, that function will be called when the response is complete.

Within that event handler function, we can gain access to the response XML object using the keyword *this*.

On some occasions, the XML.onLoad event handler function might need to have access not only to the response XML object but also to the original XML object that was sent. There is a trick that makes this possible. Simply add a reference to the original XML object to the response XML object, like xmlResponse.ref_xmlDoc = xmlDoc;.

When calling the .onLoad event handler function, the XML object will pass one parameter that will contain a *true* or *false* value, indicating success or failure (respectively).

So the apparent thing to do would be to check whether the operation was successful (with the success parameter) and then try to extract any interesting data from the response XML.

10.5.4 ASP 2.0 CAVEAT XML

When using ASP to receive XML data, one must use an XML parser. However, the MSXML 2.0 parser that is commonly installed on Windows NT 4 SP6 servers has a big problem. It cannot receive XML data! There is a bug with ASP 2.0 and MSXML 2.0 that causes the XML being received in the HTTP request to be partially corrupted.

If your web server is running on Windows NT 4 with IIS 4 and ASP 2.0 and you do not have the luxury of upgrading to MSXML 3.0; you're stuck with the problem.

Do not despair. There is a workaround. Here's what you'll need to do:

1. Get the number of bytes in the request, using Request.TotalBytes.
2. Using the total bytes value, get the entire request as a binary string, using Request.BinaryRead(bytes).
3. Use a loop to extract 1 byte at a time from the binary string and convert it from binary to text, using Chr(AscB(MidB(binRequest,, idx, 1))).
4. Accumulate the converted text bytes into a string.
5. The resulting string is your XML that was sent to the ASP from Flash.

For an example of the ASP 2.0, MSXML 2.0 workaround, see Code 10.10.

```
Dim xmlString, idx
Dim byteCount, binRequest

'— Extract the data from the ASP Request Object —
'— as binary data since IIS 4 MESSES IT UP!!!   —
byteCount = Request.TotalBytes
binRequest = Request.BinaryRead(byteCount)

'— Convert the Binary HTTP data from a binary —
'— SafeArray to an ASCII xml string           ---
xmlString = ""
For idx = 1 to byteCount
  xmlString = xmlString & Chr(AscB(MidB( binRequest, idx, 1)))
Next
```

Code 10.10   The ASP 2.0, MSXML 2.0 workaround script.

10.6   RECEIVING XML IN FLASH

The most useful feature of Flash's XML object is the XML.load() method. It can be compared with the ActionScript loadVariables() command in that it retrieves data from a URL quite easily. Let's look at how to make Flash retrieve XML from a URL and how to access the data after it's loaded.

10.6.1   LOADING XML DATA

Loading XML data into Flash can be relatively simple. At a minimum, it requires three steps:

1. Create an instance (in a variable) of an XML object:
   var xmlDoc = new XML();

2. Tell Flash to ignore blank spaces between XML tags (see the Note earlier in this chapter):
   xmlDoc.ignoreWhite = true;

3. Call the load method with a URL:
   xmlDoc.load("http://www.server.com/something.xml");

If your Flash movie needs to know when the XML data is done being loaded, it could check the xmlDoc.loaded property until it becomes true, or it could use xmlDoc.onLoad to set up a function that gets called when the data arrives.

See Code 10.11 for a simple example that loads XML data and uses the XML.onLoad property to set up a function to be notified when the transfer is complete.

```
//
//— Define a function that gets called when the  —
//— customer XML document is finished loading    —
function customerLoaded(success) {
    if (success) {
        _root.gotoAndPlay("customerOK");
    } else {
        _root.gotoAndStop("customerError");
    }
}
//
//— Create a new "instance" of an XML object —
var xmlDoc = new XML();
//
//— Tell Flash to ignore blank spaces in between XML tags —
xmlDoc.ignoreWhite = true;
//
//— Set the function for this XML object "instance" —
//— to call when data is finished loading        —
xmlDoc.onLoad = customerLoaded;
//
//— Now, start loading the XML document from a URL —
xmlDoc.load("http://www.juxtinteractive.com/deconstruction/samples/customer.xml");
```

Code 10.11   Sample ActionScript using XML.load().

10.7 SIFTING THROUGH THE DATA

Once XML data has been loaded from a URL, we must extract data elements from the XML data structure. Because the data is stored in a format that is internal to the XML object, we use the methods and properties provided to access the data. Once again, we can choose to use either the XML.childNodes[] array or the XML.firstChild and XML.nextSibling properties to navigate through the hierarchy of our data.

If we are in control of the hierarchy and order of the original XML file being used by Flash, we can get away with programming a few commands that extract the exact data element we're looking for. For example:

```
myXML.firstChild.nextSibling.nextSibling.firstChild.firstChild
```

or

```
myXML.childNodes[2].childNodes[0]
```

This puts the Flash movie at the mercy of the source XML data. If, for any reason, items were put into a different order or were added at a later date, our Flash movie would not work the way we want it to.

If we want to build in some bulletproofing, we have to jump through a few extra hoops. This is exactly the reason why we chose to use the ArrayTransport Library. We could benefit from the structure and cleanliness of XML without the hassle of extra hoops to jump through anytime we wanted to get at a data element. Although we used ArrayTransport—and there are several other similar solutions available for download from the Internet (wddx and loadXML libraries)—it can prove useful to know how to write bulletproof ActionScript to sift through XML data.

If you're still interested in using WDDX to work with XML in Flash, check out the following URLs:

http://tmug.theshore.net/cfusion/wddx.html

www.OpenWDDX.org

In Code 10.12, the example safely accesses some XML data that has already been loaded by Flash. Rather than access items in the XML data by position, it searches for nodes by name. First, we create a function named findNode, which takes three parameters: xmlNode, sName, nMaxDepth. The actual XML object can be passed to the xmlNode parameter if the search is to begin at the top of the data hierarchy. Otherwise, a reference to any valid XML node will start the search a little further down the tree.

Notice that the first time we call findNode(), we pass xmlDoc as the first parameter, yet the second time we use the first found item (oShoppingCart) as the xmlNode. The sName parameter is a string that specifies the node name for which we are looking. Finally, the nMaxDepth parameter tells the function how deep in the hierarchy of XML data to search. This is to make it run faster by not delving into the deepest depths of the data hierarchy and staying within the general region we think it should search.

The findNode() function in our example does something that might seem odd. It calls itself. When it discovers that the current node it is inspecting has child nodes, it calls findNode() and passes xmlNode.firstChild. However, this only occurs if it hasn't exceeded its maximum depth. The maximum depth is a feature we added to the findNode() function to make it run faster. It ensures that findNode() only searches a few levels deep in the XML structure because an exhaustive search through all of the nodes in a large XML document could stall a Flash movie.

When a function calls itself, it is called a "recursive" function. Care must be observed when creating recursive functions; if a mistake is made, it might create an infinite loop and crash or freeze the program. Fortunately, the example in Code 10.12 has been written with care and has been tested thoroughly. As a result, it works quite nicely.

```
// — Uses customer.xml data that has already been loaded —
//
//
function findNode (xmlNode, sName, nMaxDepth) {
   if (xmlNode != null) {
      // — See if any sibling nodes match the sName —
      do {
         // — See if the current node is a match —
         if (xmlNode.nodeName == sName) {
            return xmlNode;
         }
         // — See if any child nodes match the sName —
         if (xmlNode.hasChildNodes() && nMaxDepth>=1) {
            var oFound=findNode(xmlNode.firstChild, sName, nMaxDepth-1);
            if (oFound != null) {
               return oFound;
            }
         }
      } while (xmlNode.nextSibling != null);
   }
   // — nothing found! —
   return null;
```

continues

```
}

// — Find the ShoppingCart item —
var oShoppingCart = findNode(xmlDoc, "ShoppingCart", 2);
trace ('found shopping cart.  node name='+oShoppingCart.nodeName);
// — Find a CartItem under ShoppingCart —
var oCartItem = findNode(oShoppingCart, "CartItem", 1);
trace ('found CartItem.  node name='+oCartItem.nodeName + ', id=' + oCartItem.attributes["ID"]);
// — Find the NEXT CartItem —
oCartItem = findNode(oCartItem.nextSibling, "CartItem", 0);
trace ('found CartItem.  node name='+oCartItem.nodeName + ', id=' + oCartItem.attributes["ID"]);
```

Code 10.12   Sample ActionScript that safely accesses XML data.

10.8   MOVIE MAKER XML

When we built the movie maker, we chose to use XML as an information vehicle between the Flash movie and the web server. Because XML is a user-defined markup language, we get to make it all up. Let's take a look at the XML structure we decided on and why.

10.8.1   SAMPLE XML

To understand how the movie maker uses XML to contain all of the customized movie attributes, we should first look at a snippet of the XML. Next, we'll discuss why this structure was used and what the tags mean to the movie maker.

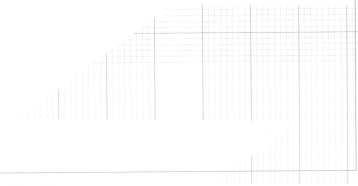

```xml
<?xml version="1.0"?>
<ARRAY index="0">
 <VALUE index="userCode" type="string">
  <![CDATA[]]>
 </VALUE>
 <VALUE index="sound" type="string">
  <![CDATA[0]]>
 </VALUE>
 <ARRAY index="1">
  <ARRAY index="1">
   <VALUE index="origclipnum" type="string">
    <![CDATA[2]]>
   </VALUE>
   <VALUE index="speed" type="string">
    <![CDATA[0]]>
   </VALUE>
   <VALUE index="blue" type="string">
    <![CDATA[62]]>
   </VALUE>
   <VALUE index="green" type="string">
    <![CDATA[100]]>
   </VALUE>
   <VALUE index="red" type="string">
    <![CDATA[100]]>
   </VALUE>
   <VALUE index="alpha" type="string">
    <![CDATA[50]]>
   </VALUE>
   <VALUE index="scale" type="string">
    <![CDATA[100]]>
   </VALUE>
  </VALUE>
 </ARRAY>
 <ARRAY index="2">
  <VALUE index="origclipnum" type="string">
   <![CDATA[0]]>
  </VALUE>
  <VALUE index="speed" type="string">
   <![CDATA[0]]>
  </VALUE>
  <VALUE index="blue" type="string">
   <![CDATA[100]]>
  </VALUE>
  <VALUE index="green" type="string">
   <![CDATA[51]]>
  </VALUE>
  <VALUE index="red" type="string">
   <![CDATA[100]]>
  </VALUE>
  <VALUE index="alpha" type="string">
   <![CDATA[100]]>
  </VALUE>
  <VALUE index="scale" type="string">
   <![CDATA[100]]>
  </VALUE>
 </ARRAY>
</ARRAY>
<!– snip –>
</ARRAY>
```

Code 10.13   nDecision movie maker XML data (partial listing).

10.8.2 XML OR ARRAYS

When a Flash movie loads in a chunk of XML data, it is left in the XML object. The only way to get at it is to use the XML object's methods and properties to dig step by step down into the depths of the data. If the program needs to dig down three levels of hierarchy to get to a data element, it takes quite a few lines of code, several loops, and a lot of if statements. One reason for this difficulty is that the XML elements are not guaranteed to be in any particular order. So the list of tracks (two levels down in the hierarchy) might be listed as 1 and then 2, or 2 and then 1.

It would not be safe for the ActionScript that attempts to retrieve information about track 2 to try accessing it with an expression like the following:

```
myXML.firstChild.nextSibling.nextSibling.firstChild.firstChild
```

Or even:

```
myXML.childNodes[2].childNodes[0]
```

It would be so much more desirable for the movie maker to work with arrays. Then, to access the second track of the first movie clip, it could use an expression like this:

```
myArray[1][2]
```

Arrays are so much more direct and intuitive than the XML data structure. But wouldn't it be tough to convert XML to and from a multidimensional array? Well, yes. But the payoff in simple dealings with the data is worth the trouble of conversion.

10.8.3 AN ARRAY XML LIBRARY

Once the XML data seen in Code 10.13 is translated to a multi-dimensional array, it is much easier to work with. For example, to access the data element highlighted in the XML code sample, one would simply access the array (named aClips in our movie) as aClips[1][2]["green"] (which might have a value of 51). In the movie maker, this means that the first movie clip that plays will have a green value of 51 (out of a possible 255) in the second track (which is the background track).

Likewise, the data element in the array that records which sound track the user selected is accessed as aClips["sound"].

Once it was decided to use XML only as a transfer mechanism for the movie maker data and to use arrays as the movie's representation of the data, it made sense to write a series of functions that could generically convert between arrays and XML. We created an external text file that could be included in the Flash movie using the *#include* directive. This text file defines a new object called ArrayTransport. The purpose of this object is to transport arrays to and from the web server, using XML as an internal data format.

Once the ArrayTransport object library was created, the movie maker could simply request that an array be loaded from the server (to retrieve previously saved movie settings) or request that the currently active array (in the Flash movie) be sent to the server to be saved. All of the gory details were taken care of by the object. We'll discuss this object more later in this chapter.

10.9 NDECISION'S USE OF THE ARRAYTRANSPORT LIBRARY

The ArrayTransport library is nothing more than a custom object written in ActionScript and saved as an external text file. It can be added to a Flash movie using the #include command. This custom object makes it possible to convert XML data to and from Flash arrays. It serves as an insulation layer between the ActionScript throughout the movie and the XML object, making it easier to work with the data from XML. Let's look at how this handy object works and how it was used in the nDecision movie maker.

10.9.1 USING ARRAYTRANSPORT TO SAVE DATA

In the movie maker, when the user clicks on the Build Movie button, it calls the function buildMovie(). This function, in turn, uses the ArrayTransport object to take care of all the XML conversion and transfer. Here are the ArrayTransport steps used in buildMovie():

1. Create an instance of the ArrayTransport object using aClips as the array to be converted to XML.

2. Use the .setHandler() method of ArrayTransport to set a handler function that will be called by ArrayTransport when the XML data has completed sending.

3. Call the .sendTo() method of ArrayTransport to send the XML version of the array to the specified URL.

4. When the settingsSavedHandler() function is called by ArrayTransport, it checks the oTransport.errorMsg property to see if an error occurred. An empty string indicates success; anything else is an error message.

5. The handler function then extracts any response data in the form of an array called .serverResponse.

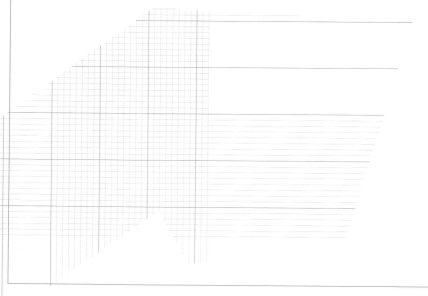

```
//---------------------------------------------------
// Purpose: Called when the user clicks on the Build Movie button in
//     the Flash movie; initiates the process of converting
//     the data from the array of attributes over to XML and
//     then sends that XML to the server for saving.
//
// Globals:  aClips == a multi-dimensional array containing
//              the movie settings.
//          sendto.yourEmail == a text field containing the
//              email address of the person who built
//              the movie settings.
//          settingsSaved == a Boolean variable indicating to
//              the rest of the movie maker whether or not
//              the settings have completed saving.
//---------------------------------------------------
function buildMovie() {

  aClips['yourEmail'] = sendto.yourEmail;
  settingsSaved = false;

  var oTransport = new ArrayTransport( aClips );
  var strServerURL = serverBaseURL + "saveSettings.asp";

  oTransport.setHandler( settingsSavedHandler );

  oTransport.sendTo( strServerURL );
  return;
}
```

continues

```
continued
//-----------------------------------------------------
// Purpose: gets called by the xmlArray library when the movie
//     settings have been saved to the server, and the response
//     array (oTransport.serverResponse) is ready to read.
//     Sets the global variable (userCode) and
//     (settingsSaved=true).
//
// Globals: userCode, settingsSaved
//-----------------------------------------------------
function settingsSavedHandler( oTransport ) {

  //-- Extract the GLOBAL variable (userCode) from --
  //--   the Server Response Array --
  if ("" == oTransport.errorMsg) {
    _level0.userCode = oTransport.serverResponse['userCode'];
    _level1.userCode = oTransport.serverResponse['userCode'];
  }
  settingsSaved = true;

  _level1.onMovieSaved(_level0.userCode);
}
```

Code 10.14   nDecision script that uses ArrayTransport to send an array.

10.9.2 HOW ARRAYTRANSPORT CONVERTS ARRAY DATA TO XML

Within the ActionScript that defines the ArrayTransport object, there
is a function called arrayToXMLString() that converts the contents
and structure of an array to XML. See Code 10.15 for a code listing.

```
//--------------------------------------------------------
// Purpose: Given any JavaScript array, converts the contents to
//     an XML string.
//--------------------------------------------------------
function arrayToXMLString(ary, xml, thisIdx) {
  var idx;

  if (xml == null) {
    xml = '<?xml version="1.0"?>';
  }

  if (thisIdx == null) {
    thisIdx = 0;
  }

  xml = xml + '<ARRAY index="' + thisIdx + '">';
  for (idx in ary) {
    if (typeof(ary[idx]) == 'object') {
      xml = arrayToXMLString( ary[idx], xml, idx );
    } else {
      if (ary[idx] != null) {
        xml = xml + '<VALUE index="' + idx + '" type="' + typeof(ary[idx]) + '"><![CDATA[' + ary[idx] + ']]></VALUE>';
      }
    }
  }
  xml = xml +  '</ARRAY>';
  return xml;
}
```

Code 10.15   arrayToXMLString() function (from xmlArray.as).

When calling the arrayToXMLString() function for the first time, all that needs to be passed as a parameter is the array that needs to be converted. The value returned by the function is an XML string.

For every element found in the array, the function adds a piece of text to the XML string. That piece of text will contain an XML tag for <VALUE> or <ARRAY>, depending on whether the element is a simple data value (scalar value) or a subarray. The index numbers or names from the array are stored in the XML as an attribute called *index*. The data type of the original array value (string, number, and so on) is stored in the XML as an attribute called *type*.

If the element is a subarray, the function adds a beginning <ARRAY> tag and then calls a copy of itself (the arrayToXMLString() function) to process the subarray. As mentioned previously, when a function calls itself, it is termed recursive. It puts the currently running instance of the function on hold while a new copy of the function is executed with different parameters. When the new copy of the function finishes, it will return to the original instance that was placed on hold so that it can continue executing. In this way, as the arrayToXMLString() function encounters subarrays, it calls itself to handle the deeper level of the array. Eventually, all of the deeper levels of subarrays are processed, and their respective pieces of XML strings are returned and pieced together.

10.9.3 HOW ARRAYTRANSPORT SENDS XML

Beyond the mechanics of converting a multidimensional array to and from XML, the ArrayTransport object merely uses the built-in XML object to send and receive XML data. The highlighted lines of ActionScript in Code 10.16 show the primary commands responsible for sending the XML data to the web server. These commands should look familiar from earlier in this chapter, when we explained how to use XML.sendAndLoad().

```
//-----------------------------------------------
// Purpose: Defines the ArrayTransport.sendTo() method.
//-----------------------------------------------
function _sendTo( strURL ) {

  //--- Make sure the caller passed a URL ---
  if (null == strURL) {
    this.errorMsg = "object.sendTo() requires a 'strURL' parameter.";
    return;
  }

  if (null == this.xmlDoc) {
    this.xmlDoc = new XML();
  }

  //--- Initialize the .transferComplete property so ---
```
continues

```
continued
//—   the loader can check when we're done —
this.transferComplete = false;

//— Clear out the .serverResponse property —
this.serverResponse = [];

if (null != this.array) {

  this.errorMsg = "";

  //— Convert the array to XML —
  this.xmlString = arrayToXMLString( this.array );
  this.xmlDoc.parseXML( this.xmlString );

  //— Set up another XML document object, for the response XML —
  this.xmlResponse = new XML();
  this.xmlResponse.onLoad = onXMLSent;
  this.xmlResponse.refToArrayTransportObj = this;

  //— Start the asynchronous data transfer with the server —
  this.xmlDoc.sendAndLoad(strURL, this.xmlResponse);

} else {
  this.errorMsg = "The object.array property is null.  "
    + "Cannot convert to XML, or send empty XML data."
}

return;
}

//— Attach this function definition to the Class, as a method —
ArrayTransport.prototype.sendTo = _sendTo;
```

Code 10.16   ArrayTransport.sendTo() method definition (from xmlArray.as).

10.9.4 USING ARRAYTRANSPORT TO LOAD DATA

In the movie maker, once the user builds a movie, a URL for that movie can be emailed out to friends and enemies. Within that URL is a unique code that identifies the information in the database that defines the settings for the movie. The viewer.swf Flash movie receives that unique code and uses it to retrieve the movie settings from the database on the web server. During the loading sequence of the viewer.swf file, a call is made to the function restoreMovie(), passing the unique code as a userCode parameter.

Like the buildMovie() function, the restoreMovie() function uses the ArrayTransport object to take care of all the XML conversion and transfer details. These are the ArrayTransport steps used in restoreMovie():

1. Create an instance of the ArrayTransport object using aClips as the array to be converted to XML.

2. Use the .setHandler() method of ArrayTransport to set a handler function that will be called by ArrayTransport when the XML data has completed loading.

3. Call the .getFrom() method of ArrayTransport to load the XML version of the array from the specified URL.

4. When the settingsLoadedHandler() function is called by ArrayTransport, it checks the oTransport.errorMsg property to see if an error occurred. An empty string indicates success; anything else is an error message.

5. The handler function extracts the loaded array data from the .array property of the ArrayTransport object (see Code 10.17).

```
//--------------------------------------------------------
// Purpose: Called when the Flash movie is first loaded, and is in
//     need of the attributes of the previously saved movie.
//
//        Retrieves the Movie settings from the server, using
//     the (userCode) to identify whose movie to load.
//     Sets the global variable (aClips) with the array.
//
// WARNING: there is a delay before the (aClips) array is loaded.
//
// Globals:  settingsLoaded
//--------------------------------------------------------
function restoreMovie( userCode ) {

  if (null == userCode || "" == userCode) {
    initSettings();
    settingsLoaded = true;
    return;
  }


  settingsLoaded = false;

  oTransport = new ArrayTransport();

  oTransport.setHandler( settingsLoadedHandler );

  var strServerURL = serverBaseURL +  "loadSettings.asp?userCode=" + userCode;

  oTransport.getFrom( strServerURL );
```
continues

```
continued

  return;

}


//————————————————————————————————
// Purpose: gets called by the xmlArray library when the movie
//    settings have been loaded from the server.
//    Sets the global variables (aClips) and
//    (settingsLoaded=true).
//
// Globals: aClips, settingsLoaded
//————————————————————————————————
function settingsLoadedHandler( oTransport ) {

  if ("" == oTransport.errorMsg) {
    aClips = oTransport.array;
  } else {
    initSettings();
  }
  settingsLoaded = true;


  _root.MovieLoaded();
}
```

Code 10.17   An nDecision script that uses ArrayTransport to load an array.

10.9.5 HOW ARRAYTRANSPORT CONVERTS
XML TO ARRAY DATA

As part of the ArrayTransport library, there are two functions that
work together to reconstruct an ActionScript array from XML. These
functions are named *XMLDocToArray()* and *buildArray()*. See Code
10.18 for a code listing.

```
var NODE_VALUE = 'VALUE';
var NODE_ARRAY = 'ARRAY';

var XML_NODE_TYPE_TEXT = 3;
var XML_NODE_TYPE_ELEMENT = 1;


//--------------------------------------------------
// Purpose: given an XML document (using ARRAY/VALUE tags),
//     converts the contents into a JavaScript array.
//--------------------------------------------------
function XMLDocToArray(oXML) {

  var ary = [];

  if (oXML == null) {
    return ary;
  }

  //-- Step past the root element to the first ARRAY node --
  var eRoot = oXML.firstChild;
  if (eRoot != null) {

    //-- Make sure this XML element is an "ARRAY" element --
    if (eRoot.nodeName == NODE_ARRAY) {
      ary = buildArray(ary, eRoot.firstChild);
    }
  }

  return ary;
}

//--------------------------------------------------
```

continues

continued

```
// Purpose: Called by XMLDocToArray() function, to recursively build
//    the array from the XML document.
//---------------------------------------------------------------
function buildArray(ary, eItem) {

  var idx = 0;
  var indexCounter = 0;
  var eChild;

  //--- Loop through the sibling elements in this level of the XML ---
  while (eItem != null) {

    if (eItem.nodeType == XML_NODE_TYPE_ELEMENT) {

      if (eItem.nodeName == NODE_ARRAY) {

        if (eItem.attributes['index'] != null) {
          idx = eItem.attributes['index'];
        } else {
          idx = indexCounter++;
        }

        //--- Call self recursively to build a sub-array ---
        ary[idx] = buildArray( [], eItem.firstChild);

      } else if (eItem.nodeName == NODE_VALUE) {


        //--- Extract the CDATA or raw text child value ---
        eChild = eItem.firstChild;
```

continues

```
continued
        if (eChild.nodeType == XML_NODE_TYPE_TEXT) {

            if (eChild.nodeValue != null) {

                if (eItem.attributes['index'] != null) {
                    idx = eItem.attributes['index'];
                } else {
                    idx = indexCounter++;
                }



                //— Save the value from the TEXT —
                //—    element into the array —
                if (eChild.attributes['type'] == 'number') {
                    ary[idx] = parseFloat(eChild.nodeValue);
                } else {
                    ary[idx] = eChild.nodeValue;
                }
            }
        }
    }


    }

    //– Get the next sibling node in this level of the XML —
    eItem = eItem.nextSibling;
}


return ary;
}
```

The XMLDocToArray() function's job is to take an XML object and start the process of converting it to an array. The array starts out empty and is passed to the buildArray() function to fill it with data from the XML object.

Given an array and a node within an XML object, the buildArray() function works through the XML hierarchy using recursion. When it encounters an XML node named VALUE, it simply adds an element to the array with which it is currently working. When it encounters a node named ARRAY, it recursively calls itself, passing that node and a new empty array. The new instance of buildArray() goes to work on the branch of the XML hierarchy building a new subarray and returns the subarray. The original instance of buildArray() stores that subarray into an element in the current array with which it is working. In this way, it works through the structure, digging deeper and wider in the hierarchy of XML nodes until it finishes processing all the nodes in the XML object.

The end result is an array that can be multidimensional. Each dimension can be a simple array or an associative array that is returned to the caller of XMLDocToArray().

10.9.6 HOW ARRAYTRANSPORT LOADS XML

Like the .sendTo() method of ArrayTransport, the .getFrom() method simply uses the built-in XML object to handle the transport of data. The highlighted lines of ActionScript in Code 10.19 show the primary commands responsible for loading the XML data from the web server. These commands were covered earlier in this chapter when we discussed the XML.load() method.

```
//----------------------------------------------------------
// Purpose: Starts the process of loading an array (via XML) from
//     a URL.
// Notes: The array does not become available immediately upon return
//     of this function.  The transfer starts running in the
//     background.  When the array has been loaded, the
//     .transferComplete property of the ArrayTransport will be
//     true.
//     example:
//         if(myAryTrans.transferComplete == true) {
//             gotoAndPlay('continue');
//         }
//----------------------------------------------------------
function _getFrom( strURL ) {

  //--- Make sure the caller passed a URL ---
  if (null == strURL) {
    this.errorMsg = "object.getFrom() requires a 'strURL' parameter.";
    return;
  }

  if (null == this.xmlDoc) {
    this.xmlDoc = new XML();
  }

  this.errorMsg = "";

  //--- Set up an event handler for the response document ---
  this.xmlDoc.onLoad = onXMLLoaded;
```

continues

```
continued
this.xmlDoc.refToArrayTransportObj = this;


//— Initialize the .transferComplete property —
//— so the loader can check when we're done —
this.transferComplete = false;


//— Tell Flash to ignore blank spaces in between XML tags —
xmlDoc.ignoreWhite = true;


//— Start the asynchronous data transfer with the server —
this.xmlDoc.load(strURL);


return;
}


//— Attach this function definition to the Class, as a method —
ArrayTransport.prototype.getFrom = _getFrom;
```

Code 10.19   ArrayTransport.getFrom() method definition (fromxmlArray.as).

10.10 SUMMARY

XML the data format can be easy to read and write. XML the technology is highly flexible and thus can be employed in any number of programming languages. XML the Flash object is a powerful addition to the medium. Although everything that is accomplished with the Flash XML object could be accomplished through the loadVariables() command, the XML object helps organize and structure information.

Of course, XML is not always the best way to send and receive data in Flash, nor should it be treated as such. It is just another powerful tool at the disposal of the Flash developer, and it should be considered seriously whenever Flash needs to exchange data with a web server.

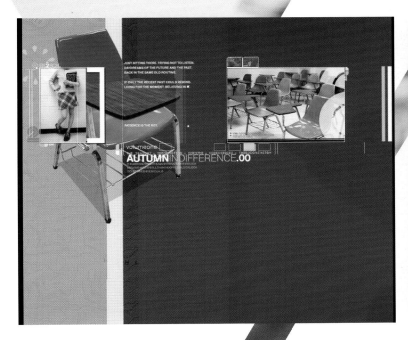

MATT OWENS

Matt Owens Interview
by Todd Purgason

Introduction
www.volumeone.com

I think that every designer on the web has a special place in his or her heart and mind for the URL www.volumeOne.com. It can be argued that Matt Owens gave birth to the personal designer site phenomenon that has spread like wildfire through the global web design community.

Matt has consistently delivered fresh and poetic views of design exploration with each seasonal issue of VolumeOne. In addition,

on the for-profit side (or should I say, for-client side) of the game, he, along with partners William Corbit and Lee Misenheimer, has delivered some amazing work, both on and off the web. We at Juxt have always intently followed Matt's work, drawing inspiration and entertainment from his visions of creative thinking and execution.

Teaser from the Interview

TP: So, we're here with Matt Owens from volumeOne and One 9ine Design. So Matt, who is Matt Owens?

MO: It's just me. We were having a discussion earlier today about who people are. I don't know how many people you've met that are doing online stuff. But everyone's sort of like... One of my immediate thoughts, if you're doing stuff online and you're posting stuff and you're a regular participant, you're in it for a reason. Like there's something about it that's important to you, you know. And I think that's, for me, being able to do design and do self-publishing and get things out there. It is the whole genesis of it in the first place, you know. But where I'm coming from, not so much as a guy that was like on some sort of multiuser dungeon as a preteen or something that's grown up with it. Just more of a graphic designer that's fallen into it. You know?

TP: Just gives you a platform to show your work?

MO: Yeah, but I mean there's a community there, too. Like one of the things I've noticed that's happened over the last five years: it's become merged into traditional design, you know. It's like, you got a giant message board that is just all designers. Those guys don't claim to do web stuff at all, and they're not really from that world, but the Internet has impacted them from a visibility standpoint, and from a community standpoint. People know who they are, so I definitely feel like it's become what was once kind of web design stuff, is now something much larger and much more complex because people are not just participating online, but they're utilizing the web to do things. Whether it's sending print work to some printer far away to, you know, having some sort of melodramatic discussion about something or another. You know?

TP: Yeah.

MO: And everything in between.

TP: Yeah, it's impacting everybody's lives.

MO: Totally. That's, I mean, that's the coolest part about it. Now you feel like the world is really, really big, and really, really small at the same time.

TP: Yeah, it's like you can touch people all the way across the world and not even know it.

MO: Or you can piss some dude like thousands of miles away off without even trying...

TP: Yeah, totally.

MO: The converse.

TP: That's pretty funny.

MO: Like the world is just one big elementary school playground where people are annoying each another.

To hear the rest of Matt's answer to this question, as well as his answers to the following questions, please go to the Inspirations section of the book's site at www.JUXTinteractive.com/deCONSTRUCTION.

QUESTIONS

02. If you were a fish/sea creature, what would you be?

03. What CD or mp3 is in your player right now?

04. What is your definition of design?

05. What was your very first impression of Flash?

06. If you were walking down the street and came across John Gay and Jakob Nielsen engaged in a fistfight, what would you do?

07. You're kind of known as the inventor of the personal design site, which has in essence become its own genre. What motivated you to create volumeOne?

08. Which issue of volumeOne is your personal favorite and why?

09. What motivated the Codex Series? And what is your vision for it?

10. Let's see...volumeOne, Codex Series, One 9ine, and the Buddy System. You must have some serious sleep deprivation issues. How do you keep from getting burnt out?

11: One 9ine is made up of yourself and Warren Corbit. Does the work break down by medium, or do you tag team projects? How does it work out for you guys?

12. How do you come up with your concepts for volumeOne?

13. All your client work is very original as well. Do you only take projects that give you creative control?

14. What is it that happens in a typical day that gives you a feeling of satisfaction when you go home at night?

15. I know you're into music. Do you find songs that inspire a visual piece, or do you develop the visuals and then find a tune that reinforces the mood you want?

16. If you could do one last project before you had to hang up your designer's cap, what would you want that project to be?

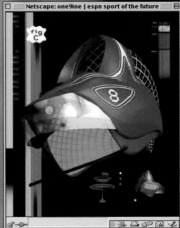

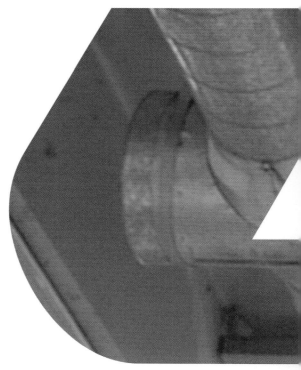

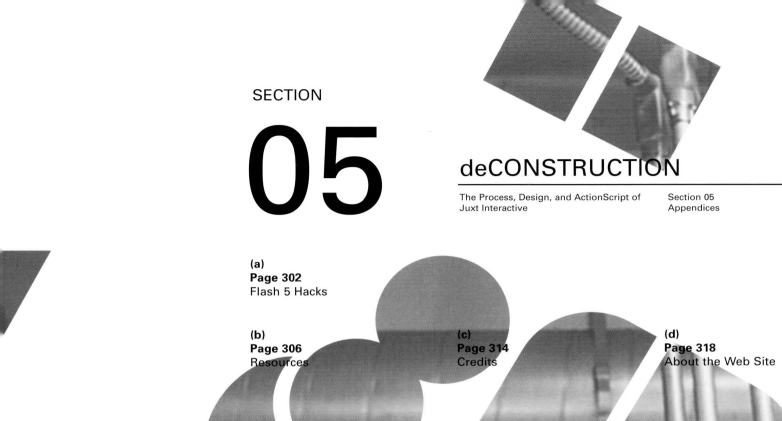

SECTION

05

deCONSTRUCTION

The Process, Design, and ActionScript of
Juxt Interactive

Section 05
Appendices

A APPENDIX
Flash deCONSTRUCTION
FLASH 5 HACKS

The following is a rundown of various issues, problems, and quirks we've run into while working with Flash 5. We've developed solutions and workarounds to these problems, and we'll share them with you in this appendix. If you have any development issues of your own that you've come across, please share them in our ongoing forum at www.JUXTinteractive.com/deCONSTRUCTION.

SOUND OBJECTS

Flash 5 introduced a new dynamic method for dealing with sound. This method is the sound object, and it gives us considerable control over what we can do with sounds. It enables us to create a sound that can be controlled through ActionScript. However, with this new method comes a new problem that needs to be addressed whenever you choose to use it. In a file that contains a sound object, Flash forces the sound to be loaded before anything else in the entire movie. This is because Flash doesn't know exactly when that sound is going to be used. Therefore, if you attach a sound that's 100K to a movie, when the user comes to that movie, before the player even loads frame 1, it will load 100K of data for that sound file. Because you can't build a preloader in the same file that communicates your loading, all the user will see is a blank screen. There is a workaround for this problem. The solution is to put your attached sounds in a separate external SWF that will be called into the main timeline. By doing this, you can communicate to the user that you're about to load a certain lump of data before you start loading in the sound object.

SHARED LIBRARIES

Another great new feature in Flash 5 is the shared library. With shared libraries, you can download elements once and use them in multiple movie clips throughout your project. Shared libraries not only help optimize files, they also contribute to efficiency and organization when working in a group environment. However, to reap the full benefit of shared libraries, they need to be managed, and just as with the sound object, you need a strategy for handling your libraries.

When you call a symbol from a shared library, Flash needs to load the entire shared library SWF before it can access the symbol you need within that library. This could compromise the movie's loading time. The best strategy for using shared libraries is to create multiple shared libraries that are small in size. This works much more efficiently than having one shared library for all your shared assets.

SHARED LIBRARY AND BUTTONS

When we started developing in Flash 5, we discovered some disappointing aspects of the application. For example, we discovered that buttons stop working when you share them via the shared library method. When you create a button and put it in a shared library, you can load it as a graphic element, but it won't respond as a button. So, to work around this issue, we create a movie clip that reacts as a button. Then we use an invisible button over the movie clip to simulate a button. We use this technique a great deal, but it would be much easier if we were able to share buttons through the library.

EXPORTING QUICKTIME FROM FLASH

This isn't necessarily a bug or a problem with Flash 5; it's just the nature of the beast. Flash is great for exporting QuickTime. You never see your Flash animation as fluid as you do when you're watching in QuickTime. This is because QuickTime renders out a frame at a time. It doesn't need to rely on the CPU like Flash. You can create rich-emotion sequences that play back beautifully in QuickTime because it's rendering a frame-by-frame movie. This kind of effect would be impossible to play back in the Flash Player on your CPU. The equivalent Flash Player file might appear choppy in playback and would create the wrong experience for the viewer.

However, there's a limitation to files created for export to a QuickTime movie. The export only renders out the frames related to the main timeline. What this means is that if you have a movie clip with its own timeline, the first frame of that clip will be rendered out continuously across all the frames in which the movie clip is on the stage. So, in QuickTime, it will look as if it's a still image. If you intend to export your file in QuickTime format, author the entire file on the main timeline. Or, if it's necessary to use movie clips, set their instance properties to graphic symbols. If looping is required, you will need to simulate it by creating a new keyframe for every loop. For example, if a movie clip is 10 frames and you want it to repeat three times, you will have a keyframe on frames 10, 20, and 30 of the main timeline.

INFINITE LOOP HANG-UP

When Flash is running and executing ActionScript, there is the potential for some scripts to take up so much CPU time that Flash lags while waiting for the script to finish running. If a script has what is known as an infinite loop (a loop that will never terminate), the Flash Player will lock up forever or until the user terminates the Flash Player. To save the user the frustration of having to terminate Flash when a misbehaving script takes over, Flash only gives individual ActionScripts 15 seconds to get their job done. If a script takes longer than 15 seconds, Flash will give the user the option of aborting all ActionScript for the remainder of the movie with the following pop-up message:

> "A script in this movie is causing Flash Player to run slowly. If it continues to run, your computer may become unresponsive. Do you want to abort the script? [Yes] [No]"

Unfortunately, the XML parser that is built into the Flash 5 Player has limits as to how much XML it can parse within 15 seconds. The parser speed limits vary from CPU to CPU, but they have been benchmarked in the range of 10–40K per second or 50–120 nodes per second. So, if you have an XML file that contains more than 150KB or 700 nodes, your Flash movie is in the danger zone for scaring your users into aborting your ActionScript.

If you are in control of the XML file format, it is advisable to remove blank spaces, tabs, and newline characters between tags to reduce

file size. You can also design your XML structures to be less hierarchical and more relational, although this strategy sometimes causes more hassles in trying to work with the data afterwards.

Finally, probably the most effective technique is to break up your XML files into logical and smaller pieces and load them in with separate calls to the XML.load() method.

XML PARSER

When software is developed, it goes through a beta-testing process. Macromedia is very responsible with beta testing and works very hard at it. But often, not every problem is discovered before software is released. With the new integration of XML in Flash 5, certain elements of XML didn't get properly tested. As a result, the players in Flash were released with some serious XML parsing bugs. A new version of the player was released some months after Flash 5 was released.

Versions "WIN 5,0,41,0" and "MAC 5,0,43,0" solve many of these problems. However, the vast majority of users already downloaded the Flash 5 Player before the new version's release. They don't understand why they would need to download a new version of the player, and this makes the problem a much bigger issue. Therefore, a lot of the XML that could be done with Flash 5 will have to wait for Flash 6. With a new release, users will have a real reason to upgrade their players.

Checking the $version variable to ensure that the version is greater than 5,0,40,0 is strongly recommended if your Flash 5 project uses XML. The most direct way to check the minor version is:

```
if ($version.split()[2] >= 40) {
    // good xml parser
} else {
    // bad xml parser
}
```

XML PROCESSING WHITESPACE

In the initial release of the Flash 5 Player ("WIN 5,0,30,0" and "MAC 5,0,30,0"), the XML parser automatically converted all whitespace (spaces, tabs, newlines) between XML tags into actual XML nodes. This dramatically increased the number of nodes found in the XML structure after the data has been loaded. Furthermore, it became confusing to the Flash developer when trying to work with an XML structure that contained useless empty nodes that must be skipped over.

Thankfully, the next release of the Flash 5 Player ("WIN 5,0,41,0," "WIN 5,0,42,0," and "MAC 5,0,43") added a feature that causes the XML parser to ignore extra whitespace. To invoke this fine feature, use the following command before using the XML.load(), XML.sendAndLoad(), or XML.parse() methods:

```
myXML.ignoreWhite = true;
```

Of course, the myXML prefix is where you use your variable name that contains an instance of the XML object.

PLAYING OLDER VERSIONS

In an effort to give more control to developers, Flash relies on developers to address the issue of degradable player versions with their own strategies. This means if the player version isn't detected beforehand, someone using the version 4 player might view the Flash 5 file, and it will play and kind of work, but will appear as if it's broken. You need to detect the player version and route people with the right version to the appropriate content, and those without to an upgrade notice or alternate site.

Checking for the player version within Flash is not as straightforward as one might expect. It's one thing to write a version checker for Flash 5 that tells you which minor version of Flash 5 Player is in use. It's another to make it properly detect a version prior to Flash 5

and take appropriate action. Flash 5 introduced the $version and getVersion() features, but they don't do much good when Flash 4 is attempting to play your Flash 5 movie.

One way to beat this is to allow the playhead to move on to a "badPlayer" frame unless a good player is detected. We add a frame to our movie that has the detection ActionScript. (Let's call this the "detect" frame and assume that it is frame 1.) We also add a frame that displays a status message to users, letting them know they need a newer plug-in to view the content. (Let's call this the "oldPlayer" frame and assume it is frame 2.) The remainder of the frames (3+) in the movie might assume that the proper plug-in is in use. So frame 1 does not have a stop() action in it. This enables the playhead to advance to the next frame if nothing in frame 1 alters its course. Frame 2 has a stop() action to show the user the upgrade message. Frame 3 has a label like "goodPlayer." In frame 1 (the "detect" frame), we use the following ActionScript:

```
function goodFlashVersion( nReqMajorVer, bNeedXML ) {
    var aPlatform = $version.split(" ");
    var aVer = aPlatform[1].split();
    if (int(aVer[0]) < nReqMajorVer || (bNeedXML && int(aVer[2])
      < 40)) {
        return false;
    }
    return true;
}
// Check for a Flash 5 player with the XML fix
if (goodFlashVersion( 5, true )) {
    gotoAndPlay("goodPlayer");
}
```

B APPENDIX

Flash deCONSTRUCTION

RESOURCES

Flash is a continuum of study, research, and exchange of ideas between users. The Internet is alive with information about the many faces of Flash. Fortunately, Flash developers are often willing to share new information with our community by posting their ideas on various sites.

This section offers a wide range of resources that further expand on the topics covered in the book. Serious Flash users will find the following list invaluable in their search for sometimes hard-to-find information. The URLs range from training to books to simple inspiration. We believe that as of this writing, these URLs are some of the best Flash resources out there.

THIS BOOK'S SITE

www.JUXTinteractive.com/deCONSTRUCTION

JUXT INTERACTIVE

www.JUXTinteractive.com

FLASH RESOURCE SITES

WE'RE HERE
www.were-here.com

ULTRASHOCK
www.ultrashock.com

FLASH KIT
www.flashkit.com

FLASH MOVE
www.flashmove.com

FLASH PLANET
www.flashplanet.com

OPEN SWF
www.openswf.org

FLASH CORE
www.flashcore.com

FLASH Q&A ARCHIVE
www.i-technica.com/flashlist/

FLASH FORUMS

WE'RE HERE FORUMS
www.were-here.com

DREAMLESS
www.dreamless.org

ULTRA SHOCK
www.ultrashock.com

FLASH KIT
www.flashkit.com

DREAM NATION
www.dream-nation.com

FLASH AND ACTIONSCRIPT

COLIN MOOCK'S MOOCK.ORG
www.moock.org

ACTIONSCRIPTS.ORG
www.actionscripts.org

FLASH 5 ACTIONSCRIPTING
www.flash5actionscript.com/

GENERATOR RESOURCES

MARKME
www.markme.com

XML RESOURCES

O'REILLY'S XML RESOURCE SITE
www.xml.com

SPECIFICATIONS AND STANDARDS FOR XML
www.xml.coverpages.org

MICROSOFT'S XML NOTEPAD
www.msdn.microsoft.com/xml/notepad/intro.asp?

MSDN ARTICLE: HOW TO ENCODE XML
www.msdn.microsoft.com/xml/articles/xmlencodings.asp

MSDN XML DOM REFERENCE
www.msdn.microsoft.com/library/default.asp?URL=/
library/psdk/xmlsdk/xml_9yg5.htm

JUXT'S FLASH 5 OBJECT/XML CONVERTER
www.juxtinteractive.com
(Click Desktops, Source Code, loadXML.)

JAVASCRIPT RESOURCES

CREATING CUSTOM OBJECTS IN JAVASCRIPT
www.wsabstract.com/javatutors/proto.shtml

DANNY GOODMAN EXPLAINS ARRAYS
www.developer.netscape.com/viewsource/
goodman_arrays.html

NETSCAPE'S JAVASCRIPT REFERENCE ON ARRAYS
www.developer.netscape.com/docs/manuals/communicator/
jsref/index.htm?content=core1.htm#1080770

THE JAVASCRIPT SOURCE
www.javascript.internet.com/

GAMES

SHOCKWAVE
www.shockwave.com

BANJA
www.banja.com

DRIVING JAKOB NIELSEN
www.urbanev.com/jakob/

FLASH GAMER
www.flashgamer.com

FLASH KIT ARCADE
www.flashkit.com/arcade/index.shtml

WE'RE HERE FORUMS
www.were-here.com/Games/index.html

EDUCATION

FIG LEAF
www.figleaf.com

LYNDA.COM
www.lynda.com/

MACROMEDIA UNIVERSITY
www.macromedia.elementk.com

EHANDS ON
www.ehandson.com

OPEN SWF
www.openswf.org

ENTERTAINMENT

HEAVY
www.heavy.com

ATOM FILMS/SHOCKWAVE
www.atomfilms.com

SONICNET
www.sonicnet.com

MP3.COM
www.mp3.com

ELVIS IN HAWAII
www.jdandme.com

AUDIO

SOUND SHOPPER
www.soundshopper.com

PROPELLER HEADS
www.propellerheads.se

GROOVE MAKER
www.groovemaker.com

MIX MAN
www.Mixman.com

RADIO FREE TOKYO
www.radiofreetokyo.com

ENDEKKS
www.endekks.com

BOOKS

FLASH WEB DESIGN
www.hillmancurtis.com/book

NEW MASTERS OF FLASH
www.friendsofed.com/books.html

FLASH STUDIO SECRETS
www.flashstudiosecrets.com

FLASH 5 BIBLE
www.flash5bible.com

DRAG SLIDE FADE
www.dragslidefade.com

O'REILLY ACTIONSCRIPT
www.oreilly.com/catalog/actionscript

FLASH TO THE CORE
www.praystation.com

GENERATOR DEMYSTIFIED
www.flashenabled.com

CONFERENCES

FLASH FORWARD
www.flashforward2001.com

OFFF CONFERENCE
www.offf.org

THUNDER LIZARD
www.thunderlizard.com

FRESH CONFERENCE
www.freshconference.com/

NEW MEDIA UNDERGROUND
www.nmuf.org

VECTOR LOUNGE
www.213.11.4.226/vectorlounge/

UCON
www.macromedia.com/macromedia/events/

FLASH INSPIRATION

FLASH CHALLENGE
www.flashchallenge.com

MACROMEDIA SITE OF THE DAY
www.macromedia.com/showcase

INSPIRATION

THE REMEDI PROJECT
www.theremediproject.com/

KALIBER10000
www.k10k.com

BORN MAGAZINE
www.bornmag.com

DESIGN PROJECT
www.design-agency.com/project

SURF STATION
www.surfstation.lu

DIGITAL THREAD
www.digitalthread.com

LINKDUP
www.linkdup.com

DESIGN IS KINKY
www.designiskinky.net

H73
www.h73.com

COOL HOME PAGES
www.coolhomepages.com

KIIROI
www.kiiroi.nu

INFRONT
www.australianinfront.com.au

AGAINST THE GRAIN
www.againsthegrain.com

ARCHINECT
www.archinect.com

FACTORY512
www.factory512.com

SHIFT
www.shift.jp.org

COMMUNICATION ARTS
www.commarts.com

ARCHITECTURE INSPIRATIONS

FRANK GEHRY
www.guggenheim-bilbao.es/ ingles/edificio/el_edificio.htm

www.lava.ds.arch.tue.nl/gallery/praha/tgehry.html

www.e-architect.com/media/releases/12%2D03%2D98a.asp

STEVEN HOLL
www.stevenholl.com/

ASYMPTOTE
www.asymptote-architecture.com/

MORPHOSIS
www.morphosis.net/

ZAHA M. HADID
www.zahamhadid.com

COOP HIMMELBLAU
www.coop-himmelblau.at/

ROTO ARCHITECTS
www.rotoark.com

LEBBEUS WOODS
www.skewarch.com/architects/woods/

TYPOGRAPHY

TYPOGRAPHER
www.typographer.com

EMIGRE
www.emigre.com

T 26
www.t26.com

GARAGE FONTS
www.garagefonts.com

HOUSE INDUSTRIES
www.houseindustries.com

FOUNTAIN
www.fountain.nu

TYPO 5
www.typo5.com

FUEL FONTS
www.fuelfonts.com

CHANK
www.chank.com

MINIML
www.miniml.com

FLASH DECONSTRUCTION INSPIRATIONS

HILLMAN CURTIS

www.hillmancurtis.com

BRENDAN DAWES

www.brendandawes.com/

FRED SHARPLES

www.orangedesign.com

JIMMY CHEN

www.typographic.com

MATT OWENS

www.volumeone.com

MIKE YOUNG

www.designgraphik.com

GLENN THOMAS

www.smashingideas.com

JAMES BAKER

www.wddg.com

JOSH ULM

www.ioresearch.com

JOSHUA DAVIS

www.praystation.com

C APPENDIX

Flash deCONSTRUCTION

CREDITS

BOOK

Authors

Todd Purgason
Phil Scott
Brian Drake
Bonnie Blake

Design

Creative Director: Todd Purgason
Art Director/Designer: Paul Venaas
Photography: Kimball Hall

FLASH DECONSTRUCTION BOOK SITE

www.JUXTinteractive.com/deCONSTRUCTION

Creative Director/Designer: Todd Purgason
Programming: Brian Drake
Sound: Todd Purgason
Copy Writer: Todd Purgason
Photography: Kimball Hall

JUXT INTERACTIVE SITE

www.JUXTinteractive.com

Creative Director/Designer: Todd Purgason
Technology Director/Programmer: Phil Scott
Designer: Chandler Owen
Programmers: Jeff Keyser, Brian Drake, Mark Fisk
Copy Writer: Rebecca Nordquist

BILLABONG USA

www.billabong-usa.com

Creative Director/Designer: Todd Purgason
Technology Director/Programmer: Phil Scott
Project Managers: Leanna Bush, Brandy Lee
Designers: Paul Nguyen, Luis Escorial, Josh Forstat,
Jennifer Redmond
Programmers: Brian Drake, Anthony Thompson, Mark Fisk
Photography: Todd Purgason
Sound Design: Todd Purgason
Client Creative Director: Ian Walter

PICKLED.TV

www.pickled.tv

Creative Director/Designer: Todd Purgason
Technology Director/Programmer: Phil Scott
Project Manager: Brandy Lee
Programmers: Jeff Keyser, Brian Drake, Anthony Thompson
Video: High Voltage Productions
Sound Design: Todd Purgason
Copy Writer: Todd Purgason
Client Creative Director: Ian Walter

BILLABONG STORE

www.billabong-usa.com/store

Creative Director: Todd Purgason
Technology Director/Programmer: Phil Scott
Project Manager: Brandy Lee
Art Director/Designer: Paul Nguyen
Programmers: Jeff Keyser, Brian Drake
Video: High Voltage Productions
Client Creative Director: Ian Walter

NDECISION

www.JUXTinteractive.com/ndecision

Creative Director: Todd Purgason
Technology Director/Programmer: Phil Scott
Art Director/Designer: Luis Escorial
Programmers: Jeff Keyser

JUXT INTERACTIVE TEAM

The team we owe this book to:

Steve Wages
CEO/Founder

Todd Purgason
Creative Director/Founder

Jeff Henning
Chief Operational Officer

Phil Scott
Chief Technology Officer

Mike Manson
Chief Financial Officer

Leanna Bush
Sr. Project Manager

John Devine
Project Manager

Brandy Lee
Project Manager

Luis Escorial
Art Director

Matt Kipp
Art Director

Paul Nguyen
Designer

Brian Dreiling
Designer

Brian Drake
Sr. Programmer/Web Developer

Anthony Thompson
Programmer/Web Developer

Scott Van Vliet
Programmer/Web Developer

Brian Miller
Intern

Lisa Brabender
Office Manager

Sue McDonnald
Bookkeeper

No longer with Juxt Interactive but instrumental in featured work:

Jeff Keyser
Programmer/Web Developer

Mark Fisk
Programmer/Web Developer

Chandler Owen
Designer

Eva Au
Designer

Josh Forstat
Designer

D APPENDIX

Flash deCONSTRUCTION

ABOUT THE WEB SITE

Additional resource material for this book is located at www.JUXTinteractive.com/deCONSTRUCTION. You will also find a link to this site from the book's title page on www.newriders.com.

This web site will give you everything you need to complete each of the projects in this book. Just access the figures on the web site and follow the instructions in this book. To make this more convenient, you will also find all the source code on the web site. In addition, we have audio interviews with each of the inspiration designers featured in the book. Other links provide added value so you can expand your digital library of resources. And, of course, we'd love your feedback, too! Please access the web site to send us your comments.

DOWNLOADS

This section of the site includes all the source files used in the book, listed by chapter.

INSPIRATIONS

In this section, we have audio interviews with each of the featured designers. These interviews range from 30 to 60 minutes each and provide an amazing perspective on today's top Flash developers. Also included are special interactives, created by each of these designers specifically for the book site.

RESOURCES

This list includes anything extra you might find useful—links to other sites, technical documents, fonts, design inspirations, and sounds, as well as many of the bitmap images used in the book.

FORUM

We really want to know what you think about the book and get you talking and sharing ideas with other readers. So join the forum, share your thoughts, and read the thoughts of others.

INDEX

Flash deCONSTRUCTION

attachSound method, 118

attributes of movie clips, 230

    changing

        with Color.setRGB(), 232-233

        with Color.setTransform(), 234-236, 239

    Color object, 231

attributes() function, 238-239

automating offline Generator, 179-181

B

ba (Blue Alpha), 235

Bandwidth Profiler, 92-94

bb (Blue Offset), 235

beta testers, 28

beta testing, 304

    Juxt Interactive process, 39

Billabong-USA.com, 13, 40

    branding, 133

    Featured Surf Riders. *See* Featured Surf Riders

    Pickled.tv site. *See* Pickled.tv site

    skate team riders. *See* skate team riders

    team riders section. *See* team riders section

Billabong store, 203-204

    forms, planning, 207

    shopping carts, 204

        checkout, 207-208, 211

        decimal points, 212-213

        movie clips, 205-206

        sales tax, 212

        setting variables for clips, 211

        shipping costs, 213

        subtotals, 212

bitmaps, compressing images, 90-91

blank spaces and XML, 269

blank.swf, 54

Blue Alpha (ba), 235

Blue Offset (bb), 235

brainstorming, Juxt Interactive process, 035

branding

    Billabong, 133

    movies, Pickled.tv site, 193-194

browser windows, opening with JavaScript, 145

buildArray() function, 288, 292

building. *See* creating

buildMovie() function, 280

buttons, 49

    shared libraries, problems with, 303

C

calculated coordinates versus hard-coded coordinates, 245

CFX_Generate, 180-181

    ColdFusion example, 179

checking for player versions, 305

checkout with shopping carts, 207-208, 211

childNodes, 262

choosing sliders, 242

clear drop versus set drop, 224

Clip 1, 224

Clip 5, 224

clip events, 105-106

    if statements, 211

    looping techniques, 106

clip parameters, 121

cluster cores, 137

code

    ActionScript for Color.setTransform(), 234

    Basic ColdFusion example using CFX_Generate, 179

Button event handlers for Orig Clips, 226

    for checkout with shopping carts, 208

    clip events, 209-210

Clip Event handlers for movie clip _root.2.alpha, 244

    for decimal points in shopping cart totals, 213

getTarget() function defined in the main timeline, 226

    for modifying movie clip properties using dot syntax, 231

    for movie clip named scroller clip, 200-201

    for moving image scrollers, 202-203

    for name clusterer, 135-136

    for nav clip, 140

nDecision video clip attribute update ActionScript, 238

    for off frame, 142

    for on frame, 140

    for paused frames, 144

    for playing frames, 143

Raw data from the web server that feeds Figure 10.2, 256

releaseTarget() function defined in the main timeline, 228

    for sales tax on shopping carts, 212

Sample ActionScript that loads and traces the structure of an XML file, 265

Sample ActionScript that uses the XML.onLoad property, 261

Sample ActionScript using XML.childNodes, 262

Sample ActionScript using XML.sendAndLoad(), 270

Sample XML document to define cascading, 254

    for shipping costs, 213

team structure, 25
ActionScript programmers, 28
creative director/art director, 27
database designers, 28
designers, 27
developers, 28
information architects, 27
programmers, 28
project manager—client, 27
project manager—consultant, 27
*quality assurance engineers/beta
testers, 28*
technology director/programming lead, 27

K

Key down clip events, 106
key features of extranets, 24
Key up clip events, 106

L

libraries
array XML libraries, 279
ArrayTransport Library. *See* Array
Transport Library
shared libraries, 83-84
line generation, 114
creating, 114-115
dynamic line generation, 114-115
Process presentation, 116-117
list count variable, 211
live sites updates, scheduling, 181
Load clip events, 106
loading
data
with ArrayTransport Library, 286
into XML object, 260-261
external movies, 051-054
XML data, 273
with ArrayTransport Library, 292-294

loadMovie command, 168
loadVariables, comparing results to
XML object, 256
loadVariables() action, 254
looping techniques, clip events, 106
loops, 55, 58
do...while loops, 57
for loops, 58, 64
infinite loops, 304
while loops, 56-57
lundstromarch.com, 11

M

Macromedia
Generator. *See* Generator
FreeHand. *See* FreeHand
maintenance, Juxt Interactive
process, 41
managing, 172. *See also* content
management
marketing, 193. *See also* branding
masks, 88
Math.round() function, 213
methods
attachSound, 118
Color.setRGB(), 231-233
Color.setTransform(), 231, 234-236, 239
for loading XML object, 260
.getFrom(), ArrayTransport, 286
getTimer(), 109
indexOf(), 212
parseXML(), 260
.setHandler(), ArrayTransport, 286
used by XML object to navigate
documents, 262, 267
window.open(), 145
XML.load(), 273, 304
XML.send, 269

XML.sendAndLoad, 269
XML.sendAndLoad(), using with
XML.onLoad, 270
modifying movie clip properties with
ActionScript, 230-231
motion
organic motion, 106-107
randomizing, 108
motion graphics, navigation
(Pickled.tv site), 198-199
Mouse down clip events, 106
Mouse move clip events, 106
Mouse up clip events, 106
movie clips. *See also* movies
attributes, modifying with ActionScript,
230-231
buttons, 49
controlling attributes, 230
Color object, 231
Color.setRGB(), 232-233
Color.setTransform(), 234-236, 239
dragging, 225
editing, 167
frames, tracking, 107-108
shopping carts, 205-206
setting variables for, 211
slider button movie clips, 119
structure for Alpha Slider, 242
structure of, 49
dissecting, 50-51
updating colors with Color object, 231
viewcart, 205-206
movie maker
controlling speed, 240-241
nDecision, elements of, 223-224
MovieClip.droptarget, slashes, 224
movies. *See also* movie clips
controlling quality, 142-145
external movies, loading, 51-54
Pickled.tv site. *See* Pickled.tv site

XML.send(), versus
  XML.sendAndLoad(), 269
XML.sendAndLoad()
    using with XML.onLoad, 270
    versus XML.send(), 269
XMLDocToArray() function, 288, 292
xmlNode.attributes[attribName], 262
xmlNode.childnodes[i], 262
xmlNode.firstChild, 262
xmlNode.hasChildNodes(), 262, 267
xmlNode.lastChild, 262
xmlNode.nextSibling, 262
xmlNode.parentNode, 262
_xscale, movie clip parameters, 230

Y-Z

-yscale, movie clip parameters, 230
_y, movie clip parameters, 230

Solutions from experts you know and trust.

www.informit.com

OPERATING SYSTEMS

WEB DEVELOPMENT

PROGRAMMING

NETWORKING

CERTIFICATION

AND MORE...

**Expert Access.
Free Content.**

New Riders has partnered with **InformIT.com** to bring technical information to your desktop. Drawing on New Riders authors and reviewers to provide additional information on topics you're interested in, **InformIT.com** has free, in-depth information you won't find anywhere else.

- Master the skills you need, when you need them

- Call on resources from some of the best minds in the industry

- Get answers when you need them, using InformIT's comprehensive library or live experts online

- Go above and beyond what you find in New Riders books, extending your knowledge

As an **InformIT** partner, **New Riders** has shared the wisdom and knowledge of our authors with you online. Visit **InformIT.com** to see what you're missing.

www.informit.com

New Riders

www.newriders.com

NEW RIDERS
GRAPHICS
CLASSICS

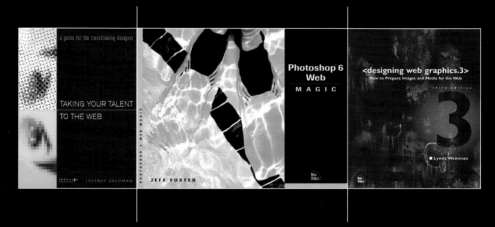

Taking Your Talent to the Web
Jeffrey Zeldman
ISBN: 0735710732
$40.00

Photoshop 6 Web Magic
Jeff Foster
ISBN: 0735710368
$45.00

<designing web graphics.3>
Lynda Weinman
ISBN: 1562059491
$55.00

The Art & Science of Web Design
Jeffrey Veen
ISBN: 0789723700
$45.00

<creative html design.2>
Lynda Weinman and
William Weinman
ISBN: 0735709726
$39.99

Don't Make Me Think!
Steve Krug
ISBN: 0789723107
$35.00

The Authors. The Content. The Timeliness.
What it takes to be a classic.

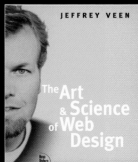
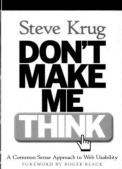

Publishing
the Voices
that Matter

OUR BOOKS

OUR AUTHORS

SUPPORT

| web development | graphics & design | server technology | certification |

NEWS/EVENTS

PRESS ROOM

EDUCATORS

ABOUT US

CONTACT US

WRITE/REVIEW

You already know that New Riders brings you the Voices that Matter. But what does that mean? It means that New Riders brings you the Voices that will challenge your assumptions, take your talents to the next level, or simply help you better understand the complex technical world we're all navigating.

Visit **www.newriders.com** to find:

- ▶ Previously unpublished chapters
- ▶ Sample chapters/excerpts
- ▶ Author bios
- ▶ Contests
- ▶ Up-to-date industry event information
- ▶ Book reviews
- ▶ Special offers
- ▶ Info on how to join our User Group program
- ▶ Inspirational galleries where you can submit your own masterpieces
- ▶ Ways to have your Voice heard

New Riders

WWW.NEWRIDERS.COM

Blending the art of design

with the magic of technology

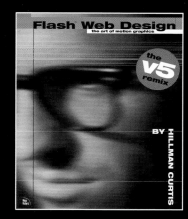

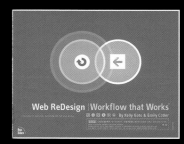

Flash Web Design:
The v5 Remix
ISBN: 0735710988
Hillman Curtis
$45.00

Flash 5 Magic with
ActionScript
ISBN: 0735710236
Scott Hamlin,
Dave Emberton
$45.00

Inside Flash
ISBN: 0735711054
Jody Keating,
Fig Leaf Software
$45.00

Flash ActionScript
for Designers:
Drag, Slide, Fade
ISBN: 0735710473
Brendan Dawes
$45.00

Generator/Flash
Web Development
ISBN: 0735710805
Richard Alvarez, et al.
$34.99

Flash Deconstruction
ISBN: 0735711496
Todd Purgason, Phil Scott
$45.00

Flash to the Core
ISBN: 0735711046
Joshua Davis
$45.00

Web Redesign:
Workflow that Works
ISBN: 0735710627
Kelly Goto, Emily Cotler
$45.00

VISIT OUR WEB SITE

WWW.NEWRIDERS.COM

On our web site, you'll find information about our other books, authors, tables of contents, and book errata. You will also find information about book registration and how to purchase our books, both domestically and internationally.

EMAIL US

Contact us at: **nrfeedback@newriders.com**

- If you have comments or questions about this book
- To report errors that you have found in this book
- If you have a book proposal to submit or are interested in writing for New Riders
- If you are an expert in a computer topic or technology and are interested in being a technical editor who reviews manuscripts for technical accuracy

Contact us at: **nreducation@newriders.com**

- If you are an instructor from an educational institution who wants to preview New Riders books for classroom use. Email should include your name, title, school, department, address, phone number, office days/hours, text in use, and enrollment, along with your request for desk/examination copies and/or additional information.

Contact us at: **nrmedia@newriders.com**

- If you are a member of the media who is interested in reviewing copies of New Riders books. Send your name, mailing address, and email address, along with the name of the publication or web site you work for.

BULK PURCHASES/CORPORATE SALES

If you are interested in buying 10 or more copies of a title or want to set up an account for your company to purchase directly from the publisher at a substantial discount, contact us at 800-382-3419 or email your contact information to corpsales@pearsontechgroup.com. A sales representative will contact you with more information.

WRITE TO US

New Riders Publishing
201 W. 103rd St.
Indianapolis, IN 46290-1097

CALL/FAX US

Toll-free (800) 571-5840
If outside U.S. (317) 581-3500
Ask for New Riders
FAX: (317) 581-4663

New Riders

WWW.NEWRIDERS.COM